Stock Market For Beginners - How To Start Investing Today

Adil Khan

Published by Adil Khan, 2024.

Table of Contents

Copyright 1

About 2

Why This Particular Book? 3

How to Prevent Stock Market Losses? 6

An Important Case Study 8

An Absolute Guarantee Of Losing Money In The Stock Market .. 16

Beware Of Dangerous Traps 25

The Only Reliable Method Of Making Money In The Stock Market 28

The Stock Market Is Not at All Risky 30

The Stock Market's One and Only Risk 33

The Only Path to Financial Success 35

Don't Ignore the Fundamentals 38

Knowledge Investment Yields the Highest Returns 39

The First Step in Choosing Quality Stocks 42

Equity Return 45

Competitive Advantage or Economic Moat 47

The Risky 4-Letter Word: Debt 50

Advancement to the Subsequent Parameters 54

How to Assess Management 56

Most Effortless Techniques for Assessing Management 58

Management Assessment 60

Second Management Assessment 70

Management Assessment 72

What Next 73

Assessment 74

Typical Instruments For Appraisal 76

Investor Misconceptions First Misconception 83

The Disadvantages Of Valuation Methods 86

The Simplest Method For Determining Value 91

Knowing When to Sell and Buy 98

Frequently Held Myths to Avoid 102

How Soon Should I Sell My Stock? Improved Possibilities ... 104

Dangerous Errors to Steer Clear of Error #1 112

How to Prevent Stock Market Losses 118

The Purchase Rate Is Not the Main Focus 122

Don't Attempt to Forecast the Market's Path 124

Market for Love Bears (Falling) 126

How to Build Your Portfolio 127

Issues with a Vast Portfolio of Stocks 130

Investor Misconception Misconception No. 1 132

Defending The Portfolio Against A Crisis In The Market............138

Avoidable Stocks: Stocks to Steer Clear 141

Recap 145

Day Trading Forex - Simple Forex Day Trading Strategy Work ...146

Enhancing Trading Signals 149

Momentum Oscillators for Effective Entry/Exit 151

Trend Tracking Entry and Exit Signals of Indicators 159

Stock Market Fundamental Analysis..165

Essential Evaluation...173

Political-Economic Interpretation 178

The Economic Cycle 182

Understanding Asset Bubbles and Protecting Yourself 184

Evaluation of the Industry...188

The Administrative 198

The Organization 206

The Annual Report..209

Profits 225

Advisability 229

Availability 232

Make Use of...237

Ability to Pay Debt..240

Effectiveness and Asset Management 244

Margin 249

Flow of Cash 254

What Next 256

Basic Analysis: Method by Method 258

Essential Analysis: Concise Overview 263

Value Investing Strategies for Stock Market Investing 264

Concerning 265

Be Sure To Create A Plan Before Trading 267

Grow from a Small Plant to a Giant Banyan Tree 268

Take Part In Little Transactions Only 271

You Should Always Aim For A Little Profit And Set An Even Smaller Stop-Loss 274

A 2:1 Profit-To-Loss Ratio Is Required 277

Engage solely in high volume stocks 279

All Investments Are Either Losses Or Winners; There Are No Good Or Bad Stocks 281

Avoid Combining Different Trade Sections 283

Control Your Avarice And Fear 286

The Sharegenius Swing Trading System 287

VWAP Technique Breakout 290

Small Trade Stop-Loss Method 292

Mastering The Mentality Of Leveraged Trading 294

Take A Break From Competing With The Market 296

Determining Profit Goals 298

When Swing Trading, Only Utilize Index Stocks 302

Neither Swing Trading Nor Intraday Conversion To BTST 303

Greed Is The Stock Market's Curse 304

Is It Possible to Sell a Poor Investment? 305

Put Aside Thoughts Of Bonuses 308

Typical Results Aren't Always Negative 310

Either Employ Swing Trading Or Properly Study How To Invest For The Long Term 311

Why Is Buying Index Stocks Justifiable? 313

NIFTY Stocks Are An Excellent Choice For Trading And Swing Trading 314

Analyze a Plunging Deal 315

What is my trading strategy for stocks? 316

An Investment Never Declines Abruptly 318

Benefits of Purchasing Dividend-Paying Stocks 320

Extracting Taxes on Income to Lower Capital Gains 323

When Trading Options, Apply The 4-Stroke Method 325

Trading In Options Was Launched By The NSE 328

Conclusion 330

Copyright

Published in the United States of America by Adil Khan,

Columbus, OH 43211 USA.

Copyright © 2024 by **Adil Khan**. All rights reserved. No part of this book may be reproduced, scanned, or distributed in any printed or electronic form without permission. Please do not participate in or encourage piracy of copyrighted materials in violation of the author's rights. Purchase only authorised editions.

Stock Market For Beginners - How To Start Investing Today

Printed in United States of America and Distributed by **Adil Khan**

First Edition: Feb 2024

Book Design by **Adil Khan**

About

So you want to start investing in the stock market? Great! I know that starting in the stock market can be very overwhelming and challenging, especially if you go at it alone (I've been there myself..)

In the beginning, I just didn't know where to begin. When I started, I made mistakes after mistake, costing me thousands of dollars. It took me years of frustration, hard work and dedication before I finally understood how to become a successful stock market investor.

In other words, I've learned the do's and don'ts of the stock market the hard way. BUT, there's a much easier way to learn investing. A way that could've saved me thousands of dollars and A LOT of time - if only I wasn't so stubborn to go at it alone. If I just decided to learn from other experienced investors, who've already achieved what I wanted to achieve.

If I just decided to learn in a couple of hours what they've learned in a lifetime. I would've had a much better start to my investing career. And that's exactly the reason I created this Book. So that you can learn in just 2 hours, what I learned in years of investing.

Why This Particular Book?

Hundreds of books exist that purport to provide an answer to the query, "How to make money from stocks." However, the majority of small and ordinary investors lose money overall in the stock market. Through my interactions with hundreds of retail investors since 2010, I've come to the conclusion that a large portion of the stock market's loss is caused by investor misconceptions. In addition, a lot of investors choose to follow "Stock Tips" in order to make rapid money. Additionally, commercial channels, print media, and social media platforms like Facebook, Twitter, and WhatsApp offer a plethora of free trading suggestions.

Nevertheless, a lot of individuals lose a lot of money in the stock market. I came to the conclusion that many people could save their hard-earned money in this market if I could explain all the reasons why people lose money. Protecting your capital should be your top responsibility as an investor. This book's first two chapters are devoted solely to capital protection. "My goal in writing this book is to protect small investors' hard-earned equity investment capital." The only way to make money is to buy high-quality stocks at the proper price and keep them for a fair amount of time. Choosing quality stocks doesn't require an MBA in finance or a comparable degree. Choosing stocks is frequently regarded as one of the world's most difficult topics. Nonetheless, anyone can become an expert in the field—all it takes is a strong work ethic, desire, and commitment to the stock market. This book contains a variety of doable strategies and realistic approaches to help you make money in the stock market on a regular basis. I read a ton of best-selling stock market books while I was in college.

Peter Lynch's book "One up on Wall Street" is one such noteworthy work. Although I found the book difficult to finish, I did learn a lot. I used to read books with a dictionary at my side since the very technical English made it very hard to understand what was being said. "One up on Wall Street" is without a doubt one of the best novels I have ever read, yet I found reading it to be excruciating and tiresome. With Benjamin Graham's other best-seller, "The Intelligent Investor," I had a similar experience. To fully understand that book, it took me two years and multiple tries. I sent it to a few friends, who all said the stock market was "boring" and gave up after reading a few pages. At this point, it occurred to me that I ought to produce a book that simplifies this difficult topic. In addition to reading books, Investopedia, a well-known website, is a great resource for knowledge.

Even in this case, the topic is presented in a way that can bore and lose the attention of many readers. I acknowledge that the stock market is a huge and complex topic, but it can also be explained in a way that is engaging and simple to comprehend so that even little investors may become more knowledgeable about it. This book is my attempt to make the enormous and complicated subject of "stock market" understandable and engaging for readers of all ages, including eighteen-year-olds from diverse backgrounds. The US stock market serves as the basis for the majority of the best-selling books written about investing. I found it difficult to connect those works to the Indian stock market while I was reading them. My contacts with hundreds of ordinary investors over the past few years have made it clear to me that creating a book focused exclusively on the Indian stock market is essential.

Occasionally, a lot of our subscribers would ask me to recommend a decent book that is solely focused on the Indian stock market and is written in simple English. This book, in my opinion, will accomplish the goal. Because of the straightforward language utilized, anyone with any background can easily grasp it. "With its exclusive focus on the Indian Stock Market and abundance of real-world examples, this book is ideal for individuals seeking to gain knowledge on the subject with little to no exertion." Thus, ask yourself the following:1. Are you seeking for simple techniques to reduce or eliminate loss associated with equity investing? 2. Do you want the value of your hard-earned money to increase gradually and regularly over time? 3. Are you trying to find an engaging book that will help you learn the fundamentals of the stock market? 4. Most importantly, do you want to invest your way into a rich and joyful life without experiencing any stress? Continue reading if you said "yes" to any of the aforementioned questions; this book won't let you down.

How to Prevent Stock Market Losses?

Introduction: Find out about stock market investing from your friends, neighbors, or family. The majority of them will try to dissuade you by calling it just another kind of gambling. A lot of people still think that the change in stock prices is illogical. Large stock market gains are simply the result of "luck". On the other hand, it is noteworthy that nearly every billionaire in the world made their wealth through the stock market, either directly or indirectly. "Indirectly" refers to putting their companies on the stock market, whereas "Directly" refers to investing in stocks directly.

Direct stock investing is how investor and philanthropist Warren Buffett, one of the richest persons in the world, made his money. Several well-known billionaires, such as Larry Page of Google, Mark Zuckerberg of Facebook, and Bill Gates of Microsoft, amassed their wealth by placing their businesses on the stock exchange. Numerous wealthy investors, including Vijay Kedia, Radhakishan Damani, and Rakesh Jhunjhunwala, made their entire fortune through direct stock investment, even in India. My query is this: how have these billionaires made their fortunes from the stock market if stock market investing is just another kind of "gambling"? It is not feasible to become a "billionaire" through traditional "gambling," even though you might win once or twice. Do you think they were merely fortunate? While luck may favor you once, twice, or even three times, successful billionaire investors have been making money in the stock market for many years.

A gambler is not likely to routinely win billions. A billionaire cannot be created solely by luck. Consequently, there must be another story. But a lot of regular people lose their hard-earned cash on the stock market! The phrase "retail investors" appears frequently in this work.

"Retail investors" are people who invest (or plan to invest) a portion of their money in the stock market and have a full-time job or another source of income. You must comprehend why, in this market, the majority of ordinary investors lose their hard-earned money while a tiny number of billionaire investors make their fortune. Understanding the causes of financial loss is the first step towards preventing losses in the stock market. I'll give an example from real life to illustrate the reasons. The following narrative may also be related to current equities investors.

An Important Case Study

During a meeting with an investor named Rohit a few months ago, I discovered to my astonishment that he had lost almost ₹10 lakh (₹10,00,000) in the stock market. He used a variety of strategies and followed numerous analysts in the last five years of the stock market, but the result was a cumulative loss of over ₹10 lakh! He has been profitable on multiple occasions. However, these isolated gains paled in comparison to his enormous total losses. His experience with the stock market is broken down into four stages.

Let's examine each stage in great depth and see exactly where he went wrong. Stage One Rohit was keen to invest but had no knowledge of the stock market approximately five years ago. A stockbroker friend of his used to be a regular trader. Although Rohit was intrigued, he was unsure about where to start. He went to his acquaintance, who assisted him in setting a demat account and trading. After that, Rohit gave someone else ₹100,000 (about one lakh) to trade on his behalf. Given his lack of experience with what to buy and how to sell, that was the best course of action. At first everything went without a hitch. His broker acquaintance would assist him in trading the stock that day and provide him with daily news-based suggestions.

Every day at the conclusion of the workday, Rohit would get a call with his profits. Following an early profit, Rohit gave his broker friend an extra ₹50,000 to trade. Why wouldn't he? Without any technological expertise, he had already made a twenty percent profit. Abruptly, the circumstances shifted. For several weeks, there was no confirmation of the trade. His broker no longer gave him calls. Rohit was concerned. Then he saw that half of everything he had started with was lost! Rohit was taken aback. It was difficult for a novice investor to absorb a 50% loss on his initial investment. Later on, he discovered that the market had experienced a severe meltdown due to an unfavorable macroeconomic environment, and that things would not be getting better anytime soon. Exasperated, Rohit gave his broker friend the order to sell everything he owned.

Upon terminating his trading account, he discovered that he had lost 55% of the money he had invested, without counting brokerage fees and other penalties. What went wrong, and where? Following your broker (or buddy) blindly in the stock market could be quite costly. Have you noticed that your broker constantly makes money, regardless of how much you win or lose? Brokerage is required for each transaction (buy and sell). Only when you trade can your broker make money. It follows that your broker will definitely push for regular buying and selling. The only thing your broker needs to do is work for him! Your broker is as driven to maximize his personal profits as you are to profit from the stock market. Hence, regardless of the outcome, maximal brokers would promote frequent trading rather than prioritizing their clients. This is where the issue appears. Your broker makes more money the more you trade and the greater the danger of loss.

I'll go into more detail about why trading frequently raises the possibility of losing money later in this chapter. To stimulate trading, large brokerage houses frequently provide their clients email and SMS stock advice. Sub-brokers have to reach minimum turnover requirements or face pressure. If sub brokers don't fulfill the minimum trading volume requirement, they risk losing their license as well. Throughout the entire process, retail investors are the ones who are most impacted. If you trade regularly in high amounts, you may have also noticed that brokers are constantly willing to lower brokerage. This is a subliminal invitation to trade more, regardless of your position, so they can profit handsomely.

Stage Two Following the initial occurrence, Rohit had closed his trading account. I was curious as to what had motivated him to return to the market. After his initial unpleasant experience with stocks, six months had passed, and Rohit had begun to routinely read a few business periodicals. Reading newspapers, surfing the internet, and watching TV shows like CNBC become obsessions for investment ideas. This occurred during a period of extreme strength in the equity market, referred to as a "bull market." The market reached new heights nearly every day, and the majority of companies were rising. Numerous pundits on TV and in print media were also airing their sanguine opinions. "This time it is different, the market will continue to rise for at least the next two or three years," was one of the many upbeat remarks made by several of them.

Rohit was keen to take advantage of this opportunity and was tempted. He quickly submitted an application for a new trading and demat account. This time, he forged a relationship with a reputable broker. He chose intraday trading because he was ready to get into the market and make some quick cash. One of the best things about intraday trading is that there are a lot of newspapers and television networks that offer free suggestions. His broker was willing to offer up to ten times the margin for intraday trading, meaning that he could trade in values worth ₹1,000 for every ₹100 in his trading account.

He committed ₹50,000, allowing him to trade up to ₹5 lakh in a single day. Everything was excellent. There was ample margin money available for trading, along with a ton of free trading advice. Rohit was profitable with these tips on multiple occasions. But the whole advantage from multiple profitable trades was erased by one or two losing trades. This is a strange issue. Gains are invariably negligible in relation to losses. Rohit was unable to pinpoint his exact mistakes. He had set a "Stop Loss" in accordance with analyst advice, but frequently the price began to rise after it touched the stop loss. He paused his trade after four months in order to figure out his total profit. The outcome was unexpected. His initial capital didn't increase at all, even though he made a number of profitable trades. Rather, he had lost twenty percent of his whole investment!

Approximately 70% of his trades throughout these four months were profitable, which is an intriguing fact. Those were times when he made money. Still, the remaining 30% of losing trades erased the entire profit. That was annoying. He kept "Stop Loss" and "Target," but in the end, he lost a lot of bad transactions and made little money on profitable ones. For instance, Rohit once paid ₹800 for a Reliance. It achieved its initial goal of ₹810, and he recorded a ₹10 profit. One more day, he paid ₹800 for Reliance and set "Stop Loss" at ₹790. But the stock fell so hard that it only touched 780 instead of 790! He was so obliged to book a ₹20 loss per share and sell at ₹780. Rohit was really irritated since he couldn't figure out why the market was acting in this manner. What went wrong, and where? From the start, Rohit made mistakes.

Trading intraday practically always results in losses. Almost no one has ever made money from intraday trading on a regular basis. There isn't a single billionaire in the world that gained their wealth just through day trading. You will inevitably lose money after making money one, two, or three times. A loss is often always bigger than a profit. Give it a shot. Consider the day:

trading advice from any analyst, anyplace. Numerous companies offering paid stock suggestions assert a 99% success rate. Pay attention to their advice, trade intraday, and monitor the outcome. As unpleasant as it may sound, the truth is that no market expert can make you money with intraday trading. Recall the subliminal motivation provided by Rohit's intermediary? His broker permitted him to swap items worth 5 lakh (₹500,000) in an intraday transaction, which equates to ten times the initial amount, even though he only had ₹50,000 in his trading account. This is referred to as "Margin Trading" and is a great method to profit—for your broker, that is! Stage Three After learning his lesson from day trading, Rohit was resolved not to make the same error twice.

Now, he was more cautious, but he was also very confident that he could make a lot of money in the stock market. The only issue was his meager financial resources. He began buying a few popular stocks, intending to hold them for several months. In ten months, his portfolio was showing increases of about 20%. After this procedure, he amassed almost 8 lakhs. He discovered an alluring offer during this period of time called "loan against shares," which allows one to use securities as security for loans. One can get a loan for as much as 70–80% of their entire net worth, depending on their stock holdings. If you are unable to maintain the minimum collateral value, banks have the power to liquidate your collateral holdings. Rohit made no second thoughts. He was receiving an annual return on his stocks of about 20%.

It was a good deal, especially when you factored in the bank loan's 10-12% interest rate. He therefore didn't think twice to take out a loan in order to purchase shares, keeping his entire investment as security. As long as the market continued its upward trend, everything was good. Rohit was pleased to see that the growth in his investment was exponential. The bank was prepared to offer more loans for each percentage gain in share value. Rohit was aiming for a more powerful role. This, however, was short-lived. The stock market abruptly made a 180-degree turn. Rohit's portfolio worth decreased by about 20% in a span of ten days. Rohit was required by the terms of the bank to maintain the collateral amount, but he was in serious trouble due to the market's subsequent correction. In order to keep collateral, he was obliged to sell a portion of his investment. The market was still falling, and things were becoming worse. The market was dominated by pessimism. Even equity experts, who only a few months before were projecting huge targets, were voicing their pessimistic opinions.

Rohit could not accept that his investment had decreased. The bank persisted in exerting pressure on him to keep his collateral in the interim. Everything was getting out of hand. In the end, Rohit sold all of his investment, mostly as a result of bank pressure and fear. He had amassed almost 10 lakhs during the previous two years, and a few months ago, he was in a strong position, but he ultimately suffered a 25% loss. "Forced selling" was the reason for the total loss. Had Rohit stayed away from the "loan against shares" plan, he would not have had to sell his equities when the market was falling. What went wrong, and where? Borrowed money stock investing is risky unless you have sufficient knowledge of the industry. You may compound your loss and enhance your gain tremendously with this exercise.

A lot of knowledgeable investors use leverage in their holdings. They are knowledgeable about risk management, know when and how much to leverage, and most importantly, they are deeply knowledgeable about the topic. Determine if you possess sufficient skill. It is advisable for individual investors to avoid "loan against share" schemes. Any investor can prosper in a prosperous market, but what sets wise investors apart from the rest is their capacity to reduce losses in a bear market, or a market collapse. In prosperous times, a lot of investors choose to "loan against shares." Once you begin to think you have mastered the game after a year or two of strong returns, the market will unavoidably teach you a lesson. During market crashes, leveraged positions can potentially lead to bankruptcy. Thus it is always preferable to stay away from the same. Phase Four: Rohit decided enough was enough. Following three failed attempts, Rohit intended to work with a seasoned stock tip source. He found a lot of names when searching the internet.

Many of them displayed amazing prior results and boasted a success percentage of 90% or more. Rohit signed up for a three-day trial with a number of stock tip providers since he was perplexed. They began making him a lot of calls after the trial. One such service provider claimed that by using "Futures and Options," he could profit from market fluctuations as well as up and down swings. It surprised Rohit. He has lost money in the past, mostly during a market collapse. The prospect of profiting during the market's collapse was alluring enough to draw his interest. He was excited to pay for the stock tips provider's services. The only issue was that they demanded an exorbitant subscription price. He hesitated before making a choice. Still, they called him over and over, urging him to enlist. Even three "trial calls" were agreed upon. Positively, every call made reached its objective.

Additionally, they guaranteed a monthly return on their "Futures and Options" trading call of 100% or more. Rohit was persuaded. He purchased the "Futures and Options" package at a steep subscription cost. To start, Rohit was willing to invest 5 lakhs (₹500,000). From the first contact, he had ₹3 lakhs (₹300,000). It was surprisingly displaying a 50% rise in just 15 days. He made the decision to invest more money after realizing the potential of "future trading." He was looking forward to the next call because he had made good money on the prior one. He put more money on the following trading tip. The uncertainty that comes with Futures & Options (F&O) was something he was unaware of. F&O can undoubtedly yield exceptional returns, but it can also result in "unlimited loss." You can profit 50% to 100% on every right wager, but an incorrect wager can result in a 100% loss.

For Rohit, this is what transpired. In 15 days, he had lost 90% on the second "trading call" and gained 50% on the first. What went wrong, and where? For retail investors, trading "Futures and Options" is the worst choice they can make. Your entire life's savings could be lost. A lot of analysts and stock tip providers will tell you that trading F&O can yield a 100% return in as little as one month. I would like to know why they don't trade themselves. Selling "tips" is unnecessary if you can generate a 100% monthly return on your own analysis. You can become a billionaire in two to three years after repaying a bank loan of 10 lakhs if you can secure a 100% monthly return. However, there isn't a single person who used "Futures and Options" trading to become a billionaire. One thing to learn from this is to ask the above question to any stock recommendations source who entices you to trade "Futures and Options" (F&O).

Many stock tip providers are boasting such exceptional profits from their trading calls, as one may discover with a basic online search. But the truth speaks a different language. Avoid falling for their tricks and avoiding stock tip providers that make extravagant returns claims. F&O is primarily intended for hedge funds and institutional investors. Large corporations and wealthy people use F&O to hedge their positions. One excellent way to hedge is through futures trading. Retail investors typically experience a great deal of disappointment when they jump into F&O expecting tremendous returns.

An Absolute Guarantee Of Losing Money In The Stock Market

In summary, the topic at hand is "Trading in the stock market will most likely result in losses for retail investors."

In this context, "trading" includes intraday, futures, options, and any other activity in which you buy stocks with the intention of selling them for a profit within one to fifteen days. "Retail investors" are people who invest a portion of their savings in the stock market while working a full-time job in another field. Why trading is a surefire method for average investors to lose money Hedge funds and institutional investors are the target audience for trading. Nobody else can reliably make money like them. As a retail investor, you can profit from one, two, or three profitable trades, but one bad trade will wipe out all of your gains.

Retail investors should avoid trading for the following reasons, as it is a surefire way to lose money: You lack the necessary time and experience. To regularly make money from trading, one needs a great deal of knowledge, expertise, patience, and self-control. You don't possess that level of expertise, discipline, or experience, admit it. Most significantly, because they already work a full-time job, retail investors are unable to commit a significant amount of time. Trading takes a lot of time and mental energy, taking up a whole day. If, as a retail investor, you think you are smart enough to trade, you should quit your job right away and apply to become a professional trader. In the industry, there is a severe lack of competent expert traders!

When determining profit and loss, take taxes and brokerage into account: Let's say you buy a stock for ₹100 and sell it for ₹110 a few days later. It looks like you received ₹10. The real number is different, though. You must pay brokerage, Security Transaction Tax (STT),

Service Tax, and an exchange fee for each transaction (buying or selling). In addition, you must pay the government 15% of your profits in short-term capital gains tax. Usually, these costs are ignored when determining profit or loss. Let's figure out the net profit and loss in two distinct scenarios. Assume that the buy price in the first transaction was ₹100 and the sell price was ₹110, for a gross gain of ₹10. In the second, there is a gross loss of ₹10 due to a purchase rate of ₹100 and a sell rate of ₹90. I'm taking into account 1% of total turnover as brokerage + STT + service tax + exchange charge to make the computation simpler. Therefore, for each 100 ₹ that you engage in either purchasing or selling, you must pay ₹1.

The outcome shown in the above table is unexpected. Whereas a gross loss of ₹10 becomes a net loss of ₹12, a gross profit of ₹10 becomes merely ₹6.5. Hence, a 10% gross profit equates to an only 6.5% net gain, whereas a 10% loss results in a 12% loss. Do you use this method to compute net profit and loss? This is an additional explanation for trading losses. You are up against the odds. Making money regularly is nearly difficult with the way the system is set up. Only the government, stock exchange, and brokers are able to profit from trading on a regular basis. You have to pay them everything each time you trade. Is it truly your goal to increase their wealth? The reasons why free trading advice is risky Why would someone give away free money-making suggestions, or stock tips? Do you receive any free high-quality goods or services in other spheres of your life? Naturally, no! These days, even pure drinking water is an expense!

Everything has a cost, even reading the newspaper and watching movies. Retail businesses (Big Bazaar, Pantaloons, etc.) sometimes give out free gift cards. Why? Their goal is to entice their current clientele to return for more expensive purchases. There are dozens of free trading advice available every day if you tune into any business channel. Additionally, your broker is happy to offer free trading advice. Every day, dozens of websites provide free trading tips. Facebook, Twitter, WhatsApp, Telegram groups, and many other platforms offer tips. There would be a very extensive list of companies offering free trading suggestions. None of them engage in charitable work. None of them wish to become wealthy for you. Let's examine their motivations in more detail: Motive #1: After giving free trading advice to their paying customers, many operators do the same for free. As a result, they manipulate stock prices, benefiting only their paying clients. Let's say I own the websites paidtips.com and freetips.com.

One is for tipping paid clients, and the other is for clients who receive no charge. Customers are unaware, though, that the same individual or organization is running both websites. I therefore give tips to my paying clients before everybody else. I am sending the same to free subscribers after their purchase. The price increases as long as free subscribers purchase the same stock. In addition, I advise paid clients to make a "Profit Booking/Exit" call. Free subscribers are consequently forced to the top. As a result, my paying subscribers are making a profit at the expense of receiving free clients. My goal is to get paid additional money from customers that have already subscribed! This makes it simple to manipulate the price of small- and mid-cap companies with little trading volume. Motive #2: In order to ensure a seamless exit at a healthy profit, operators frequently provide complimentary tips. Here is an actual case study.

I got an SMS on July 23 and 24, 2014, saying, "Sure-shot purchase call — purchase Naisargik (BSE code -531365) at ₹175. Aim for ₹350 in a few weeks. I was unfamiliar with the name of the company, which operates in the microcap sector. Both days had extremely high trading volumes, and the stock price had increased dramatically. Based on the trend, it appeared that thousands of retail investors received the identical SMS from the operator, and many of them ended up buying the stock. The most unexpected information is that three operators sold about 120,000 amounts for ₹19,769,661 (about 2 crores) over those days.

Thus, operators were offering thousands of ordinary investors an SMS to purchase shares with the "guaranteed" goal to double their investment! The stock entered a freefall phase during the following ten days, with a price drop to below ₹100.

Because there were no more buyers, the rate became locked at this low level. As of this writing, the stock is trading at about ₹4. Thousands of ordinary investors vented their frustrations on the moneycontrol.com forum after losing 90% or more of their investment. Check out the BSE website's historical statistics and the moneycontrol.com message board debates to see for yourself. You'll discover the evidence behind the whole incident and discover how thousands of gullible investors lost their hard-earned money! There is no one to save them. These days, with smartphones and the internet, these kinds of activities are typical. The next time you receive a communication like this, exercise caution! Why it's sometimes riskier to use sponsored trading advice

Free trading recommendations can result in you losing your investment, but what about paid tips? Unexpectedly, paid recommendations might bring much more suffering because you run the risk of losing both your membership money and the money you invested.

Just perform a simple web search. Numerous trading advice providers will catch your eye with their impressive track records, 50%–100% monthly profits, and free trial periods of a few days. Let's examine how using a free trial might be a trap for anyone. How do paid stock tip schemes operate? Let me create a stock tip website and advertise, "Our most recent stock trading strategy, honed over a decade of intense research, can predict the stock price movement with 99.99% accuracy." Check out how you can profit greatly from our incredibly accurate trading calls by signing up for our 4-day free trial of intraday advice. A "4 days free trial" will entice a lot of eager investors to sign up right away. To carry out this fraud, a database of demat account holders' email addresses and phone numbers can be purchased. I can get 5,000 dealers' mobile numbers in this way. Think of Rohit as one of the five thousand subscribers. I'll send out one SMS trade call every day. I will now begin my "4 days free trial."

First-day tip: Today will see Reliance Industries advance. Purchase Reliance to make money today. Reaction: Dependency increased significantly. Although Rohit is feeling fine, he is unsure and perplexed. It can just be a matter of luck. In any case, there are three remaining free trial calls. Watch what transpires. Second Day Tip #2: Today is the day that reliance will fail. Profit from an intraday short sale. Selling first and then purchasing at a reduced price to generate a profit is known as a short sell. Reaction: Dependency significantly decreased. Fantastic, Rohit is astounded by the show. This specific stock declined even as the market went higher—exactly as the tip suggested! The trade call must be having issues. His self-assurance grew. Rohit can definitely invest some money if the following advice is successful. He is now eager to hear from the next caller and confirm the performance. Third-Day Tip #3: Today will be a negative day for Reliance. Profit from an intraday short sale. Reaction: Reliance dropped a lot! Now, Rohit is taken aback and amazed. He finds it unbelievable that he got 100% correct calls for three days in a row.

It's an incredible strategy. According to the fourth and last free trial tip, he is now prepared to trade. He's already begun to figure out when he can turn a significant profit on his investment. He is eagerly awaiting the last gratuity. Tip 4: Today is the fourth and final day, and reliance will increase. Purchase for a day's profit. Reaction: In an attempt to make some quick cash, Rohit had put down ₹100,000. Since there was no upward movement in morning trade, he was initially anxious. But during afternoon trading, the price actually increased, and he made a healthy profit! He was ecstatic to book the full profit as per the call. He made the decision to heed the advice at all costs, guaranteeing that he would make a sizable sum of money quickly. He was prepared to liquidate his other holdings in order to use the full amount for trading calls. Now that Rohit has access to the tips, he can see how following them over the next year or two will help him become a millionaire. The 4-day Free Trial Tips have ended. Rohit had already felt the enchantment, as had many others.

Calls that were made four times in a row were accurate. It's incredible to have a 100% success rate over four days. "You already experienced our 4-day trial and noted how accurately we predict stock price movement," reads the next SMS. It took us years of arduous study and research to establish an approach this extremely accurate. Our daily trading calls would cost ₹30,000 for six months if you wanted to continue. For just ₹50,000, you can also sign up for our one-year plan, which is discounted. The same amazing accuracy as our "4 free trial calls" is what you can anticipate. The profit from our trading calls will cover the full cost of the subscription in a few weeks. Even though the subscription fee is hefty, Rohit is so impressed that he signs up and begins daydreaming about becoming a millionaire in a matter of months.

The following day, the recommendations continue, but there's a problem. Not all of the tips are effective. Of ten intraday calls, five are operational and the remaining five are not. It frustrates Rohit. He is facing significant losses after having already made a big investment. Whenever he attempts to make up for the loss, the opposite occurs. The loss keeps getting bigger! Rohit fell victim to a stock advice fraud. Let's see how this con operates now. I had five thousand subscribers at first. I split them up into two groups, Group A and Group B, each with 2,500 members. I make calls to Group A to "buy" and Group B to "sell." The stock price will now either increase or decrease. Consequently, one group will profit. I've already identified the right answer. The "Buy" call to Group A was accurate because the stock increased. I keep Group A and throw out Group B. I'm repeating the process with 2,500 subscribers (Group A) at this point. Send a "Buy" call to one group of the 2,500 and a "Sell" call to the other. One has to be right. Once more, I keep the group that profited and delete the group that was given the incorrect trading call.

After four days of doing the same thing over and over, I had 312 people in my group who got all four of the right pieces of advice. Among the 312 people is Rohit. You can now envision how individuals fall victim to these frauds. It is easy to follow up and collect a final subscription payment by calling those 312 "Target" subscribers. Even if half of the 312 users—156—choose to pay for a six-month subscription, it still leaves room for earning ₹46,80,000, or around 46 lakhs (156*30,000 = 46,80,000). Therefore, it's no laughing matter to get 46 lakhs by defrauding others. The best thing about this tactic is that the individual who received the incorrect call doesn't get any more SMSs or calls after that. 312 of the original 5,000 members are consistently receiving the right call, making them easy pickings! By the way, never ever attempt any such ruse to con someone out of quick cash. Never forget the "Law of Karma," which states that "whatever we put out into the universe, comes back to us." Many traders who offer trading recommendations in real life would boast success percentages between 90% and 95%. Simply type "Intraday Tips," "Trading Tips," or "Stock Tips India" into an internet search engine, and more than 50 websites giving these "Free trials" will come up. It's interesting to note that a lot of them boast amazing prior results and success rates of 90%, 95%, or even 100%.

Additionally, stock tip providers may call you to invite you to sign up for their trial services. Such calls are rather typical in a bull market. I used to get a lot of calls like this. I was first curious as to how they obtained my phone number. It dawned on me later that a lot of businesses sell their customer database. It's likely that our mobile numbers are sold to different stock tip providers once we register a trading account. These days, I respond to these operators with phrases like "I don't trade" or even "I have no interest in stock trading at all." Recognizing phony stock tip sources Recognize the sources of trading advice. Intraday, short-term, futures, and options trading are all included. Be wary of claims of large returns. A claim of a 50% or more monthly return is undoubtedly false. Only pick stock advisors who offer comprehensively reasoned investment advice or knowledge-sharing lessons. The majority of trading tip providers don't offer any reasoning. All they say is "Purchase with target and stop loss."

Inquire as to the reasoning behind the call. Check to see if they can respond to your queries satisfactorily or if they dodge them. Don't let the amazing results and the testimonials of a select few clients captivate you. They too may be untrue. New techniques are being developed to deceive gullible investors. Many operators may also be exhibiting screenshots of significant trading profits to entice new investors. Not that any of those are frauds, mind you. On the other hand, if you start two trading accounts and trade long (buy) in one and short (sell) in the other, one of those two accounts will win handsomely every day. Therefore, by opening two trading accounts, even a novice trader can provide a daily screenshot of substantial trading profits. Don't let the profit screenshot fool you into falling for such traps! Verify an advisor's background and expertise in the stock market before choosing one.

Beware Of Dangerous Traps

temptation from neighbors, coworkers, or pals "Hey buddy, I made ₹10,000 in the stock market today!" A similar letter might be sent to you by friends, coworkers, or neighbors. In a bull market, these kinds of remarks are typical.

The truth is that your acquaintance will not message you as enthusiastically when they lose money; instead, they will mostly share their successes. It's in your nature to enjoy brag sessions about accomplishments with people you know. Sharing failure, on the other hand, is difficult and embarrassing. "My son placed first in his class" is a proud and easily shared statement. Telling friends, "My son failed math," is not as simple. Similar to this, "earning ₹10,000 in a single day" in the stock market is a source of pride. In summary, a claim like "I made ₹10,000" only tells a portion of the tale. Avoid investing in the stock market based solely on incomplete information. Your friends' success story shouldn't encourage you because they can be hiding their losses. In particular, avoid taking advice and reading articles from social media accounts since they are probably not the whole story. Your broker's seduction If you trade often or in volume, your broker will give you a lower brokerage. They'll always be prepared to provide traders with large margin funds.

They might make claims like, "You have ₹20,000 in your trading account," in an attempt to persuade you. Not a problem. To profit more, you can purchase shares for ₹50,000 and sell them within three days. If you're planning an intraday trade, several brokers allow you to trade up to ₹100,000. They fail to convey that you should be "earning for them," not "earning for you." Your broker may also send you email or SMS alerts with trading recommendations. Have you ever seen your broker present a two- to three-year holding term investment idea? They are unable to provide this since if you purchase now and retain them for two or three years, their brokerage business will cease to exist. Actually, though, this is the right thing for you to do! Wealth can only be built through time. Frequent trading will just raise your risks of losing money in the near term and boost the broker's profit.

Temptation from purported experts Any impostor may pass oneself off as a stock analyst in a bull market. Thousands of self-described analysts may be found on social media thanks to the internet. There will be an abundance of stock suggestions on television, in newspapers, and on websites whenever the market rises. Almost all analysts will paint a positive picture and advise you to buy stocks. Remarkably, in a free-falling bear market, the same analysts change their minds. The worst thing is that these analysts will even suggest staying away from the stock market during bear markets out of concern that it may decline even deeper. In actuality, one of the ideal periods to invest is during a bear market because quality equities are accessible at a discount. Furthermore, if you choose quality stocks, the movement of the market as a whole rarely matters. Avoid being overly influenced by any analyst. The stock recommendations provider is tempting me. These days, receiving calls and SMS alerts from different stock tip providers is normal. Ads with a strong visual appeal are very popular.

I've already shown you how any stock tip service can trick you with a free trial. Always be on the lookout for high return guarantees. Numerous providers of trading tips assert that their trading technique yields a monthly return of 50% or more. If that was indeed the case, stock trading would be the source of wealth for every billionaire in existence today. The truth is a little different. Overconfidence Assume, at the end of your first year of investing, that you started in a bull market and were able to generate a 45% return. Every stock you bought was doing well. In a scenario like this, you can begin to believe you have a firm grasp of the material. You continue to increase the amount you invest since your confidence level rises along with the market. Right now, you're acting too hostile. The market crashes out of nowhere, and a protracted bear market ensues. The bear market is what distinguishes wise investors from foolish ones. If you notice that your portfolio is yielding returns that are higher than average in a bull market, resist the temptation to invest aggressively.

The movement of the stock market is not linear. Making money is simple during a bull market, but challenging during a downturn. Learn how to make money in all types of markets if you want to be a successful investor.

The Only Reliable Method Of Making Money In The Stock Market

Investing in a solid company and holding onto your stocks for the right amount of time are the only ways to profit from the stock market on a regular basis. Look up the information of any billionaire equity investor worldwide. They have one thing in common, that's for sure. They invested for the long term and picked reputable stocks. The richest person in the world and most successful investor in history, Warren Buffett, amassed his wealth over more than 50 years of equities investment with an annualized return of 22%. He didn't dive right into futures and options or intraday trading.

Consider this: a consistent 22% yearly return over 50 years becomes a billionaire, however these purveyors of trading tips claim returns of 50% or more each month! Not most likely! Forget about short-term trading, intraday trading, and futures and options. Recall that there are no shortcuts to becoming wealthy.

In reality, all quick-money-making schemes are money-losing schemes. The only way to make money is to invest in quality stocks and hold them for the right amount of time. It is simpler to say this than to do it. These are the apparent queries: What is meant by "stocks of high quality"? How can I choose outstanding stocks? First of all, how can I identify a quality business? What is the appropriate time to hold? When should I buy and sell stocks? How should I put together my portfolio? In the second section of this book, I shall address each of these queries. Let's examine the "risk" associated with equities investing first. You will discover whether or not stock investment entails danger, as well as strategies for reducing risk, in the upcoming chapter. Things to Bear in Mind ➢ The sole route

The key to making money in the stock market is to invest in reputable companies and stick onto them for the right amount of time. ➤ Short-term trading in any form is not a reliable way to generate consistent profits. (Intraday, trading on margin, futures and options, etc.) ➤ You cannot make rich from intraday, F&O, or short-term trading, nor can your broker, stock exchange, or government! ➤ Refrain from succumbing to alluring tales or impressive historical records or screenshots while investing in stocks.

Check the advisor's credentials for expertise and experience. ➤ Never use borrowed funds to make stock investments (margin money, loans from friends and family, etc.). There's a big risk associated with it.

The Stock Market Is Not at All Risky

Rather than making stock market investments, many investors would rather retain their money in a bank account. "Risk" is a popular explanation for this. Speaking with a friend a few days ago, he said, "There is no such assurance in the stock market, but keeping money in the bank at least assures that it won't lose value." While the return on investment from the stock market is unpredictable, banks provide a consistent rate of return. What if I told you that bank deposits are not as secure as you may believe? Allow me to present "inflation," a quiet murderer.

Bank fixed deposits will undoubtedly yield an annual interest rate of between 6% and 8%, but have you ever thought about this in light of taxes and inflation? Inflation, to put it simply, is the rise in the cost of products. For instance, the cost of groceries will increase over the course of a year compared to what it is now. It can also be seen as a fall in your money's purchasing power. If two kilograms of rice cost ₹100 now, you won't be able to buy the same amount for ₹100 in a year. Therefore, in a year, today's ₹100 is not worth the same. In summary, a one-year investment of 100 rupees in a bank fixed deposit yields around 107-108 rupees; yet, the same daily costs will require 107-108 rupees. Taking taxes into account will make the situation worse. Interest earned on a fixed deposit held by a bank is entirely taxed. The tax rate is based on your taxable income. It can reach as high as 33%+ for an individual in the highest tax bracket! You will pay about 10% in taxes on the interest income, even if you are in the lowest tax bracket. A fixed deposit will provide a negative return when taxes and inflation are taken into account.

The irony is that interest rates on bank deposits are inversely correlated with inflation rates; that is, as inflation rises, so do deposit rates, and vice versa. I want to do some simple math. You must first pay income tax on whatever money you save from your earnings. Assume that you are in the 10% tax band and that your income is 100 rupees. The remaining (100–10) 90 rupees would be deposited in a fixed deposit with an annual interest rate of 6-8%. The yield on a fixed deposit will stay between 4% and 6% after interest taxes, since the principal amount is not taxable but the interest income is subject to taxation based on tax slabs. We must now calculate the amount that inflation will be. In context, 10 lacs kept in a bank account will yield about 7.5 lacs after a year when 8% interest, 9% inflation, and the highest tax bracket of 33% are taken into account. You pay income tax on your investment before making any further stock market investments. You would earn enough money with an annualized return of 12% or more to outpace both taxes and inflation. When combined with taxes and 6%–8% inflation, any investment (bank or post office deposit) that yields less than 9% annualized interest is providing a negative return.

To comfortably beat tax + inflation, an annualized return of at least 10%+ (12%+ for the highest tax rate) is needed. Therefore, bank deposits are unable to provide a profit when combined with taxes and inflation. The concerning aspect is that only 3-4% of Indians have any exposure to the stock market, but over 50% of family savings are held in bank accounts. It may occur to you that diversity is the purpose of investing in fixed deposits. Fortunately, there are plenty of tax-efficient debt investment options that provide diversification as well as a consistent yield. The issue is that a lot of people are ignorant of this. Furthermore, many people are not even aware of the lethal combination of taxes and inflation as mentioned in the preceding paragraph because personal finance and the stock market are not taught in schools or colleges. Only an emergency fund is kept in a bank account by me. I put the remaining portion of my savings in stocks. I simply store money in a bank account in case

I suddenly need it for unforeseen expenses; I don't keep it there for returns or diversification.

The Stock Market's One and Only Risk

Purchasing stocks is similar to operating a vehicle. Everyone is not a skilled driver at first. You must become a proficient driver. What would happen if you decided to forego the instruction and start driving on the first day? You have a reasonable probability of being involved in an accident. In the same way, you will always lose money in the stock market if you have no prior information. Money could occasionally be earned, but it would depend on luck. You need to know a great deal about the issue in order to make consistent money. An experienced driver must drive cautiously to prevent an accident. To prevent loss, experienced investors should likewise use caution in their choices and feelings related to their investments.

Following traffic laws can reduce your odds of getting into an accident, and investing in stocks can reduce your chances of losing money by adhering to specific guidelines. There is no formal educational requirement to drive. An MBA in finance, a CA degree, or a comparable degree cannot guarantee success in equities investment. The strategies of profitable investing are accessible to everyone, regardless of background or area of expertise. Although basic, it's not easy. "Simple" in the sense that minimal intellectual capacity is needed. "Not easy" in the sense that it calls for years of practice, self-control, commitment, and a desire to learn. You won't likely outpace inflation if you steer clear of equity investments. Deposits at banks and post offices yield flat or negative returns that are adjusted for inflation and taxes. There are only a few investment options that can yield returns over inflation, such as stocks and real estate.

Over the past few decades, stocks have outperformed other investing options in the long run, both globally and across all asset classes.

Therefore, isn't "zero exposure" to stocks just plain carelessness? By not investing in stocks, are you not taking a significant risk?

The Only Path to Financial Success

Only real estate and the stock market have historically demonstrated the ability to provide long-term returns that are higher than those of inflation. Since real estate investing takes large sums of money, small investors cannot participate in this industry. The stock market is the only avenue for professionals and those on salaries to build wealth. When it comes to investing, everyone should choose the stock market over real estate for the following reasons: Investments in stocks can be made with as little as ₹5,000. You cannot, however, invest in real estate with such a small sum.

The convenience of stock investment is greater for any retail (small) investor. The stock exchange is heavily controlled. Price discovery is therefore far more obvious. The market regulator, SEBI, has taken a number of actions to protect small investors' interests. But price discovery in real estate isn't always clear-cut. Compared to real estate, equity investing offers more liquidity. Stocks are available for purchase at any time, and they can be sold right away. There isn't any duty. You can decide when to sell them—after a minute, a month, a year, or ten years. But you can't buy land in real estate and sell it the next day. All across the world, stocks are available for purchase and sale. The emergence of online trading has rendered physical presence superfluous. A single mouse click can be used to buy or sell. That being said, real estate investing is not the same. With so many benefits and an above-inflation return, stocks ought to be included in every investor's portfolio. Refusing to invest in equity puts your retirement savings at jeopardy.

Ironically, compared to other nations, retail involvement in the Indian stock market is the lowest. The main causes are ignorance and widespread misconceptions. I spoke over the phone with a novice equity investor a few years ago. A rough transcript of our talk is provided below. Trader: I discovered your website a few days ago and perused the information regarding your stock advising service. How much profit can I anticipate if I use your approach? Me: Over the long run, you should anticipate an average annualized return of between 20% and 30%. Investor: Just a yearly 20%–30% return! Me: How come? Isn't 20% to 30% adequate? Investor: Other offers range from 30% to 50% per month. Me: 30%–50% per month! So why do they not engage in independent trading? To be honest, I think a 25% annualized return is plenty. Trader: Since the market is now rising and I want to take advantage of this, I can't say that you are my top option.

Me: Well, my recommendation would be to avoid dealing with anyone who is offering an incredible 30%–50% monthly return. Sorry to trouble you, investor. I do not think that the stock market is worth considering at an annualized return of 25%. You can't come with me. Me: Alright, no problem. Three months later, the same person contacted to inform me that he had lost ₹2 lakhs in trading after having followed the company that had guaranteed a 30%–50% monthly return. I complimented him instead of being shocked that he took three months to learn the lesson, even if it cost him two lakhs. I want to ask you a question now. For this loss, who would you blame from the aforementioned incident? Both the advisor and the stock market will be held accountable by a large number of people! Few would hold the investor accountable. However, in actuality, only that investor bears responsibility for the result. The 7%–8% interest rate on bank fixed deposits is enough to satisfy investors, but the 20% annualized return on the stock market makes them unhappy! You might make considerably more than 20%–30% in a bull market, but that kind of return isn't sustainable and can't be replicated year after year. If your average annualized return stays between 20% and 30% over a period of 15 to 25 years, you can easily become financially independent.

Never forget that Warren Buffett, the most successful billionaire investor in the world and formerly the second richest person in the world, amassed his wealth over more than 50 years with just a 22% annualized return. Conversely, a lot of novice investors enter the stock market expecting a 30%–50% monthly return; when they lose, they blame the market! At times, they go so far as to call equity investing just another type of "gambling" and discourage people from making stock investments!

Don't Ignore the Fundamentals

One of the main causes of the widespread misconceptions about the stock market is a lack of sufficient understanding. Just consider how long it takes us to finish our official education—roughly 12 years. From elementary school to upper secondary education, the path is fairly difficult. After completing our higher education, we select our job route. It takes an additional four to eight years to finish both graduation and post-graduation. After a demanding 18 to 20 years of diligence and commitment, we at last landed a job. You have to put in the 18–20 years of education regardless of whether you work for yourself or are employed by a company.

Your entire income is the product of your 18–20 years of arduous labor. However, it may surprise you to learn that investors aim to make money in the stock market right away! Following five years of study in the MBBS program, doctors practice for a few additional years. Lastly, people can profit financially from their vocation. Nonetheless, a lot of individuals try to make money in the stock market from day one! What would happen if you go through with a crucial medical procedure without the necessary knowledge and experience? Who is to fault for these outcomes? Sadly, when it comes to the stock market, investors tend to leap in without much information, lose money, and then point the finger at the advisor, the market, the business media, etc. Investors, excluding themselves, are willing to place blame anywhere.

Knowledge Investment Yields the Highest Returns

All that a stock represents is a portion of the company's ownership. Think of yourself as the proprietor of several neighborhood eateries. Would you, as a restaurant owner, think about regularly purchasing and selling your establishments? Would you consider selling a restaurant and then repurchasing it at a later date, if your firm experiences a brief downturn? Remarkably, a lot of investors are willing to follow suit in the stock market. Just a 10% increase in stock price tempts investors to book profits, but a 10% decline in price incites fear. Your risk of losing money will increase as you trade more. You can limit yourself from trading frequently if you can see yourself as a co-owner of the company.

We do extensive study before investing in televisions, costly cell phones, or cars. I vividly recall spending at least thirty thousand dollars before I bought my first car.

Over a three-month period, he spent forty hours online, made three trips to the dealership, and then spent some time tracking automobile price movements constantly. I then talked to my family, went for a test drive with a different acquaintance, and bought the automobile. Do you carry out this kind of thorough study before buying a share? When was the last time you bought a costly item, such as a laptop, mobile phone, car, or other electronic device? You make an effort to gather data from reputable sources, the internet, etc., and make decisions based on that data. However, do you use a little portion of your time to conduct research before investing in stocks? Prior to making any investments in the stock market, you should improve your expertise.

This book is committed to assisting you in doing that. You will begin to learn about several facets of equity investment in the upcoming chapter, all presented in an approachable manner with plenty of real-world examples. Like I said, it's easy, but not simple. It is more important for you to learn "What NOT to do" than "What to do." I want to point out at the end of this chapter that you have already started along the path to learning "How to avoid loss and earn consistently from the stock market." I promise that if you stick with it, equities investing will get a lot simpler, easier, and more lucrative. Things to keep in mind ➤ It's riskier to avoid equities investments than it is to invest in them. ➤ When combined with taxes and 6%–8% inflation, any investment that gives less than 9% annualized return—such as a post office or bank deposit, for example—really produces a negative return.

To beat taxes and inflation, an annualized return of at least 10%+ is needed. ➤ Investing in stocks is the easiest way to build money over the long run. ➤ Investing in stocks is comparable to operating a vehicle. It gets easier if you can grasp the material. ➤ The main cause of common misperceptions and the lowest number of retail stock market participants is ignorance. All a stock represents is a portion of the company's ownership. Consider yourself the company's owner.

➤ Before thinking about investing in equity, invest in knowledge.

The First Step in Choosing Quality Stocks

Where Should I Begin? You will find different stock suggestions in the stock market from various sources. Prior to making an investment in any stock, you could wish to assess the stock's quality; nonetheless, the amount of information and financial indicators could overwhelm you.

There are hundreds of metrics, ranging from valuation to balance sheet ratios. Which one should I think about first? What ought to come first? Since profit growth is the most readily available and conspicuously displayed figure in the financial statement, many investors begin by focusing on it. If you start with profit growth and focus too much on it, you will make a significant error. Profit figures are easily manipulated by any business. Moreover, genuine cash flow is not guaranteed by a large profit. In the books, a company may show a million dollar profit even when its cash flow is negative. Furthermore, external debt may provide the fuel for successful expansion. To put it briefly, increased profits do not guarantee the caliber of a company. Check out the formerly well-known, over 100-year-old tour business Cox & Kings. The company reported strong earnings growth through March 2018. In actuality, their consolidated profit growth rate for the fiscal year that concluded in March 2018 was 153%.

But by August 2019, the stock price had dropped from 270 in January 2018 to just 10, representing a loss of more than 95%. The profit statistics were later shown to have been falsified. There are countless instances of strong profit growth in spite of stock prices that plunge 70–90% in a matter of years! The sales figure is what many investors look at next. This presents an additional issue.

Growth in sales does not guarantee a profit for shareholders. It's impossible to predict how much of a sale will be converted into cash or whether it will increase margin. Above all, sales figures are also subject to manipulation. Assume you run a restaurant and serve a large number of patrons each day. This would result in enormous sales. But ultimately, what matters most is how much money you keep. It's possible that by concentrating on cost optimization, your rival is making significantly more money with fewer sales.

Proprietary small firms, with their fixed sorts of expenses and a single source of income, are very simple to grasp. However, the income and expense structures of the corporations that are listed on the stock market are intricate. There are numerous revenue streams, different categories of expenses, and most importantly, they may have multiple subsidiaries. The outcome of all of this is a complicated financial statement. It is simple for firms to inflate or deflate numbers since they can report a variety of incomes and expenses from a variety of sources. Additionally, balance sheets are prepared by large accounting firms. As a result, interpreting the figures for those companies is even more difficult. Many huge corporations manipulate profit figures because they anticipate that novice investors will prioritize profit growth.

The majority of the financial results only highlight the figures related to profit and sales growth. Thus, it stands to reason that businesses will exert every effort to maintain earnings and sales growth at the highest level in order to prevent needless stock price fluctuation. It follows that businesses will undoubtedly make every effort to maintain those growth measures at a level that prevents needless stock price volatility. Consistent stock price movement facilitates promoters' smooth fundraising. Therefore, investors shouldn't prioritize these measures because promoters would never want a dramatic swing in profit and sales figures. The crucial question now is: what will be our top priority if we place the least importance on profit and sales growth figures? The return on equity (ROE) is the response. It is your responsibility as a shareholder to monitor the promoters' use of shareholder funds. Do they add value for themselves or for their shareholders? Let's take a closer look at return on equity.

Equity Return

The Most Crucial Factor Let's say that two eateries are located nearby. You can choose to put money into any one of them.

Restaurant A is turning a thirty percent profit on its one hundred investments. With $1,000 in capital, Restaurant B is turning a profit of $200,000. In the event that all other factors stay the same, which company would you rather invest in as an investor? Based only on the facts, it can be shown that Restaurant B reported a bigger profit. But Restaurant A operates more effectively. Restaurant A will make a profit of Rs. 300 if they invest Rs. 1,000 as they made a profit of Rs. 100. Put simply, Restaurant B has a 20% return on investment, while Restaurant A has a 30% return. Consequently, investors will inevitably come to favor Restaurant A. In a similar vein, you should think about the underlying business's efficiency before purchasing any stocks. Return on Equity is a useful metric for assessing managerial effectiveness.

The amount of net income returned as a percentage of shareholders' equity is known as return on equity. Return on Equity (ROE) is computed as follows and is represented as a percentage: ROE = Net Income/Shareholders' Equity It assesses a company's profitability by disclosing the amount of profit it makes from the capital of its owners. When comparing two comparable businesses, investors would prefer a return on equity (ROE) of 18% over 12%. The term Return on Equity has several different uses. The same information is included in this book's later sections. For my part, I like equities with rising return on equity (ROE) or businesses with ROEs above 20%. Recall that not all businesses with a ROE of less than 20% would necessarily experience a decline in profits. Now, what causes the business to record a higher ROE is the question. The phrase "economic moat" contains the solution.

Competitive Advantage or Economic Moat

Financial decisions shouldn't be made exclusively on the basis of data. It is not reasonable to assume that a business that is very profitable will continue to be profitable in the future. High-growth businesses frequently find it difficult to stay profitable. The explanation is simple: rivalry grows stronger when success increases, and the greater the profits, the more intense the competition. It goes without saying that more restaurants will open in the area if your extremely successful eatery draws large crowds of customers. It will eventually get harder to keep the same level of profitability. As a result, companies that are very profitable typically see a decline in profitability over time as rivals take market share.

Let's now examine how businesses establish an economic moat. The most popular strategy is to provide a superior good or service than those of the competition. Consumers are willing to spend a little bit extra for superior goods or services. You can charge more if you can set your goods apart from competitors. Features, technology, specifications, durability, look, and anything else are examples of differentiating aspects. The issue is that improved features or technology in any product are not long-term viable. The rationale is that rivals will never stop trying to create better items or technologies. Moreover, creating better products comes with high R&D costs. The product will consequently cost more. The client can start to notice prices. Because of the cost advantage, the market leader may be displaced by its rival.

Consider Nokia as an example: Between 1990 and 2010, Nokia dominated the mobile phone industry. Nokia mobile phones were renowned for their high quality and longevity. Over time, Samsung began producing a nearly identical product at a reduced price. Afterwards, Samsung surpassed Nokia to become the market leader with the release of the Android operating system.

In addition to the actual product differentiation, a powerful brand name influences the customer's perception of the product differentiation. Even if the product isn't better than others, buyers will still be willing to pay more for the name brand. Establishing a reputable brand takes time. But popular brands don't necessarily serve as a wide economic buffer. One such instance is Apple Inc. Apple charges a high price for its MacBook and iPhone. The most expensive Android-based phone costs 15%–20% more than Apple's iPhone. Nonetheless, there aren't any appreciable functional distinctions between the two. All brands do not, however, need to develop a sizable economic moat. Consider the well-known airlines Jet Airways and Kingfisher. Because of the way the airline business is set up, it is challenging to charge more for the brand alone.

Encouraging high switching costs or customer lock-in is one of the strongest and most sustainable competitive advantages. It can be very simple to identify brands, superior products, and cost advantages from the outside, but it can be challenging to pinpoint the precise reason behind a customer's loyalty to a specific good or service. The term "switching cost" describes the elements that make it challenging for a client to move to a competitor's goods or services. Money, time, or convenience are just examples of the variables. Customers won't switch to the competitor's goods or service fast if the switching cost is significant. It is therefore easy for the business to expect more from its current clientele. There is a switching cost moat for CRM providers like Sales Force, Veeva, Freshdesk, and accounting software companies like Tally and Intuit (QuickBooks).

It is exceedingly cumbersome for a corporation to switch accounting software once it has set up accounting in Tally, and doing so would also need additional expense for employee training. Remember that switching costs don't always have to be financial. The quintessential instances of a great economic moat that don't require any financial switching costs are Facebook and WhatsApp. There were dozens more social networking sites besides Facebook. The majority of them had to shut down their businesses. The massive online company Google was also compelled to close Orkut, a social networking site. Although leaving Facebook doesn't cost anything, the networking effect makes switching impossible. Numerous free mobile conversation apps are available. But why would I use a different messaging app when all of my friends are already on WhatsApp?

It is quite tough to switch to another platform because of the powerful networking impact that results. Because of the networking effect, Google, Facebook, WhatsApp, Instagram, Twitter, LinkedIn, and so forth are all excellent instances of moats. How Can a Competitive Advantage or Economic Moat Be Identified? Determining the economic moat is entirely arbitrary. Analyze the client base, supply and demand situation, and elements that make your product or service unique. Economic moat identification cannot be done using a precise methodology.

Return on Equity (ROE), however, provides a rough picture. "A signal of sustaining economic moat is increasing ROE over the last five to ten years with stable or improving operating margin."

The Risky 4-Letter Word: Debt

At different points in our lives, we all choose to take out different kinds of loans. Our dream house is easier to afford with a home loan. Our desire to own an automobile is fulfilled with a car loan. In actuality, all consumer goods such as televisions, washing machines, and cell phones can now be purchased with simple interest payments. It is not good or evil to borrow. Everything is dependent on the borrower's financial situation. Nearly all businesses, like individuals, must borrow money. It might be for the need for working money, occasionally for the acquisition of real estate and equipment, or for other business expansion.

Debt is necessary for a firm to grow. Nevertheless, bankruptcy could be the outcome of having too much debt or exceeding one's means. As a result, it can reduce the wealth of all stockholders. Therefore, we must determine if the company can afford to repay the whole debt without jeopardizing its earnings or ability to conduct business as usual. Because analyzing the balance sheet itself is a complex procedure, analyzing a company's ability to repay debt is a difficult, time-consuming undertaking. My goal is to offer a solution that is simple to comprehend. Taking out a loan is the simplest way to grow any business. A business owner should be willing to borrow $1,000 in order to realize a profit of $200 if they can make $20 on a $100 investment. In a similar vein, borrowing is necessary for corporate growth.

The issue arises from borrowing too much. Imagine you are making 10% profit margin but having to pay back 12% interest on the loan amount. Higher sales in this situation will increase your loss because you are losing 2% on each sale. Thus, debt can occasionally turn disastrous. There are many ratios available for analyzing a company's debt position, including the Debt to Equity Ratio. Ratio of interest coverage Present Ratio Fast Ratio.

Of all those ratios, the debt to equity ratio is the one you should really grasp. I won't go into all of the things because doing so will get confusing and challenging for small investors to apply. Let's begin by defining the debt to equity ratio. The definition of the debt to equity ratio does not need to be committed to memory. It will suffice to know how to apply it to accomplish your goal. The definition of debt to equity ratio is given below: A company's financial leverage is gauged by dividing its total liabilities by the equity held by investors, a process known as the debt to equity ratio. It shows the percentage of debt and equity the business is employing to finance its assets.

Total Liabilities / Equity is the debt to equity ratio. Examine a stock's debt to equity ratio prior to purchasing it. The ratio can be found on a number of financial websites. You must review the ratio from a minimum of three prior years.

A red signal is indicated by a debt to equity ratio more than 1 (and increasing continually). It highlights the possibility that the business would have challenges soon. Avoid investing in these businesses. There is inherent risk associated with investing in high-debt companies (notice that the debt-to-equity ratio does not apply to banking and financial companies). Various sets of ratios are available for the analysis of financial and banking stocks. Let's examine the companies with high debt to equity ratios and their stock price performance in the accompanying chart.

The table above shows a noteworthy outcome. Over a one-year and three-year period, all of these companies produced negative returns, while the market index, or Sensex, which measures overall performance, produced positive returns. Therefore, businesses with a high debt load (and continuing to do so) perform poorly in all market conditions, regardless of whether the market is in a bull or bear phase. In 2019 and 2020, the majority of these companies will have generated an additional 80–90% negative return from their 2014 levels; a few will have even reached zero, and a few will have gone bankrupt and been acquired by a stronger player (not comparable to the acquisition of Ruchi Soya by Patanjali or Bhushan Steel by Tata Steel).

Avoid investing in companies with a debt to equity ratio of 1+ (and rising) and declining ROE and interest coverage ratio. Using any year's data point—2010, 2018, or 2025, for example—you will discover that these equities can only produce positive returns if debt levels drop quickly in tandem with rising ROE and interest coverage ratios. Without it, the majority of these businesses eventually demolish the wealth of their shareholders. "Avoid the lethal combination of decreasing interest coverage ratio, ROE, and a 1+ (and rising) debt to equity ratio."

Advancement to the Subsequent Parameters

Hopefully, it is now evident what the first factor is when evaluating any investment choice. There are a ton of stock suggestions available thanks to the Internet and social media. Don't just mindlessly obey them. Determine the trend of the Debt to Equity ratio and Return on Equity (ROE) after obtaining a stock concept. Analysis of profit and sales growth is to follow. The stock should be discarded if the ROE is less than 12% (and declining) and the debt to equity ratio is more than 1 (and rising). Additionally, keep in mind that it is preferable to utilize a combination of numerous other ratios, such as the interest coverage ratio, current ratio, quick ratio, etc., to analyze the debt position of any organization. I won't be going over them all here, though, as that will make things very difficult for regular investors.

My goal is to provide small investors with a fast, simple solution. When analyzing a company's efficiency and debt load, the debt to equity ratio, interest coverage ratio, and return on equity (ROE) are usually enough (excluding banks and financial enterprises). You can watch a live demonstration of how I use a pre-formatted Excel sheet to assess any stock with these ratios in a matter of minutes in our video lesson series, which is available on our website. The live demonstration portion can only be accessed in video format; it is not accessible in any book (text format).Going forward, we will cover simple, useful methods for assessing management with various perspectives and real-world examples in the upcoming chapter.

Points to keep in mind: Businesses can readily manipulate sales and profit statistics. Therefore, the metrics for profit and sales growth shouldn't be the top priorities. ➢ A plethora of stock ideas are at your disposal. Simply perform a basic test (at least trend of debt to equity ratio, interest coverage ratio, and ROE) before investing. The most crucial factor in stock analysis is Return on Equity (ROE). The greater the return on equity (ROE) of an investment option, all other things being equal. ➢ A multibagger return can be obtained by investing in businesses with sustained economic moats, which increase ROE while maintaining or growing margin.

Businesses can build an economic moat by providing superior goods or services, making use of their strong brand, leveraging the networking effect, or keeping clients away from rivals. An important indicator of an economic moat is rising ROE over the previous five to ten years along with better operating margin and cash flow. Steer clear of equities that have both a rising debt to equity ratio (greater than 1) and a declining interest coverage ratio with a return on equity (ROE) of less than 12% (and declining over the last three years).

How to Assess Management

Difficulties in Assessing Management Effectiveness I had perused numerous best-selling books regarding stock investing. I learned from those books how crucial it is to assess management quality before purchasing any stock. As everyone knows, incompetent management may destroy a successful company, but competent management can turn a failing one around.

"How do you judge whether the management is good or bad?" is the key question at this point. To be honest, no best-selling book ever answered my question. Numerous of those works are credited with creating the concepts of factory/plant visits, founder discussions, management visits, etc. Do you believe that a retail investor may visit the factory or have a conversation with management? Let us say that you own twenty distinct equities in your portfolio. Eight distinct cities house the headquarters of the twenty companies. Is it feasible for you to visit all those cities and meet with the management before making an investment? It must be nearly difficult for millions of small investors to meet with management before making an investment in a company. Regarding the analyst's interactions with management, I am also very skeptical.

Assume I am a senior research analyst at a reputable brokerage business and you are the CEO of a corporation. Will you admit to any shortcomings in your business throughout our meeting? Your main goal will be to get my approval so that I may write a strong research report, which will increase the stock price. Ultimately, as the CEO, you stand to gain the most from the increasing stock value. My skepticism regarding the management visit stems from the obvious fact that management would always attempt to present a positive image to equities research analysts. There are numerous instances of well-known companies losing a significant amount of money despite numerous company visits simply by trusting the management's statements.

One of the most well-known instances is the significant loss that renowned brokerage house Motilal Oswal suffered from their several hundred crore investment in Manpasand Beverage in spite of numerous management interactions. However, because you are not alone at the Annual General Meeting (AGM), going is significantly more beneficial. The whole management team is available to answer questions, as are a sizable number of investors. Additionally, participating in a conference call is preferable than visiting a business. Many businesses have conference calls following the release of the results, allowing different analysts to speak with the management face-to-face. A clear image is provided by the management's responses to various questions posed by the analyst community.

However, I am aware that not every retail investor is able to attend every AGM.

Small villages, remote from big cities, are home to millions of small investors. Furthermore, the majority of retail investors work "day jobs." When is the meeting that I should be at every time? If this sounds like you, I can help with some easy fixes!

Most Effortless Techniques for Assessing Management

I'll outline the quickest and easiest method for learning about the credibility of the management. You may assess these straightforward and simple-to-understand techniques from the comforts of your own home! I've put these techniques through a rigorous testing process so you can gain a great deal from my knowledge.

We only need three inputs to accomplish our goal: Pattern of Shareholding, Dividend History, Tax Rate, and Return on Equity (ROE) Let's start by examining how easily accessible the data is. With the development of the Internet, ordinary investors can now easily get this kind of data. Each listed business notifies the appropriate stock market of its shareholding pattern. At the conclusion of each quarter, all corporations are required to reveal their shareholding pattern. Thus, any listed company's shareholding pattern can be found on the BSE website (www.bseindia.com). Through "block deals" or "bulk deals," promoters or institutional investors buy equities off the open market. It is also required to report these transactions. This implies that you may quickly obtain comparable statistics from the exchange website at the conclusion of the trading day.

Both the tax rate and return on equity (ROE) are easily obtained from the company's financial statements. Basic math is needed to calculate ROE. On many financial websites, calculated ROE is accessible, though you should always double-check the information. You may easily see dividend history on the websites of the BSE and NSE. With just one click, you may view the dividend history for the previous ten years. Thus, we have all of these evaluation criteria for the management right in front of us. All you really need is an internet connection! Now, let's talk about each of these factors individually, beginning with the analysis of shareholding patterns.

Management Assessment

Analysis of Shareholding Patterns Generally speaking, shareholding patterns fall into two categories: Promoters and Promoter Group: The people who incorporated the business are known as promoters. They may be an entity (or group of individuals) that is domestic or foreign. Members of the promoter group who possess shares are also their relatives. Public Group: Shareholders that fall under the public shareholding pattern are those who are not promoters. This group includes individuals, insurance firms, mutual funds, banks, money managers, FIIs, DIIs, and others.

Companies or people, other than the promoters, that hold more than 1% of the total share capital need to publish their details. Let's examine the effects of a company's performance as a function of shareholder behavior. Promoters increasing their stake – Nobody knows the company better than its owners.

Assume that you are a company promoter that is publicly traded. You will not buy your own company's shares on the open market if you don't have strong convictions. So, promoters increasing stake via open market purchase is a positive signal. During 2013, I had invested in a micro-cap stock, Fluidomat, based on a similar theme. Throughout the year 2012, 2013 and 2014, promoters were consistently increasing the stake via open market purchase, i.e. purchasing from retail investors.

The company manufactures fluid coupling that has a wide application in the infrastructure sector. Being a small-sized company, there was not enough information in the public domain. There were no management interviews/guidance, no conference calls, and no public appearances. Further, not a single brokerage or research house had active participation on Fluidomat. There was zero institutional shareholding. There is always some risk involved with investing in an unknown micro-cap because you don't have enough information. But, I had invested since, over the previous few years, the promoters had steadily increased their ownership (along with high ROE and minimal debt).

Eventually, the plan paid off; the stock produced a return of more than 300% in just a year after the investment! As long as the promoters continued to increase their ownership, the plan was to hold onto the shares and then sell them when they stopped increasing book profit. Investing in unidentified microcap stocks might be dangerous, but in this instance, the promoters' buying habits reduce that risk. Since the company's owners are also purchasing from the open market, it seems like you're not the only one investing in this business. Promoters may raise their investment for a variety of reasons, but the end effect is almost certainly going to be favorable. It is not necessary for a retail investor to delve deeper into the reasons behind Promoters' stake increases because, in most cases, the outcome will be favorable.

It's not always a good thing when promoters increase their interest through equity dilution (preferential issue). "A higher percentage of promoter ownership increases confidence, which leads to price appreciation or downside protection of the stock price." Promoters cutting back on their investment: This could have a favorable or negative impact on the stock price. Promoters' forced sales could result in a significant decline in the value of the shares. The "forced selling" will be covered later in this chapter. Let's take a peek at things from a different perspective first. A lower promoter stake indicates a lower level of trust among the promoters in the company, indicating a lack of optimism over the future. Can anyone forget the Satyam controversy? The promoters and their group held just 10.70% of the total shares. By the end of December 2008, it had decreased to 2.70%. Then, in January 2009, the share price fell by 77.7%. In this case, the promoters knew about the financial mishandling well before anyone else did. They gradually lowered their investment before making the scandal public.

Steer clear of businesses where the promoters own little stakes in the company or where they frequently reduce their investment by a significant amount. Reducing the promoters' stake isn't always a terrible thing, though. This is because promoters themselves are entitled to share in their company's profits. If they sell a portion of their stake, it might not be all that horrible. In addition, they have been in the business of making money for the past ten, twenty, or even fifty years! For instance, Page Industries' promoters reduced their ownership between 2012 and 2015, although the company's stock price increased by more than 200% over that period.

Another example is Atul Auto, one of my ventures. In November 2013, the promoters decreased their ownership. I was concerned at first, but after doing some research, I learned that one of the promoters had sold his portion of the company to an institutional investor. A major institutional investor's first entry is usually a hint of good times to come. Due to the institutional investor's entry, I had raised my investment. The outcome was profitable. In the following year, the stock yielded a return of over 150%!

However, it is generally viewed favorably when banking and financial company promoters dilute (lower) their stake in order to raise money. Money can be thought of as a raw resource used in the banking industry. A business can lend (give loan) more and make more profit if it has more money. Therefore, although it may decrease the promoter holding, banks and financial companies' fundraising efforts are generally beneficial.

When promoters cut back on their stake, you should thus investigate more. Either a negative or favorable outcome is possible. Investment banks, commercial trusts, insurance firms, mutual funds, pension funds, and money managers are examples of institutional investors. Their substantial share purchases have a significant influence on the fluctuations of the stock market. They are regarded as experienced and well-informed. Small investors thus follow in their footsteps.

There are two categories of institutional investors: DII (Domestic Institutional Investors) and FII (Foreign Institutional Investors). Foreign Institutional Investors' (FII) effects International institutional investors are regarded as the company's darlings. The stock market is driven by them. They are thought of as wise individuals making wise investments.

A larger FII stake is seen favorably, and a smaller FII stake indicates a lack of FII confidence in the business. FIIs only invest money when they are positive and confident about the company's future, therefore it is seen positively if they grow their investment.

Similar to promoters, the sale of shares by FIIs does not necessarily indicate a fundamental weakness in the company. Their selling could be the result of political or economic upheaval, legal issues in their native nation, or just their desire to earn a profit. Whatever the cause, if they dump large amounts, the stock price drops precipitously. The multibagger return key is: Finding a stock that FIIs can identify as a favorite in the near future is the secret to successful investment. A stock price could increase by three to four times or more in a year or two in such a scenario. As an example, in December 2012, I made an investment in Ajanta Pharma. The stock was not being watched by brokerage houses at the time, and institutional players were not giving it enough attention.

Institutional investors began to show interest in the company gradually as its fundamentals improved, its financial performance was solid, and its prognosis for the future improved. FII's investment climbed by 3.81% between December 2012 and March 2014, making up approximately 184% of the total growth in FII holdings. It seems to make sense that within two years, the stock price has returned more than 500% (more than six times) since then. Thus, you may raise doubts about your ability to purchase a stock before FIIs (or institutional investors) do. Domestic Institutional Investors' (DII) effects DII is made up of a nation's institutions or organizations, including banks, insurance providers, mutual fund houses, etc.

As was already mentioned, money managers are aware and skilled individuals that closely monitor all business operations. As a result, they select the stock after doing a thorough investigation and meticulous observation. Therefore, a higher DII investment is advantageous for any stock.

You must combine the buying patterns of FIIs and DIIs to obtain a more comprehensive image. Put succinctly, you must adhere to the combined component of institutional operations. The stock price rises in response to increased holdings in this sector and vice versa. Don't, however, give up on your investment just because an institutional investor does. They can sell because of their own requirements in addition to the company's fundamentals. "A sharp increase in the stock price follows an increase in institutional holdings."

Impact of the Individual Investor Although a large number of people—thousands or even crores—make up the shareholding pattern, individual retail investor transactions have no effect on stock prices since the shares they own are tiny in relation to the overall number of shares. If you locate a business where institutional and promoter shareholding is declining but individual shareholding is rising, you should be cautious as this could be a warning indication of impending disaster.

In brief

Whenever promoters increase their interest through an open market transaction, the stock always benefits greatly. Promoters cutting back on their ownership may have good or negative effects. Entrepreneurs (or first investors) sometimes have to book a profit. On the other hand, the stock price will suffer if promoters are obliged to sell off any interest. The stock price benefits from institutional investors' increases in holdings, particularly mutual funds and FIIs. However, there may be a stock price correction if institutional investors' maximum allowable investment limit reached its cap. There is a negative correlation between institutional investors' reduction of stake and the stock price.

Combine the holdings of mutual funds with FIIs (Foreign Institutional Investors) when taking institutional investors into account. The general public's or retail investors' incremental shareholdings have negative effects, and vice versa. Why is it risky for shareholders to pledge their shares? In a similar vein to how we obtain loans to satisfy our need or desire to become property owners, promoters likewise acquire money by pledging their shares as security. Retail investors should always be cautious when pledging a high number of shares. It can result in an abrupt decline in stock value. Let's examine a few different facets of pledging. What is a share pledge? Because shares are regarded as assets, banks view them as security when granting loans. The act of the promoters keeping their own firm shares as security for a loan is known as share pledging. They take out a loan to finance the company's operations or to meet their own requirements.

Shares are pledged through banks or non-banking financial entities. Why is it so hazardous to pledge shares? The last resort available to promoters seeking to obtain capital is share pledges. It indicates that no one else is prepared to lend money since the company either has a poor outlook for the future or is heavily indebted and may be facing further financial difficulties (in which case pledging is the last remaining option). Pledges don't generate problems when stock prices are rising since promoters may rely on the optimistic value of their investment. Since lenders (banks and NBFCs) are also rather confident in the increasing value of the investment, they don't give it much thought. When the stock price declines steadily over an extended length of time, the issue arises.

Collateral value decreases as share price drops. That indicates that the shares, which were valued at, let's say, 100 Cr at first, are now only worth 50 Cr. Promoters are compelled to pledge more shares in response to the lender's request for additional collateral in order to safeguard the loan amount and reduce risk. The lender has the right to recoup their money by selling the pledged shares on the market if they fail to do this. Thus, pledging may even result in promoters losing ownership of the business. A comparable circumstance involved Vijay Kantilal Sheth from Great Offshore. 2009 saw Mr. Vijay ultimately relinquish ownership of his company as a result of the substantial level of pledges. By committing more than 99 percent of his stock, he had raised Rs 200 crore.

Promoters frequently promise to use their shares to fund acquisitions, pay off debt, and grow their company. When share pledges exceed a particular threshold, they become exceedingly dangerous, and the corporation is left with no other option. Promoters who have given up a sizable portion of their ownership are typically heavily indebted. An illustration of this is Shah Alloys. Of the total shares held by the Shah Alloys promoters, 98.71% are held as collateral. Throughout 2005–06, the company traded between 150 and 170 levels, reaching an all-time high of 252 in May of that year. A sharp decline in the company's stock price occurred after significant share pledges.

This company's debt is accruing rapidly. Falcon Tyres is an additional example. In mid-June 2009, the promoters pledged around 78% of their shares. After a year, strict requirements compelled promoters to promise almost ninety-one percent of their ownership. Promoter ownership was required to be reduced to 31.62% by September 2012, with 97% of the share held as collateral. The stock price of the company experienced a significant decline due to a rise in share pledges and a decrease in promoter stake. Numerous instances (including well-known ones like Zee Enterprise, Fortis, etc.) exist where a company's stock price plummets dramatically as a result of strong promoter pledges. Why do promoters choose to pledge their shares if it is so risky? When there is a downturn in the economy and borrowing becomes more expensive, fundraising becomes extremely challenging. But in order to grow the company, money needs to be raised.

The easy way out in this situation is to pledge shares. Additionally, a corporation that is currently heavily indebted will not be able to obtain additional loans without collateral. The only remaining alternative in such a situation is share pledging. What must investors do in order to pledge their shares? Steer clear of companies whose promoters are increasing the number of shares they have pledged. Investors must closely monitor the proportion of shares that promoters have committed to buying. The company's earnings could be completely destroyed by an increase in pledged shares, leaving no opportunity for future earnings growth. High share pledges are followed by high debt. Thus, repaying the lenders takes up a large portion of the profit.

The ability to share dividends is reduced or eliminated, which has an impact on ordinary investors. Share pledges unnecessarily increase stock price risk. A company of any caliber could fall prey to such circumstances.

A significant number of shares being pledged often results in an abrupt drop in the stock price. Why then should you take a chance like this? Steer clear of these stocks. The list of businesses that pledged the most and increased stake of their promoters as of August 2014 is as follows. Over the course of a year and three years, every company on the list underperformed the market (Sensex). The Indian equity market saw a tremendous bull run in 2014, even though the majority of the businesses with a high (and rising) share of promoter pledges produced a loss for investors.

You will see that many of these companies saw additional stock price declines of 70–90% in 2018–2020. Some of them became insolvent, and taken over by other parties, leaving prior investors with nothing. You can compile a list of companies with high promoter pledged shares (and growing) for educational purposes, then track their performance over time. "Avoid investing in companies whose promoters have pledged more than 30% of the company's holdings, and where that percentage is rising."

Second Management Assessment

History of Dividends and Tax Rate The true cash outgo is tied to taxes and dividends. Those numbers cannot be changed by an accountant. Sales and revenue statistics can be manipulated in a number of ways. It is not possible to manipulate tax and dividend calculations, nevertheless. A "dividend" is just a portion of the profit that is distributed to the shareholders. You have the right to dividends (if any) as a shareholder based on your ownership. Businesses have two options: they either pay a dividend to shareholders from their profits, or they can reinvest all profits back into the company. Since shareholders receive the dividend in cash in the end, it is nearly impossible to change the dividend figures.

Businesses that have been paying dividends continuously for the past ten to twenty years have probably got a strong business. The company is likely on a "real" growth track if the dividend has increased annually during the preceding five years. A further indication of management that values shareholders is a higher dividend payout. Don't, however, take the dividend distribution percentage alone. A capital-intensive company may choose not to pay dividends in order to sustain growth if it needs further investment. "A higher dividend payout ratio in conjunction with a rising dividend rate validates the management's friendliness toward shareholders." As of 2020, the corporation tax rate in India is approximately 25–26% (before, it was approximately 33%). Thus, until 2019 (at the latest), businesses should declare a tax rate of between 30% and 35%.

You must look farther if that isn't the case. Calculate the tax rate on average over the next five to six years and see if it aligns with the corporation tax rate that is most common. Numerous businesses (such as those in the pharmaceutical, chemical, and IT industries) are eligible for tax breaks for producing a specific range of goods or for locating in a specific area. The corresponding corporations' annual reports contain mentions of tax incentives. In the absence of any tax incentive, a company's continued reporting of a lower tax rate over a few years raises concerns about the caliber of its management and corporate governance.

Management Assessment

ROI, or return on equity The most potent ratio is return on equity. It may also shed light on the caliber of management and reveal whether or not businesses are falsifying their financial statements. Reliability and high ROE are signs that the management is making good use of the capital.

In order to manipulate an account, you must either inflate the spending side of the income statement or overstate the assets section of the balance sheet. The best part is that any such event will immediately result in a decreased return on equity. Let's say you need to understate expenses and inflate revenue (sales figures) since you are overstating profit. Your imaginary profit must now be kept in the balance sheet's "assets" section. You are decreasing Return on Equity by doing this. Thus, businesses that falsify their financial statements are unable to continuously report high ROE. Never disregard the average ROE over the previous five years. An average ROE of more than 20% during the last five years suggests that the company is unlikely to be distorting its accounting. Businesses with an average ROE over 20% over the previous five years offer enormous upside potential in addition to mitigating negative risk. Stocks with higher ROE would outperform their peers while all other financial parameters stay the same.

What Next

Stocks can yield multibagger returns when excellent business and management are combined. Infosys is among the most well-known instances of this combo. Other examples include ITC, HDFC Bank, and Tata Consultancy Service (TCS). Early on, figuring out such stocks is like striking gold. Examples of excellent management combined with poor business practices abound, such as Tata Steel and Tata Motors. They are a business that cycles. The economic cycle and macroeconomic variables affect the return on these stocks.

No travel or in-person meetings with management are necessary to complete any of the aforementioned management evaluation tests; they may all be completed from the comfort of your home. Additionally, all of the ratios and numbers are freely accessible online. If you are having trouble getting the last eight to ten years' worth of data in one location for a speedy assessment of your organization, you may want to look at the video lesson series.

IMPORTANT NOTES ➤ Before purchasing stock, small investors find it nearly impossible to visit the factory or management. There are management analysis options that you may complete in the convenience of your own home! ➤ The stock price benefits greatly when promoters increase their share through open market purchases. ➤ Promoters have a number of reasons to reduce their ownership. It may affect the stock price in a favorable or negative way. ➤ Avoid investing in companies whose promoters have promised over 30% of their shareholding, or even more. ➤ A notable increase in institutional holdings leads to a notable rise in the stock price. ➤ The correlation between tax rate, dividend history, shareholding pattern trend, and ROE provides valuable insights about the caliber of management and company governance.

Assessment

Why valuation matters For the following six years, an investment made in Infosys in March 2000 had a negative return.

Until 2013, investments made in Larsen and Toubro (L&T) in December 2007 yielded a negative return. Many people rank the software behemoth Infosys among the best businesses in the world because of its transparent management practices and track record of steady growth. Between 2000 and 2006, Infosys maintained its debt-free position and outperformed return ratio while reporting over five times growth in revenue and nine times growth in net profit. For the last six years, a company that has been growing rapidly, has a spotless balance sheet, and enormous free cash flow has produced a negative return!

What explanation is there for this? It illustrates the fact that the best firms in the world aren't always the greatest investments. Infosys was trading at a price to earnings ratio of more than 100 in March 2000. In addition to reflecting the fundamentals of the company, the stock price also reflects the irrational actions of market participants. Excessive optimism frequently causes the stock price to move into unsupportable territory. Infosys' stock was driven to a P.E. of more than 100 during the "dot com bubble." Do you find another customer to accept an even higher price if you acquire high-quality goods at an unreasonably high price? Of course not. With Infosys, precisely the same thing took place. Any stock's valuation must be supported; otherwise, you will not be able to profit from your investment.

The reasoning behind L&T is the same. Even though L&T is one of the top infrastructure companies in the world, from 2008 to 2013, it had negative returns. Therefore, if you buy at the incorrect price, the best company in the world could not be a wise investment choice. We have studied the analysis of businesses and their management up to this point. Investing success requires that you purchase a quality business at a competitive price. Finding a fantastic company is only the beginning of a profitable investment process. Finding the appealing price brings the procedure to a close. We will learn how to determine an appealing valuation for any company in this chapter.

Typical Instruments For Appraisal

P.E. ratio, or price to earnings ratio One of the most popular and straightforward valuation techniques is the price to earnings ratio, or P.E. ratio. It contrasts the stock's earnings per share with its current market price. P.E. ratio is therefore equal to current market rate / earnings per share (EPS). The ratio is straightforward to compute.

Any financial website will readily provide you with the computed P.E. ratio. The P.E. ratio can be calculated either forward or trailing. While forward P.E. takes into account the analyst's projection of the EPS for the upcoming year, trailing P.E. ratio takes into account the EPS of the preceding four quarters. While most brokerage companies give ahead P.E. in their research reports, most financial websites report the trailing P.E. ratio. The Price to Earnings ratio is meaningless on its own. You cannot consider a stock to be undervalued simply by glancing at it and looking at its low P.E. (say 9). Before making a final selection, a number of other considerations should be taken into consideration. It is impossible to determine if a stock is overvalued or undervalued without considering every other component. Thus, never rely solely on the P.E. ratio.

Take a logical judgment by combining the P.E. ratio with other considerations. The easiest way to use the price to earnings ratio is to compare it to its historical average. This is the most effective way to use the P.E. ratio. A stock's P.E. can be compared to its historical P.E. during the previous three or five years. A fundamentally sound stock may be a wise investment if you discover that it is trading significantly below its historical average. Verify that there haven't been any changes to the company's operating environment or business model. Compare with its industry peers: The P.E. of a stock can be compared to the PE of other companies in the same industry or business. In general, a stock is more appealing from a value standpoint if it trades at a P.E. lower than its industry rivals. Don't rely too much on this parameter, though. This is due to the possibility that two businesses in the same industry could expand at different rates, have distinct balance sheets, and have different cash flows, all of which could affect the P.E. ratio.

L&T and IVRCL Infra, for instance, are in the same sector of business. However, compared to IVRCL Infra, L&T is in a better position to manage future risk, debt levels, and growth. Thus, L&T's demand for a higher premium valuation than IVRCL Infra is reasonable. Why does the P.E. Does the ratio exist? The historical P.E. levels of different companies vary. While stocks from the infrastructure or real estate sectors frequently trade at considerably lower P.E., some stocks (mainly from the Pharma and FMCG sectors) always trade at a higher P.E. Let's examine the reasons behind this now. What motivates them? Greater P.E. is demanded by strong growth. - A higher PE is always required for strong growing enterprises. A company is likely to maintain its current pattern of growth if it has been consistently outpacing its peers in terms of growth across the market cycle.

As a result, investors are willing to pay more for its potential growth. For many years, HDFC Bank, for instance, has routinely recorded growth rates of 30% or higher throughout the market cycle. It follows that the bank will undoubtedly demand a greater P.E. multiple than its competitors. Business Model: Money is everything. Businesses with significant cash flow are less indebted. Furthermore, these businesses have no trouble meeting their working capital needs. These businesses naturally demand a greater premium, which raises the P.E. multiple. FMCG giants Hindustan Unilever (HUL) and Nestle are excellent examples. These stocks consistently trade at a higher PE level, as you will discover. Examine their debt load and cash flow to determine the solution. Conversely, adhere to Larsen and Toubro (L&T), a key player in the infrastructure sector. Their capital-intensive business strategy forces them to incur significant external debt in order to finance their ongoing operations.

An increased capital requirement results in a reduced valuation. Despite the fact that both Larsen & Toubro and HUL are well-established businesses that lead their respective markets, you will discover that Larsen & Toubro is trading at a lower valuation than HUL. Issues with the P.E. ratio Tricks in accounting "E" refers to earning, or simply reported profit, in the P.E. ratio. The issue, though, is that it's simple for a business to falsify its stated earnings. There are various accounting gimmicks that allow a business to exaggerate—or understate—its profits.

One-time income/charges: Income from the recent sale of an organization's assets or other venture is reported as a "one-time gain/profit". The income statement's footnotes contain references to these one-time earnings and expenses.

The P.E. ratio is lowered by one-time income since it can readily exaggerate earnings and profit. In a similar vein, one-time expenses have the potential to have a negative impact on reported earnings, which raises P.E. Therefore, if assessing a stock using the P.E. ratio, pay particular attention to the income statement's footnotes to find such information. Cyclical businesses Businesses that experience boom and bust cycles need to be closely monitored. Companies classified as cyclical are those whose profits sharply rise for a while before declining over time. This continues in an unending cycle of boom and bust. These businesses are referred to as cyclical firms. One such example is the vehicle and auto industries. Companies that are cyclical include Tata Motors, Maruti Suzuki, TVS Motors, and others. Therefore, if a cyclical company's P.E. is low, be mindful that there's a good chance that

Earnings will decrease. The future is always discounted in stock prices. A low P.E. could portend a dismal future.

The P.E. ratio is the most widely used valuation method because it is simple to calculate, even if it has a number of disadvantages and restrictions. Any financial portal will have the calculated ratio available. But one shouldn't base an investing decision just on the P.E. ratio. Be ready to tolerate higher P.E multiples if an asset-light company is expanding more quickly than its competitors and producing significant cash flow with favorable return ratios. P.S. ratio, or price to sales ratio Another fundamental assessment method is the price to sales ratio. It is calculated by dividing the stock's current price by the share sales. It's easy to figure out: just divide a company's market valuation by its stated total sales.

Benefits: - This ratio's primary benefit is that total revenue, or sales, or the "S" component, is rarely manipulated. Accounting fraudsters are more concerned with increasing net profit than revenue. Thus, it is quite uncommon to see a P.S. ratio modified, in contrast to the P.E. ratio. Compared to earnings, sales are less erratic. Businesses with cyclical trends may report erratic profits, but not necessarily cyclical sales. Drawbacks: - The primary drawback of this ratio is that profitability is not guaranteed by total sales. Even with growing sales, a business may still be losing money. Gaining more sales could make this loss even more significant! The net profit margin differs between businesses. P.S. ratio for a low margin company would be much lower. The majority of merchants have low P.S. ratios due to their poor profit margins. Conversely, companies with strong profit margins—like those in the software industry—trade at a high P.S. ratio. Thus, consider the industry the company operates in while evaluating the P.S. ratio.

Best Use: - P.S. ratio is more helpful when analyzing stocks of cyclical businesses, like those in the building and automobile sectors. Any turnaround company can benefit from the ratio. P.B. ratio, or price to book ratio Another crucial tool for valuation is the price to book ratio, or P.B. It contrasts the share price of the company with its book value, which also stands for net worth. In theory, book value per share is the amount that would go to each shareholder in the event of a full corporate liquidation. - Stocks for banking - Ideal Use: For financial equities or banking, the ratio is highly helpful. Bank balance statements contain enormous amounts of liquid assets. The nicest thing is that most assets are regularly revalued because they are mark-to-market. Therefore, a bank's book value is fairly current and gives a better indication of the bank's current net worth.

Capital-Intensive Business: This ratio is a better way to assess businesses with large amounts of tangible assets. A factory, a plot of land, or any other tangible asset, however, is included on the balance sheet at the price the company paid for it, which is frequently not the asset's current value. As a result, the outcomes could be interpreted incorrectly. Cons: - P.B. ratio is essentially meaningless for software businesses in the service sector. Take Infosys as an example; they are generating value with intangible assets like their database, industry reputation, and brand name. The balance statement does not list these intangible assets. For this reason, book value should not be used to assess software companies or businesses whose intangible assets account for the majority of their revenue.

Inaccurate Measure: As was previously said, tangible assets might not have been valued at the going rate in the market. The value that a company paid for a factory or a plot of land is shown on the balance sheet, which is frequently less than the asset's current market worth. Additionally, all businesses own certain intangible assets that are challenging to quantify. For instance, L&T is a prominent participant in the industry thanks to its strong brand name. Nonetheless, it is impossible to pinpoint the precise worth of a brand name. Combining ROE and P.B. ratio: - Return on Equity and Price to Book Value are related (ROE). The company with the greater ROE will have a higher P.B. ratio if the two companies are equal elsewhere. There's an easy explanation for this. The business should compound its book value more quickly if it can generate a larger return on equity. Businesses whose P.B. ratio and ROE don't correlate should be carefully examined.

Similar to all ratios, the P.B. ratio has a number of benefits and drawbacks. This ratio is not as important for software companies or the service industry, but it is helpful for analyzing banking and non-banking finance company stocks and other capital-intensive enterprises.

Investor Misconceptions First Misconception

Cheap stocks are inexpensive, whereas pricey stocks are costly. I have spoken with thousands of investors over the past few years, and I have observed one strange myth. Here are some instances of this myth: I recommended a stock in March 2013 that was valued at Rs. 1200. I was surprised to learn that after putting out the idea, people were asking questions like, "How can a stock priced at ₹1200 generate multi-fold return?" "Please send me some inexpensive stocks; I don't want to invest in such expensive stocks." Since the stock has already reached ₹1200, is there still potential for price growth? The stock reached an all-time high of ₹2300 in less than a year. There are several instances where a stock that was considered "high-priced" yielded a return that was multiplied. In July 2010, Page Industries was trading at about ₹1,000.

The identical stock was trading about ₹7,000 by the end of 2014. Return seven times in four years! Think about MRF, a well-known tire manufacturer. Around ₹3,000–3,500 was its trading range in January 2008 (the apex of the bull-run). It shot up to ₹28,000 by the end of 2015! This represents an eight-fold return from a "so-called" expensive investment in just seven years. That's not all; by year's end 2018, a single MRF stock was trading for between ₹70,000 and ₹74,000. On the other hand, a large number of inexpensive equities (those priced under ₹10) regularly underperform the market. In 2011, Shree Ashtavinayak Cine Vision, a popular penny stock, sold for about ₹7. The stock price plummeted to ₹0.70 (70 Paisa) in just two years—a 90% drop in just two years! The stock had ceased trading at both the NSE and BSE exchanges by 2014. Kingfisher Airlines, Rei Agro, and 3i Infotech are a few examples of inexpensive equities that routinely perform poorly.

Even if the price of a two rupee stock rises to ₹ 5 or 6, one would assume that it might easily yield a multifold return. However, people overlook the possibility that the stock could drop to ₹1, which would result in a 50% loss. As was the case with Shree Ashtavinayak Cine Vision, things could very easily go worse and result in a 100% loss. There are numerous instances of equities that are no longer traded on the stock market yet once traded at a price of about ₹1-2. Therefore, don't believe that the cheap stock can't drop any lower! I still get inquiries for ₹10–20 stocks a day from new investors. A component of their approach is making larger investments in cheap stocks. It is challenging to persuade novice investors that pricing is nothing more than a number.

Compared to a substandard ten rupee stock, a fundamentally good thousand rupee stock has a better chance of double your investment. After all, how many stocks you own is irrelevant; ultimately, only return matters! The simple assumption that "low-priced stocks are cheap" might result in significant losses. This fallacy claims thousands of novice investors. Never forget that the stock price is only a number. Nothing more. Investing in stocks with a low price to earnings ratio is referred to as value investing. When I first started investing in equities, I looked for companies with low price-to-earnings ratios, low price-to-book ratios, and high dividend yields. I quickly came to understand that value investing is more than just locating cheap P.E. stocks. Stupid investors overemphasize statistically low-priced stocks and refer to this practice as "value investing."

This is a significant and frequent error. In terms of statistics, stocks with low P.E., low P.B., and high dividend yield appear inexpensive. Although it can appear like you're shopping for a deal, the majority of these stocks come from dubious companies, or their potential for future profit development is uncertain. Future profits growth directly affects valuation. A corporation ought to fetch a higher price if it can expand at a rate of thirty percent each year. Premium pricing is justified by quality. In real life, we wouldn't think twice about shelling out more money for a high-quality item from a reputable brand. To obtain good quality, pricing cannot be sacrificed. What makes you hesitate to invest in stocks, then?

The Disadvantages Of Valuation Methods

The discounted cash flow approach, or DCF for short, is a financial analysis technique that uses future earnings estimates to determine a company's current worth.

According to DCF analysis, a business is worth all of the money that investors could one day be able to purchase from it. Because the cash in the future will be worth less than the cash in the present, it is referred to as "discounted" cash flow. The opportunity is deemed favorable if the value determined by DCF analysis exceeds the present cost of investing. There exist several valuation techniques apart from DCF approaches, such as asset-based valuation, liquidation value method, and reproduction cost method. I will not go into great detail about DCF or any other method since, while these techniques are nearly flawless in theory, they are useless in practice. DCF is just a mechanical instrument for valuation.

Using this approach, you may forecast the company's future cash flow by looking at its historical performance or business plan. Is it realistic to project a company's cash flow for the next three to five years? The world of business is ever-changing. Your estimation may be totally derailed by changes in government regulations, technology, or the level of competition. How many analysts were right about the future cash flow from mobile phone companies between 1998 and 2000? Online learning service Educomp gained prominence from 2005 to 2007. Numerous analysts projected that there was enormous development potential and that there would be a quick multiplication of return. Nevertheless, the stock's price crashed by 90% after 2008. In what ways can one forecast the cash flows of commodities businesses such as steel, cement, or others?

How do you calculate the strategy for capacity expansion? Is there any assurance that the new capacity will be used to its fullest extent? Is it possible that in the future the competitors won't take their market share? In a similar vein, it is impossible to forecast the cash flow of FMCG or pharmaceutical industries in the future due to variables including changing demographics, increased competition, and regulatory environments. To put it briefly, it is nearly impossible to forecast a business's cash flow for the next five to ten years. Furthermore, the intrinsic value might vary significantly even with little input changes. A small mistake in one of the assumptions can have a significant impact on the outcome. The DCF approach has minimal to no practical significance because of its extreme complexity. The examples that follow demonstrate how little use standard valuation approaches have in real-world scenarios.

Cons with real-world examples: Astral Poly Technik, a small-cap company in the plastics industry, traded at about ₹230 in June 2013, with a P.E. range of 35–40. You would have come to the conclusion that the stock was "highly overvalued" if you had tried to support the valuation using the DCF approach, or any other way. In August 2014, the value of the shares reached ₹800! Over three times the return (250%) from a stock that was supposedly "highly overvalued" in less than a year, with a P.E. of more than 50! Numerous equities, including Page Industries, Eicher Motors, and HDFC Bank, are subject to the same problem. For the entire 2014 year, Page Industries quoted at 55+ P.E. In spite of the fact that no single valuation approach could have called it "undervalued" or even "reasonably valued," the company produced above-average returns during the ensuing three to four years. Another prominent large-cap bank that exemplifies this idea is HDFC Bank.

When compared to its competitors, HDFC Bank has always traded at a premium. In their research reports, numerous experts have expressed a "Cautionary" outlook for HDFC Bank's valuation during the past ten years. These reports are untrue, though, as the stock has a stellar track record of giving investors returns of 25% or more compound annual growth over decades. The conclusion is drawn from the cases of Astral Poly Technik, Page Industries, Eicher Motors, and HDFC Bank that more than one valuation method or formula is required to make an investment choice. You will learn sophisticated valuation techniques in business school, such as the DCF, asset-based valuation, liquidation value, and reproduction cost approaches. You will pass up a lot of excellent chances to make money if you continue to rely heavily on these strategies. Why the valuation method is ineffective Not a science, but an art, is valuation. It is not like a numerical issue that a few formulas can address.

The nature of the stock market is dynamic. Predicting a stock's future potential is similar to valuation. Predicting the future always involves a lot of "what ifs." Handling such uncertainties requires manual involvement. To handle this, a simple formula or a carefully designed excel sheet is insufficient. A quick online search will yield a variety of pre-made spreadsheets using the DCF valuation approach. Technology has advanced to the point where finding software to compute the evaluation is simple. Any existing formula for any stock can be used to independently confirm whether or not a valuation based on a formula is accurate. I can state with certainty that no infallible formula will ever be created, not even in the far future. It's easy to understand why.

Assume that any such calculation determines that a stock's fair value is Rs. 100. Since practically all investors have access to the internet these days, if that formula turns out to be excellent, it won't take long for it to become popular among all investors. All investors would eventually use the same formula to determine the fair value of a specific stock. The stock price will stay unchanged after this. Recall that the price at which a seller consents to sell a stock to a potential bidder is all that the stock price represents. There are always two parties involved in a purchase or sale, regardless of price. After each and every market player determines the fair value at, say, Rs. 100. Will there be a lone buyer at Rs. 101? At 99, will there be a single seller? No one will make an order for anything above that once everyone in the market is aware of the same fair value.

The stock price never rises above Rs. 100 as a result, all buy and sell orders stay at that level, and the market stops. Therefore, the existence of an infallible formula for calculating fair value will never allow the stock market to function. Put differently, don't waste time attempting to find the ideal formula for resolving value conundrums. The stock market would never operate at all if there were such a formula!

The Simplest Method For Determining Value

I try to explain difficult topics in a way that is understandable. The following techniques are simple enough for anyone to use. There are two parts to my method of valuation. First, the historical average is compared, and then P.E. is compared to the average growth rate. Let's investigate the potential benefits of merging the two. Valuation is compared to its own historical average. One may clearly see this by comparing valuation to its own historical average.

Assume that a specific stock's average price-to-earnings ratio over the previous five years has been 20, and that throughout that time the stock has fluctuated between the P/E range of 15 and 25. As a result, whenever the P.E. ratio drops below 20, provided that the company's business prospects do not drastically change, you can consider making a purchase. When it reaches approximately the 23–25 level, you might investigate the profit booking possibility. This is the most straightforward method of determining valuation—as long as the company's business outlook has been stable over the preceding few years and no significant changes are anticipated anytime soon. Let's now examine a different aspect of our valuation technique: comparing P.E. to average growth rate. I have already gone into great depth about P.E. ratio. Since EPS is what matters most to shareholders and profit growth frequently doesn't translate into EPS growth, let's now take a look at the average EPS growth rate over the previous three years.

The EPS growth rate and profit growth will be different in the event of share dilution. If a business grows at a rate of ten percent per year, what would the reasonable price multiple be? The response will change according to investors' tolerance for risk. You can spend up to two times the average growth rate just to be safe. Stated differently, ensure that the current P/E ratio does not exceed double the average EPS growth rate over the previous three years. It is comparable to the idea of the Price to Earnings Growth (PEG) ratio, which is computed by dividing the earnings growth rate by the P.E. ratio. Price to Earnings ratio / Earnings Growth rate is the PEG ratio, therefore. The only change is that I'm taking the average EPS growth rate over the last three years into account. I can sum up the different results as follows: If there are no significant business changes anticipated in the near future, one can investigate purchasing opportunities when the PEG ratio is less than 2. One can investigate the possibility of profit booking whenever the PEG ratio exceeds 2. PEG ratio needs to be closely monitored if it stays excessively low, such as less than 0.3.

This can be a fantastic opportunity to purchase, or it might be a "value trap." A deeper understanding of the valuation can be obtained by combining the PEG ratio with previous valuation. Detailed example: Let's look at the case of Yes Bank to get more clarity. Yes Bank experienced a steady average EPS increase of almost 34% between 2010 and 2014. The stock primarily moved in the P.E. band of 6–22 over that time, with an average P.E. of about 14. So, the following can be concluded: Discount of 20%–40% off the average P.E. bands 8–11: The best time to invest P.E. band 12–17 is around average (mediocre investment opportunity). P.E. band 17–22 is the upper range (explore selling opportunity) Greater than 50% off the average — P.E. band 6–8 (Needs careful consideration) Therefore, the stock will have the finest investment opportunity in the P.E. band of 8 to 11, according to the technique. Yes Bank was observed to be trading in this value zone twice between 2010 and 2014, in August 2013 and December 2011.

P.E. was averaging 10 during December 2011 and the first part of January 2012, when the stock price was approximately ₹240. This is a fantastic investment opportunity based on the valuation approach. It makes sense; by December 2012, the stock price had returned about 95% (reported at ₹470). P.E. ratio was approximately 18, or the top band of the average, at ₹470 in price. hence suggesting a chance to book a profit. Important Note: Yes Bank split its stock after 2012, hence the stock price listed in 2020 and 2025 won't be there if you look at the historical price chart. This holds true for each stock price that is discussed in this book. When a stock is split, given a bonus, or gets rights, the historical price chart is changed proportionately throughout.

In August of 2013, the stock price was approximately ₹280 and P.E. was circling around 10. The stock price briefly fell below ₹250, and P.E. approached 6. Determining the precise bottom is not the goal. Determining the precise top and bottom is not necessary for successful investing. Using the appraisal approach, ₹280 was a very good investment. It makes sense—the stock price achieved a return of more than 100% in less than a year.

It's interesting to note that the PEG ratio stayed below 0.5 over the whole purchasing opportunity zone. The PEG ratio will be less than 0.5 for any price below 17 PE with an average EPS growth rate of 34%. As a result, the procedure is made simpler because the low PEG ratio and lower end of the historical average valuation correspond. The fact that the business prospects should be steady over the coming years is one crucial factor to take into account. In the middle of 2018, the RBI removed Yes Bank's founder, Rana Kapoor, from his CEO role. Yes Bank expanded at a very rapid pace while Rana Kapoor was in charge.

The entire company prospect changed when Rana Kapoor resigned, making the historical valuation comparison procedure irrelevant. The previous P.E. ratio is no longer relevant because the catalyst for past EPS growth—in this case, Rana Kapoor—was eliminated. The historical comparison approach will be effective once more if the company continues to grow steadily and has stable leadership for a minimum of three to five years. Assuming that company prospects stay the same, we can summarize our approach to valuation as follows: ➢ Purchasing opportunities can be investigated if the current valuation (P.E. and P.B. ratio) is less than or stays around the average of the last five years and if the current P.E. is less than twice the average EPS growth of the previous three years (PEG ratio < 2). ➢ If the present valuation is in the highest range of the past five years average and the current P.E. is double the average profit growth rate over the last three years (PEG >2), investigate selling/profit booking opportunities. ➢ In-depth attention is necessary if the current valuation (P.E. and P.B. ratio) is lower than the average of the previous five years and the current P.E. is less than half of the average profit growth of the prior three years (PEG ratio < 0.5). That can be a "value trap" or a fantastic investment opportunity. ➢ The consideration time can be changed in order to evaluate any cyclical organization.

Based on the situation, you can take into consideration any time frame in place of the 3 or 5 year average value. Limitations – There must be restrictions because this is one of the simplest approaches. The method's first drawback is that it only functions in the absence of a change in company prospects. Past data is useless if business prospects significantly change, as they did at Yes Bank when Rana Kapoor left. Due to our dependence on profit or EPS growth rate, the second drawback of the strategy is that it cannot be applied to organizations who are losing money. Therefore, it won't give a clear image of the success stories. However, only two to three of every ten losing businesses are able to turn things around. Furthermore, the turnaround time may take longer than anticipated.

Suzlon, for instance, began disclosing losses in FY2009. In 2012–2013, a lot of analysts predicted a turnaround, but it never happened. Numerous thousands of investors remain stranded on Suzlon. In a similar vein, Bajaj Electricals turnaround from a losing company took longer than expected. As a result, a lot of investors were locked into that stock for a long time. It's wise to avoid such stories unless you have a strong enough belief and a thorough understanding of the industry. Benefits of our approach to valuation: The aforementioned approach is simple to use in contrast to the DCF method, asset-based valuation method, or any other valuation method. Neither the usage of a spreadsheet nor any challenging assumptions are required.

Future cash flow and the discounted rate are not required to be predicted. Predicting future cash flow based on the current company model would need a significant investment of resources because it would require a thorough understanding of the dynamics of the whole sector. Predicting the future also has a higher risk of mistakes. A single, tiny mistake can have a compounding effect and significantly change the outcome. All other traditional methods of appraisal rely on assumptions for their input data. As a result, the likelihood of an inaccurate output rises. On the other hand, our approach uses the historical data as an input. Because the input data cannot be erroneous, the outcome is significantly more accurate.

Have no fear about a high P.E. ratio. Numerous international corporations are present, such as Abbott India, Nestle India, HUL, Sanofi India, Pfizer, and Honeywell Automation. Historically, these firms have traded at a P.E. of greater than 50. The PEG approach might not be effective for these equities, but the historical valuation method can be used to investigate potential purchases. Don't base your valuation decision just on the P/E ratio. In certain cases, if a 50 P.E. stock has superior future prospects and solid fundamentals, it may be less expensive than a 10 P.E. stock. It's interesting to note that the majority of these multinational corporations (MNCs) with historical P.E. ratios of 50 or higher are debt-free, have excellent cash flow, a large promoter ownership, and have zero shares pledged. Put differently, a firm with weak fundamentals and significant debt will never command a PE ratio of 50 or higher over the course of three to four years. Therefore, a high P.E ratio by itself shouldn't be a signal to steer clear of any fundamentally sound stock. Recall that a 50 P.E. stock can rerate even higher in the direction of any number, provided that the business prospects remain favorable.

Only high P.E. can de-rate, which will lower the stock price, if the company's performance deteriorates or its profit margin continues to decline. Thus, the most important factor is a company's core strength rather than its valuation. Investment loss can be minimized if a fundamentally sound company's valuation is incorrect. But, there could be a significant loss on your investment if you choose a business that is essentially failing. Last Remarks: Valuation is an art, as I have stated previously in this chapter. Therefore, don't assume that you will grasp the material right away. Any art demands discipline, practice, and a willingness to study in order to be mastered. You must invest time and effort. Acquiring an MBA degree or any other credential won't be very helpful in learning valuation since the subject is not like solving a mathematical formula. Avoid trying to find a flawless formula to determine the fair value of any stock since, as previously mentioned, the stock market would not be able to continue operating if there were such a formula. You are not required to commit any intricate valuation formulas to memory.

Just put the two easy techniques—comparing the historical average and PEG ratio—that were covered in this chapter into practice. You can become a better artist as you get more experience.

Knowing When to Sell and Buy

The second important question that crosses our minds after choosing high-quality equities is: precisely when and how should we buy? If the stock price increases after the purchase, the situation becomes more complicated. You'll be torn between holding it and buying more since you think your average cost price will go up. For instance, in December of 2012, I made a ₹ 250 investment in Ajanta Pharma. (Note: Ajanta Pharma changed its face value from ₹ 5 to ₹ 2 in March 2015. The price listed above does not take into account any later adjustments or the split of the shares. My original plan was to buy more amounts soon, however 40 days after I made my purchase, the stock price greatly increased and reached ₹440! I wasn't sure if I should add anything further at this point.

Within 40 days of my acquisition, the stock had returned 75%, and I couldn't help but wonder, "Is there still room for further appreciation?" Will adding extra quantities at ₹440 not impact my total return? I was unable to buy larger quantities because of numerous identical queries. To be honest, I lacked the bravery to purchase larger quantities. But my original thought was different. The upswing wasn't accidental; the fundamentals supported it. The enhanced future perspective and the better-than-expected quarterly result were the primary drivers of the price rise; nonetheless, I was unable to contribute more. Let's now examine the repercussions. Ajanta Pharma exceeded the 1500 threshold in 2015. Gain of almost 400% over the initial purchasing price.

Let's now examine two distinct scenarios and determine profit in each: First Scenario: My initial acquisition The second scenario: Buying again at different points in time (at higher rates) First Situation: This is the most straightforward way to figure out profit when there isn't a "repeat buy." A single investment of $250,000 for 1000 shares at a price of $250 each results in a profit of $1,250,000 overall. (For further information, see the comparison table.) Second Scenario: Let's now examine the scenario in which a customer makes repeat purchases during the trip. To be honest, after making my initial buy, I got the opportunity to enter three more times, and each time I realized that the stock could be bought.

In August and October of 2013, I had the opportunity. Despite having adequate cash on hand, I was unable to carry out the plan.

If I had made repeat purchases on those three occasions, the detailed purchase pattern is displayed in the chart below. Total Profit Calculation: The difference between the two scenarios' profits demonstrates how much I lost out on receiving a higher return from this exceptional business. The first case has a larger profit in percentage terms, but the "repeat-buy" scenario has a far larger profit in absolute terms. I was able to get much more. I was able to identify a "true" gem, but I was unable to maximize my profit from it. These kinds of opportunities are rare and difficult to come by. Therefore, we ought to try to take advantage of this chance if we can identify it.

Even after a 100% or 200% price rise, one should not be afraid to buy more if the fundamentals are still there and getting better. Important Note: If the stock has a split, bonus, or other event, the stock price given in the book may not match up with future dates. On the financial website, there is a split/bonus adjusted historical price chart. For instance, Ajanta Pharma split in March 2015, moving from a Face value of ₹ 5 to a Face value of ₹2. As a result, the historical price turned one-fifth, a change that is not shown in the table. If the stock experiences a split or bonus in the future, the historical price will also fluctuate proportionately, something that the book is unable to depict. Advice for Investing If the outlook for the business improves further, a fantastic stock can still be bought even after it has appreciated in value by 100%. It's never too late to invest in an exceptional firm with significant growth potential. As long as you can identify a "true" gem, timing is irrelevant. You won't be let down in the long run, even if you buy a good stock during a bull run. All that is required is that it be a genuine "quality stock."

This remark will be made clearer by using the example of a well-known "high quality" stock ITC. Assume you bought ITC during the height of the bull market in 2007–2008. Let's examine the effects on the performance of your investment: Over the following two years, the stock had a positive return, even from the January 2008 top of the bull run. As a matter of fact, the stock returned 100% of its 2008 peak value during the following four years! Thus, quality is the most important factor. It needs to be a very "Great" Stock. With hindsight bias, one can still dispute the aforementioned point of view. If, on the other hand, you can find a "truly" outstanding evergreen business (albeit they are uncommon), then entry time becomes less significant. A successful company does well in every economic cycle. Great companies will continue to operate at a high level for an extended length of time, regardless of the level of inflation or the direction of the interest rate cycle. As there are so few stocks of these gems, finding them might be challenging. As a result, they consistently trade higher than their peers. The greatest endorsement for these stocks comes from the fact that they barely decline in value even during a market correction. Conversely, during the bear phase, equities with ordinary or weak fundamentals see a substantial correction.

Important Point: No one can pinpoint the precise high and low points of a stock (or market cycle) during a given time frame. A stock cannot be continuously purchased at the low price and sold at the high price. It's just a matter of chance if you can pull it off once or twice. Repeating something repeatedly is nearly impossible. You as an investor don't have to worry about the timing any longer. You should be more concerned with quality since high-quality equities can still help you build wealth even after a 50% or 100% rise.

Frequently Held Myths to Avoid

First misconception: Investing in stocks that are within 52-week high range is not a secure bet. I suggested La Opala RG, a stock, for ₹52 in March of 2013. At that point, the stock was trading close to its all-time high. Some of my clients responded to this advice in the following ways: "I don't like to invest in equities that are close to lifetime highs. Give me some good names that are undervalued and near the 52-week low. "The stock has already reached its peak for the lifetime. Thus, how can you anticipate a favorable outcome at this juncture? "Is it safe to buy a stock that is in its lifetime high range?"

For the next two to three years, the stock maintained its trajectory, reaching the new all-time high. Over the following 18 months, the stock increased by more than 480% from the recommended price range. The price of the stock was ₹ 310 in September of 2014. Approximately six times gain in a year and a half. Throughout this voyage, the stock repeatedly reached lifetime highs, setting new records. Those who refrained from investing due to the lifetime high range stayed mute during the entirety of the remarkable comeback. I was also guilty of this kind of bias in my early years of equity investment. While stocks that consistently reach new all-time highs may not initially appear like a good investment, the truth is that if a firm can maintain its current rate of growth, it has the potential—no, I must say will eventually—to consistently reach new all-time highs. Particular attention should be paid to stocks (mostly small- and mid-cap stocks) that reach new lifetime highs in bumpy or negative markets.

These might turn out to be excellent investments. erroneous belief #2: Stocks with a 52-week low range are more likely to rise. The internet has made it simpler to discover equities that are trading close to 52-week lows. These equities pique the interest of many investors. Not many people think of these equities as "undervalued." Marking a stock is "undervalued" based only on the market price would be a grave mistake. A dramatic decline in stock price does not guarantee a dramatic rise. Consider Educomp as an example. The stock generated a return of about ten times between 2006 and 2008. In the middle of 2009, the stock price crossed the 1000 threshold. In the ensuing year, it fell to about 500 levels. Several investors bought in after such a drop, thinking it would rise to its former heights. The following ten years, from 2010 to 2019, saw the stock consistently reach new all-time lows. Educomp was accessible for just one rupee as of December 2019. Imagine, a thousand to one! One of the biggest destroyers of wealth during the past ten years is Educomp. Many investors lost money because they put their hard-earned money in the stock each time it hit a new low.

Investing in these stocks and labeling them as value buys is a grave mistake made by investors. In the market, there is a common notion that "what falls down must go up." The saying "what falls down may fall sharper in the future" is regrettably true. A 52-week low in stock price can be sustained year after year without concern due to deteriorating business fundamentals. There are numerous other examples other than Educomp, such as Unitech, Kingfisher Airlines, IVRCL Infra, Lanco Infra, etc. Following such a freefall, a large number of smallcaps and midcaps even disappeared from the stock market. Thus, never base an investment decision solely on the "52-weeks low" criterion. Learn why a stock is trading at a 52-week low. An underperforming company can consistently lower stock prices. Avoid becoming ensnared. Later on, getting out of these kinds of situations becomes difficult. Even in a bull market, it is always prudent to avoid equities that are frequently setting new 52-week lows.

How Soon Should I Sell My Stock? Improved Possibilities

Investing has only one goal: to maximize return while taking measured risks. You should switch to the superior investment option if you can find any better ones than the one you currently own. Holding a stock for a few years or because it produced a nice return in the past is not enough reason to keep it. Investors frequently develop strong emotional attachments to their holdings, making it very challenging to sell. ITC generated about four times the return between 2009 and 2013. However, the stock turned range-bound in mid-2013. Based on my estimation, ITC will not be able to produce a return comparable to four times over the next four years (2013-2017). Therefore, switching to different equities will provide better return prospects. In 2011, I made an investment in ITC.

I sold all of my shares at a 60% profit in the middle of 2013 and put the money back into Yes Bank. My return would have been restricted to 60–65% if I had stuck with ITC; but, switching to Yes Bank allowed me to earn 60% and thereafter 50%. Without a doubt, one of the highest-quality stocks is ITC, which is also fundamentally superior to Yes Bank. Yes Bank is not a defensive bet, but ITC is. Yes Bank and other midcap banking stocks are extremely erratic. There are numerous reasons not to switch from ITC to Yes Bank. However, all I was thinking about at the moment was the possibility of a higher return. ITC had become pricey following a few years of run-up, and the valuation did not keep pace with its profits growth. Conversely, Yes Bank maintained the lowest level of non-performing assets (NPA) in the industry while growing at a rate of more than 20% annually throughout economic cycles, and the bank's valuation was also appealing. Similarly, I had profitably sold off all of Yes Bank over the course of the following two years in order to reinvest in a superior opportunity. Avoid developing an emotional attachment to any asset. Past winners are not guaranteed to perform in the same way going forward.

Even if the stock has historically yielded multifold returns, don't be afraid to move on to more promising prospects. Purchasing Mistake If, after purchasing any stock, you later determine that your initial purchase was a mistake, sell the stock as soon as possible. Let's say you paid ₹100 for a stock, and three months later it was only worth ₹80. You discover during this time that your purchase selection was incorrect. It could be the result of incorrect estimates of financial ratios, incorrect assumptions, or bad advice followed. For any reason, you ought to leave as soon as possible. Whether the stock has increased or decreased by 20% from your buy rate is irrelevant. It gets simpler to quit in these circumstances if the stock price is 20% higher than your buy rate. In contrast, though, if you discover that the stock has dropped 20%, it becomes extremely tough to sell. Investors anticipate a resurgence to sell close to the original purchase price and make up for the loss. However, this is a risky strategy that is likely to increase the extent of your loss.

2012 saw the ₹30 purchase of Unitech by one of my clients. The stock price fell by thirty percent in June 2013 and was trading at about ₹20. I told him at the time to book a loss on Unitech because its fundamentals were getting worse and put the money back into PI Industries. He sold Unitech and recorded a 30% loss after first delaying it. Furthermore, he bought PI Industries with the money he had recovered. Unitech fell to ₹14 by the end of 2013, whilst PI Industries produced a return of over 90%. Had he stayed with Unitech in the hopes of becoming better, he would not only be feeling regret now but would have also missed out on such fantastic profits from PI Industries. The valuation is over inflated. If a stock's valuation rises too high, it's time to sell. The issue is in the lack of fast-forward guidelines to determine if the valuation is excessively high. When used alone, the Price to Book (P.B.) or Earnings (P.E.) ratios are unable to reveal anything about valuation. While a business with a PE of 10 may be overpriced, a stock with a PE of 50 may not be pricey. The identical topic was covered in the "Valuation" chapter. "In general, you can consider a stock to be overvalued if it is trading at a significantly higher price-to-earnings ratio than it has historically traded at with no improvement in the stock's future prospects." A different approach is to monitor market capitalization.

The company's own market size speaks volumes. Examine the market's overall size in relation to its market capitalization. Let's use an example to better grasp this. The whole telecom industry had a market value significantly smaller than that of telecom giant Bharti Airtel, which had a market valuation of about 200,000 crores in 2007–2008. Thus, you should be on the lookout anytime a stock's market capitalization surpasses that of the entire industry. Similar demands for abnormal market capitalization were made by real estate businesses like DLF and Unitech in 2007–2008, which is a surefire indicator of stretched valuation. Eventually, the price collapse will be apparent. In this instance, the same thing took place. Unitech reached a lifetime high of ₹546 in January 2008. However, the stock price fell by about 95% in the ensuing ten years (after January 2008), and by the end of 2019, it was only worth one rupee! Find out the size of the industry as a whole, the company's total revenue, and then compare it to the market cap.

Is there still space to expand? Is there a general feeling of excitement about a certain stock or industry? If so, the stock price will eventually plummet. So, as soon as you notice these signs, you should leave.

Shift in the Foundations Business foundations can frequently shift suddenly. Deccan Chronicle Holdings Ltd (DCHL), for instance, owned a number of well-known periodicals and newspapers. In their particular niche, they were the market leaders. Later on, though, they began to diversify in unrelated areas. The leisure, retail, and bookstore chain Odyssey was purchased by them for approximately 60 crores. Consequently, in January 2008, DCHL paid $107 million to acquire the Deccan Chargers, an IPL cricket team. The fundamentals had changed and were no longer sound, therefore anyone holding the stock at this point merely because of its market leadership in newspapers had to have sold it right away. The company's unrelated diversification led to massive debt accumulation and eventual bankruptcy. When compared to its all-time high of ₹270 in December 2007, the stock price dropped to ₹3! Yes, just ₹3! Loss of 98% in 7 years.

In a similar vein, you should sell a high-growth stock right away if the growth outlook changes later or if an outside event makes growth challenging. When your original rationale for buying a stock no longer holds true, sell it. Educomp was regarded as one of the "sunrise sector's" fastest-growing businesses from 2006 to 2009. This stock attracted a lot of attention from investors due to its strong growth rate and superior stock price return. Between 2006 and 2008, the stock produced a return of around ten times. But after 2009, everything absolutely altered. Growth slowed, and the business had reached the end of its potential. Despite this, a lot of investors decided to hold it in 2010 due to its allegedly "attractive valuation." Investing in a high-growth stock and

One of the biggest blunders an investor can do is to keep holding it despite the low valuation. It might totally destroy your fortune. Examine the shares of Educomp. Almost 99% of the stock price has been lost from the 2009 peak. By the close of 2019, the value of the stock plummeted to barely one rupee! There are countless instances where a shift in the fundamentals rendered the investment thesis entirely erroneous and so called for a total withdrawal.

If fundamental changes cause a "high growth stock" to lose momentum, investors should sell it right now. Investing in such stocks can only increase losses. Management Transitions: Excellent management has the power to transform an average company into a remarkable one, and poor management has the power to turn a successful company into a failing one. A shift in the leadership position is one of the significant occurrences that investors should take into consideration when making judgments. Among the most popular instances is Infosys. The company reached various new heights under the direction of N. R. Narayana Murthy. Subsequently, Infosys began to lose its luster after Mr. Murthy left the board. After Infosys was displaced, Tata Consultancy Services (TCS) emerged as India's most valuable IT company. Infosys' growth was slower than that of its contemporaries. During the same time frame, the stock price underperformed as well. Since Mr. Murthy had set the standard so high, it was challenging for his successors to keep it there. There are numerous such instances where a fantastic business has fallen from grace simply as a result of a purchase by another entity or a change in the core management.

Formulate a Preliminary Exit Strategy When Purchasing Stocks: The right investment necessitates a planned withdrawal strategy. It should be easy for you to leave if your buying purpose is apparent. For example, if a stock has been growing at a pace of more than thirty percent, you should sell it when the growth slows. Never give it another thought. If the growth rate slows down and the stock price drops, don't rate the same stock as a "value buy." For instance, BHEL (Bharat Heavy Electricals Limited) was regarded as one of the high-growth stocks from 2004 to 2007. After 2009, the growth rate decreased, and a lot of investors gave the stock a "value buy" rating. If your investment was made with the expectation of growth, it would be best to sell as soon as you notice the first indications of a downturn. Likewise, if you buy a stock based on a subject such as the depreciation of the rupee or the interest rate cycle, you ought to sell it as soon as the cycle turns around. Whether you are in profit or not is irrelevant. India's currency saw significant depreciation in 2013. In these circumstances, sectors focused on exports benefit the most. Since they earn in dollars and spend in rupees, the information technology industry has benefited the most from the rupee's depreciation, which has improved their profit margin.

The cycle began to reverse in 2014. After a severe devaluation, the rupee steadied at about 60 to the dollar. Investors who bought IT stocks only on the basis of the "rupee depreciation" thesis need to have sold them by now. If you have specific motives for investing, selling becomes considerably simpler. Therefore, create an exit strategy before investing and adhere to it strictly. Don't Remorse After Selling: "I am losing 50% because the stock price increased by 50% after I left the company," is a common admission made by investors. A similar situation happened to me when the price significantly increased following the exit. Because of a strong monsoon, I made an investment in PI Industries (Agri Input Company) in June and July of 2013 for about ₹130. The business was offered at a fair price, had a solid balance sheet, and was expanding at a good rate. But "better monsoon forecast" was the main factor in my entry. The monsoon has been exceptional this season, just as predicted. Nearly all of the agriculture-related businesses did well. The following three quarters saw great performance and results from PI Industries as well. After investing, I was sitting on a 100%+ gain in just eight months. Moreover, the Meteorological Department predicted low rainfall and maybe a drought-like scenario in March 2014. I sold all of my shares for about ₹260 without giving it a second thought, making 100% profit in ten months.

My investment in PI Industries was based on the expectation of a strong monsoon; but, as the drought developed, this expectation was weakened. So I turned to leave. But as time went on, the monsoon projection was shown to be inaccurate. The weather department's prediction of a dire situation didn't materialize. PI Industries kept up its fantastic performance. The stock price was trading at about ₹500 by the end of 2015. An additional 100% profit on my selling rate. What then ought to be the next step? Should I feel guilty now that the stock has doubled from my exit point? Of course not! Even if the stock price rises 500% from my exit level, I won't worry. I simply carried out the predetermined plan that I had created. Thus, I'm content with it. There's no use feeling sorry. Dozens of stocks double in value annually. But you don't have to take advantage of every chance to earn money! After selling, don't regret it. You have to acknowledge that no one can know who is at the top and when to let up. It is nearly impossible to time the market. You might occasionally be able to get out at the top, but it is entirely dependent on luck. It is a fact that you cannot purchase at the exact lowest price and sell at the exact highest price.

In general, clearly state your motivation for buying the stock before making an investment, and put it in writing. Continue to keep an eye on those reasons for purchases, and when those reasons change, sell. Selling decisions are more difficult and perplexing in the early years of an investment profession, but if you document every buying rationale, eventually they will be simpler. "Be sure to record the reasons for the purchase; this will greatly assist you in making the selling decision."

Dangerous Errors to Steer Clear of
Error #1

Purchasing equities from prior bull markets: Purchasing previous winners provides comfort to many investors. For instance, in 2012, I was contacted by an investor who had experienced an 80% loss on his portfolio. An examination of his portfolio in detail revealed that he had bought equities that dominated the market during the previous bull run from 2010 to 2011. His portfolio included stocks from companies like Unitech, DLF, BHEL, JP Associates, etc. There was a massive bull run in the Indian stock market from 2005 to early 2008. The top performing stocks were real estate and infrastructure. Stocks that led the bull market and were highly preferred by investors included Unitech, DLF, BHEL, and others.

It burst around the beginning of 2008. These equities' 2008 peak prices had fallen by 50% to 80% by 2009. It's possible for previous winners to run up, but it's difficult to replicate the same pattern. Regretfully, a lot of investors were caught off guard during this slight decline. The unexpected figure is displayed in the chart above. Even Infosys required six years to reach its peak performance. Wipro reached a record-breaking high in March 2000. It was still unable to reach the prior peak even after 15 years. You can see a few well-known large-cap names in the graphic above. Aside from them, hundreds of small- and mid-cap stocks that led the previous bull run have just disappeared from the market. Numerous smallcap software companies disappeared after the dot-com bubble. Those names are difficult to remember. Thus, avoid equities from prior bull markets with caution. Additionally, it's best to avoid touching smallcap stocks that led the prior bull run.

Error #2: Prolonged detention of losers The excitement of winning is always eclipsed by the fear of losing money. While avoiding losses is always the goal of investors, many of them make serious mistakes along the way that increase their losses. What would you do, for example, if you bought a stock for ₹100 and it dropped to ₹50 a year later? The majority of ordinary investors either add more to average out their purchase price or hold the stock in the hopes that it would return. Sadly, both are fatal errors that will only increase your loss. To better illustrate the dilemma, consider the following example: One of my clients' portfolios caught my attention when I was looking over it. Suzlon, a single stock that made up over 40% of his shares in his portfolio, was experiencing a 50% drop! I questioned him about why the allotment was so high.

It was a startling answer. At each dip, he increased his stock holdings steadily to average his purchase price. He spent ₹1,46,000 on 1,950 equities in this manner. As of 1,46,000/1950, the average buying price per stock is ₹ 75. He kept buying in order to average out the purchase rate per share, even though he was aware that the company fundamentals might not improve anytime soon. His buying rate per share was originally ₹90, but after making multiple repeat purchases, it dropped to ₹75. Ironically, even though he was able to average out his acquisition cost, he continued to multiply his loss throughout this process. He held the stock for two years and made multiple purchases before selling it all at ₹30 per share. Let's now compute his loss taking into account two distinct scenarios: Scenario 1: This was his first state, where he made multiple purchases to average his acquisition cost. The original situation results in a total loss of ₹ 87,500, as seen in the table above. Had he stopped after the initial purchase, ₹ 60,000 would have been the whole loss.

An astounding 27,500-dollar difference! Even though he reduced his average buy cost, he made a serious error in the process.

Conversely, a stock loss of 10%–30% does not justify an investor's sale of the shares. Nothing to be concerned about if the foundations hold true. In a bear market, even the highest-quality stocks are susceptible to a 10%–30% price correction. Keeping too long in order to reduce loss I discovered that one of my clients was sitting on a loss of almost 50% of their investment in BHEL (Bharat Heavy Electricals Limited) during another examination of their portfolios. This business used to be regarded as blue-chip. But things took a turn for the worse after 2008. I recommended that he leave BHEL and read a book on loss. It hurts to sell a stock at a 50% loss, but I told him to get out before it hurts any more. Regretfully, the customer put out a different argument. At the time of the chat in 2012, the stock price was approximately ₹250. He had bought it for around ₹500 in 2010. He identified as a long-term investor and predicted that he would be able to recoup the loss in two to three years.

The stock was showing a 50% loss in his portfolio after two years of holding, but he was still willing to hold for an additional two to three years to make up the deficit! What would be the net gain even if the stock price reached the 500 levels (his initial buy rate) in an additional two years? After four years of investment, there was no net gain! Wouldn't it be wiser to register a 50% loss and use that money to reinvest in higher-quality equities in order to make up for the loss? I didn't get this message through. He decided to stick onto his shares instead of selling the stock as a result. A year later, in 2013, the stock price fell even lower to the 170-190 mark. I received another call from the client at this time. This time, he was irritated by the significant loss. ₹500 to ₹170. After that, the loss went from 50% to 66%. That was also my recommendation. Selling a failing company and reinvesting the proceeds into excellent stocks with strengthening fundamentals is always a wise move.

Whatever your notional loss, sell losers and close the difference with winners. At ₹170, the client eventually sold his whole position. He ultimately suffered a 66% loss. He might have limited his loss to 50% if he had sold at ₹250. Investors often retain losers for extended periods of time and take early profits from wins. You must take the opposite action. Retain the winners to optimize your profit and divest from the losses. Trying to minimize loss by holding on too long will ultimately backfire. I have no doubt that many of you have encountered this kind of problem when making investments. How ought one to proceed? If the justification for the purchase has been shown incorrect or is no longer valid, withdraw from your investment. When selling, don't check your purchasing rate. If not, you'll become stuck. When you discover that the current market price is less than your buy rate, your emotions will prevent you from selling. This is an issue that many ordinary investors face. They wait for a recovery even if they are aware that something is amiss. They anticipate that eventually the stock price would approach the purchase rate, allowing them to either minimize the difference or recover their loss, but the opposite occurs. Loss gets bigger still!

While losing money hurts, it can be devastating to let the loss grow. Error #3: Sell winners too soon. Say your portfolio consists of ten equities. Six stocks are showing a 20%–30% loss, while four are showing a 20%–30% rise. Which order of importance should be used when selling?

Retail investors tend to keep the losers and rush to book gains. As a result, they continue to accumulate low-quality stocks and discard high-quality stocks. You might think that eventually the losers will turn things around and continue to hold. Not everything that falls will always rise. That which falls today can fall again tomorrow if the underlying business is weak. Losers deserve your whole attention. Why is the price of the stock declining? Is this a temporary occurrence or is there a good reason? The market's general weakness may force the stock price to correct. This kind of adjustment is only momentary. Nonetheless, the price adjustment resulting from the underlying decline is irreversible.

It needs to be distinguished. Verify your investment justification again. You could be mistaken from the start. Later on, your supposition can turn out to be incorrect. In any event, don't be afraid to book a loss if you were mistaken. Recognize your errors and put that money back into high-quality stocks to help you recover. Error #4: Offloading to purchase at a reduced price - During a price correction, a lot of investors sell their profitable stocks at a higher price only to buy them again at a lower one. The stock price rises during this period, frequently with no correction. Why sell your investment at the first sign of profit if you think it has potential? Should the stock price correct without a shift in the underlying factors, it is preferable to make more investments at lower prices. Avoid timing the market. It is possible that you will not be able to reenter at a lower level after selling. You're holding out for a lower level, and when it happens, the stock makes a U-turn. The stock price has never fallen into the range you were hoping for, and you are currently in line. There may be a significant loss of opportunity. Thus, avoid selling in order to repurchase at a loss. "Trade like an investor, don't invest like a trader!"

How to Prevent Stock Market Losses

Don't Check the Daily Stock Price: Thanks to the internet's accessibility and smartphones, stock quotes are constantly at our fingertips. Investors frequently check the stock price quote two or three times a day. If the invested equities are in the green, you get instant delight; if they are in the red, the opposite occurs! The example that follows will demonstrate how obsessing about everyday price movement can have a detrimental effect on oneself. I had proposed Can Fin Homes in May 2013. The same was bought by Ramesh (new name), for ₹150 (price not modified with bonus/split).

Regarding the future of the housing finance sector, he was optimistic. In Tier II and Tier III locations, the company mostly provides home loans to salaried persons. They had no non-performing assets because of stringent lending procedures (NPA). Everything was alright. But over the following four to five months, the stock price stayed range bound. In August 2013, it sank to about ₹115 levels. Ramesh kept up his routine observation of the stock price. He used to have complete faith in the stock, but after four to five months of poor performance, he began to have doubts. In October 2013, he eventually sold all of his stake at ₹145. He was relieved that he would not have to endure any substantial losses. He just lost ₹5 on each stock when he sold it.

Ten months after his sale, the stock price shot up to between ₹420 and ₹460. Consequently, nearly three returns in ten months! Ramesh had nothing to do at this point. What, therefore, went wrong with him? Even though he was extremely optimistic about the company's future, he still could not bear the thought of its temporary collapse. When the price dropped from ₹150 to ₹115, his whole conviction vanished. He was considering leaving at the lowest possible loss of ₹115. He sold the entire position, therefore, when the price recovered to ₹145. Subsequently, in the following ten months, the identical stock produced a return that was tripled (200%). His initial belief in the firm was therefore validated. He could have averted this by not keeping a frequent eye on the stock price. In July and August of 2013, another consumer, Rohit (name changed), had the good fortune to enter between ₹115 and ₹140. He made investments, with an average purchase rate of about ₹125. The potential for future business also won Rohit over.

He held the stock calmly during the correction phase, in contrast to Ramesh. His perseverance paid off. His investment yielded a 100% return in April 2014. The price of the stock was roughly ₹250. But he tensed when he saw a 100% return in nine months. After reviewing the foundations, he saw that they were getting better. Most crucially, the valuation remained low even after a 100% return. Same as him, Rohit used to monitor the stock price every two or three hours. He expressed concern that the stock would decline further from its recent peak of ₹250, even though it had recovered 100% in just nine months, as it corrected around ₹230. At ₹250, he sold all of his shares with the intention of reentering at ₹200. The fact that he had already secured a 100% return in less than nine months made him delighted. Never did the stock correct to ₹200. Rather, it passed the ₹300 barrier in less than a month. Since he sold his whole investment at ₹250, Rohit had intended to re-enter at ₹250, hence it was challenging for him to re-enter over ₹250.

The stock didn't correct at all, and in the following month, it crossed the ₹400 mark. The price of the shares was approximately ₹450 in October of 2014. Had he focused solely on the business progress, management interview, and quarterly result, as opposed to monitoring the stock price quote two or three times a day, he would have seen a return of over 200% today. In conclusion, regular stock price checks might have the following effects on your investment: Early booking of profits The excitement of making a significant profit is always outweighed by the dread of losing money. Regular price monitoring may compel you to record small profits in excellent equities that, in the long term, could double your investment. Early departure: Humans are emotional creatures. It is quite hard to acknowledge that you have lost money. It is difficult to maintain conviction in a company, regardless of the fundamentals, if it doesn't move during the course of eight to ten months or if it stays below our invested price.

Regularly checking prices in such a scenario may result in an early withdrawal (see Can Fin Homes, example #1). Ignore any short-term fluctuations in price. A solid stock will only follow the fundamentals over the long term, but it may swing either way in the short term. You must routinely check on your investments as an investor. Observation does not imply adherence to the current quote. You must behave like an owner of a business. It's sufficient to keep a careful eye on news pertaining to business and industry, quarterly results, and management interviews. Never forget that a stock price might move 10%–30% in the short term without any apparent reason. Don't base your investing choice on cyclical price fluctuations. It would be preferable if you could give up on tracking the daily stock quote. Many investors compute the unrealized gains/losses in their total portfolio in addition to monitoring daily price movement. The development of "Portfolio Trackers" has made it simple to determine the portfolio's total profit or loss on a given day or instant.

My trip taught me many valuable things, one of which is to "never ever calculate profit/loss until you are selling a stock." Recall that the market owns the full profit or loss until you are selling! You do not own it. Whereas the unrealized loss in the portfolio makes us unhappy, the unrealized gain makes us happy. But none of these feelings aid in our improvement as investors. Humans are emotional creatures. Even when you know a loss is unreal, it nevertheless impairs your ability to make logical decisions. Because of the unrealized loss that impairs rational thought, most investors are unable to take advantage of the bear market (a declining rate to buy more). However, if a department store sells groceries and clothes and gives a 30% discount, the same investor will buy more! Similar to this, most investors greatly increase their investments during a strong bull run (when the price rises every day) due to the satisfying feeling of the unrealized gain.

Maybe the stock market is the only area in the world where customers choose to buy more at higher prices and shop less during the discount period! "As long as you own stocks, never compute profit/loss. Only compute it after the sale.

The Purchase Rate Is Not the Main Focus

Because of the resurgence of the information technology industry and better fundamentals, I bought HCL Technologies in 2011 for about Rs. 500. At the time, I was two years into a four-year bachelor's degree. I was short on cash when it came to investing. The happiness of earning ₹2000 was surpassed by the anxiety of losing ₹1000. I once looked up the daily market price. As long as the stock was trading over 500, I felt confident in my decision to buy. Three months later, the stock price began to decline and eventually dropped to about Rs 400.

I started looking for specific reasons why I was incorrect because I was so nervous, but I was unable to come up with enough. Even if the company's quarterly results were positive, the stock price was underperforming. I used to monitor the stock price almost twice or three times a day to see if there was any progress being made. A definite sign that an investor is moving away from fundamentals and becoming overly fixated on his buy rate and the current market price is when they check the stock price two or three times a day. The stock price began to rise over the following few months, gradually approaching 450. I was relieved at this point that my loss was healing gradually. I used to figure out my notional loss every day. I eventually sold all of my stocks for about Rs. 450. I felt relieved to have focused on my loss. My joy was short-lived, as I discovered that the stock price increased to Rs. 1500 over the following two years following my sale! Therefore, even though I chose the appropriate stock at the right moment, I was unable to profit three times.

This is a prime illustration of how, by concentrating too much on the present market price, I missed three returns. I made the mistake of not viewing my investment as a share of the company, and the market made me realize how foolish that was. Lessons Learned: Applying knowledge differs greatly from possessing it. Even though I was well aware that a stock is simply a portion of the underlying company's ownership, I chose not to act upon this knowledge. If I had solely concentrated on the financials and fundamentals of the company, I could have made three times the return. Rather, I was overly preoccupied with my buying rate and the going rate. If you have symptoms such as monitoring the stock price two or three times a day, you may not view your stock investment as "partial ownership in that business."

Don't Attempt to Forecast the Market's Path

We make investments in specific stocks. None of us trades the Sensex or Nifty index. You'll see, surprisingly, that a lot of investors are more curious about the general direction of the market. Like you, I get a lot of these questions from our customers. such as, "How long will the market continue to move higher?" "Do you believe there will be a market crash soon?" "How do you see the market in the near future?" "What is your short-term goal for the Sensex?" Interestingly, long-term investors are the ones asking these questions, not day traders. Their focus lies more in the movement of the market than in the underlying values of the equities they own. Recall that you are making investments in specific companies, not the Sensex. The future prospects of that specific company determine the whole return on your portfolio; the Sensex movement has no bearing on it. You can now see that the stocks in my portfolio will yield a profit if the Sensex increases by 20% over time.

In a similar vein, my portfolio will have a negative return during the market crisis. Take a look at these instances: In 2011, Page Industries produced an 80% return while Sensex produced a negative return. Not just Page Industries, but also a number of FMCG and Pharma firms generated returns of over 50% in 2011 compared to the Sensex's negative return. We will also observe this kind of volatility if we look at well-known large-cap stocks that are included in the Sensex. Major FMCG company ITC produced a return of about 20% in 2011, whilst Sensex produced a loss. The Sensex was range-bound between 2010 and 2012, yet equities like Page Industries, Kaveri Seeds, La Opala Rg, and others produced returns that were more than double that amount. The aforementioned examples indicate that, with some difficulty, an investor may still make money in a bear market provided he makes the right investment in the right company at the right time.

On the other hand, financial losses can occur even in a bull market. Prominent large-cap stocks such as Suzlon, Unitech, DLF, and so on are excellent examples. It makes no difference if the market is rising or falling. Long-term profits might be expected if you invest in a solid company with promising prospects. Similarly, you would lose money if you invest in low-quality stock even during a robust bull market. The sole responsibility of an investor is to choose underlying strengths and promising futures for their companies. It is pointless to invest time and effort in predicting the general market trend. Limit your attention to company-specific activities. Examine the company's financial statements, business strategy, and outlook closely. Any stock's return is independent of changes in the Sensex.

Give up on analysts who consistently suggest new Sensex targets. Recall that the primary concern is the fundamental business at hand.

Market for Love Bears (Falling)

When the market as a whole is experiencing positive conditions, many investors favor purchasing equities. The market forecast follows the path of the market as well. Over the business channel, newspapers, internet, etc., you will discover a bullish stance while the market is rising. You will observe a completely different viewpoint on the same platform if the market corrects itself in a matter of days. As a result, a lot of investors always favor making investments during a market upswing and selling equities during a downturn. They wind up purchasing high and selling low during this process. It should go without saying that in order to succeed in investing, you must buy low and sell high. Still, very few investors really put this into practice.

You have to enjoy a bear market or a declining market in order to realistically implement the same idea. Fear and greed are the two main roadblocks. Fear of losing money stops people from making logical decisions during a market correction. It is your responsibility to manage "fear" while others are marketing. In an extended bad market, investment opportunities are rare. A chance like this only comes around once or twice every ten years. During this time, even investment in inferior businesses yields a respectable return in the long run! Because many companies are available at a throwaway price during these periods, stock selection also gets easier. Thus, don't pass up any such chances in the future.

How to Build Your Portfolio

A Balance between Excessive and Diversification. Selecting the right stock is simply one aspect of a successful investment; another is portfolio allocation.

Even while creating a portfolio might appear simple, one of the trickiest aspects of investing is knowing how to allocate it properly. I have examined numerous investor portfolios over the past few years, and I have found that about 80% of them are badly built. Poor portfolio building, rather than poor stock selection, is the primary cause of losses for many retail investors. Even still, one of the investment topics that gets the least attention is appropriate portfolio development. It was just a few days ago that I was reviewing a portfolio. Even if four of the 40 stocks in his portfolio were showing 200%-300% profit, his portfolio as a whole was displaying a loss! It's pretty annoying as well as surprising. Such poor performance can only be attributed to "over-diversification."

Almost all financial advisors will advise you to diversify your holdings. I agree, but the issue is that a lot of investors are unaware of what diversification really entails. Diversification and over-diversification are not the same thing. Excessive diversification can destroy your hard-earned money, even while it can help you build wealth systematically. Appropriate Diversification: Having a large number of equities in a portfolio is not a need for diversification. For diversification, many investors build an equity portfolio of 40–50 stocks, or perhaps more. You are making a serious error if you are one of them. A portfolio with 80 stocks might not be sufficiently diversified, but one with just 10 stocks might be. To make this point clearer, let's look at an example.

Twenty equities make up the portfolio above. The top five stocks in the portfolio, which make up 42% of its overall value, are banking firms. There are two main industries besides banking: fast-moving consumer goods and autos. The FMCG industry has the highest weight, followed by banking. The rest is captured by the automotive industry. The car sector also includes auto auxiliary. As the second portfolio illustrates, the whole industry is made up of just ten stocks. This portfolio seldom contains two stocks from the same industry. Which portfolio is more diversified, let's find out? What is the Appropriately Diversified Portfolio? Although the second portfolio is more diverse, it only consists of ten stocks compared to the first portfolio's twenty stocks from three major industries. The explanation is because in the second scenario, all ten equities were from ten separate sectors, whereas in the first case, despite having 20 shares, all were from only three sectors.

The first portfolio will be most impacted by the economic downturn because the majority of its stocks are in the banking, automotive, and real estate sectors. These are the industries that suffer the most from a downturn in the economy. In contrast, every stock in the second portfolio is from a distinct industry. Stocks from various industries help to ensure that, even during a downturn, your portfolio will be less impacted. It is improbable that all ten of those sectors will perform poorly at once.

Issues with a Vast Portfolio of Stocks

Having a sizable stock portfolio makes some investors feel proud. If you belong to that group, consider the issues that come with having a portfolio like that.- Having trouble accurately following the stocks It is crucial to monitor every stock in your portfolio on a weekly basis, or more frequently if you are not following the advice of any experts.

Monitoring does not entail daily stock price checks. You should invest at least 30 minutes a week in a single stock to follow (at least) quarterly results, all business-related news, competition status, management interviews, and conference calls. Now, if your portfolio consists of 60 equities, it will take 1800 minutes, or 30 hours, per week, or about 4.5 hours every day. Currently, a working person cannot dedicate four and a half hours a day to anything other than their full-time job or business. adversely impact your total return - Let's say your portfolio consists of more than 60 stocks. If four or five of these equities produce an annualized return of more than 100%, your total performance will also be subpar. The benefit could be minimized by a negative or flat return from other low-quality stocks. Never forget that there are always far fewer high-quality stocks than there are low-quality (or mediocre) stocks. Excellent investing chances don't come around very often.

Less than 0.5% of the 5,000+ listed firms in India have stocks that generate 100%+ annualized return (multibaggers); 10%–15% of the stocks have 20%+ annualized returns; another 10%–25% have returns of 10%+; and the other 60%–70% of the equities either yield negative returns or remain flat. Therefore, there's a good chance that many of the 60+ stocks in your portfolio have mediocre or bad fundamentals. The wealthiest investor in the world, Mr. Warren Buffett, has consistently maintained a portfolio of ten to fifteen equities. The Indian billionaire investor Mr. Rakesh Jhunjhunwala has limited 90% of his holdings to 10–12 stocks, even though he owns 40–42 stocks. The question now arises: how many stocks at a time are adequate to hold? The response differs depending on the investment.

Retail investors should generally keep 10–20 high-quality equities in their portfolio at any given time. The number may increase for extremely knowledgeable, skilled investors, but the majority should be limited to 10–20 stocks. Actively following 50–60 companies won't be a problem, though, if you are a full-time investor with 8–9 hours to spare each day.

Investor Misconception Misconception No. 1

Big-cap companies consistently provide security and a consistent stream of income. There's a common misperception that big-cap equities are always safe to invest in, whereas small- and mid-cap stocks are riskier. Furthermore, the majority of investors think that small and mid-cap companies are extremely volatile, while large-cap stocks give a consistent flow of return.

If I come to the direct conclusion that excellent small- and mid-cap stocks can provide more safety, a higher dividend yield, and a higher return than large-cap stocks, that will be difficult to swallow. Now, let's look at a few actual instances: State Bank of India (SBI) is a well-known, blue-chip banking firm with a big market valuation. It is India's biggest bank as well. Conversely, City Union Bank (CUB) is a regional bank with a modest size. Let's examine how SBI and CUB's prices have performed over the course of several economic cycles. 2010 arrived as a relief year following the 2008–09 financial crisis. In the event of an economic recovery, the financial industry is the first to react. In 2010, the return created by City Union Bank (CUB) was approximately 90%, whilst the return generated by State Bank of India (SBI) was approximately 27%. In the same time frame, the Sensex increased by 14.20%. Let's now examine the performance for the year 2011. In 2011, the Indian equity market had a dismal year. SBI underperformed and produced a negative return of -40%, while CUB earned a moderately negative return of -5% against the Sensex's -25% return.

As we get to 2012, the Sensex increased by 30%. In the same time frame, SBI generated about 35% while CUB generated about 52%. You will see the same picture if you compare the performance in

2013, 2014, or any other year. State Bank of India was consistently surpassed by City Union Bank in all market cycles, whether bull or bear. Thus, a quality small-cap banking stock (CUB) has consistently beaten the large-cap and the biggest bank in India, regardless of market movements! Some analysts may advise against investing in small-cap stocks, citing the fact that they rise more quickly in bull markets and decline more quickly in bad markets. There is a widespread misperception that although small-cap stocks can result in "unlimited loss," they can also give a higher return.

But the example given above paints a completely different picture. One could contend that the CUB and SBI case is an anomaly. Now, contrast Maruti Suzuki with Suprajit (small-cap car stock); contrast Ajanta Pharma with Sun Pharma; contrast TCS with Eclerx. You will always find high-quality small-cap firms beating large-cap stocks, whether it is in the automotive, pharmaceutical, IT, or banking industries. The sole requirement in this case is that "quality small-cap" and "quality large-cap" be compared. You are unable to account for low-quality small-cap equities such as Rei Agro and IVRCL. It should be noted that none of the stocks featured in the book are suggestions for stocks. I'm not saying that if you own Sun Pharma, you should switch to Ajanta Pharma right now.

There is no assurance that the quality of these small-caps will stay "as it is" in the future; all of these names are merely examples. The key factor to take into account in this case is "quality small-cap" stocks, which typically outperform their large-cap counterparts.

A lot of investors would rather have a 60% allocation in large-cap stocks, 20% in midcap stocks, and so forth. I would never recommend segmenting your portfolio according to market capitalization. The big cap of today might turn into the small cap of tomorrow (Suzlon, for example), and vice versa. The only equities in your portfolio should be "quality stocks." A 100% exposure to "quality mid-cap and small-cap stocks" is acceptable. Secondly, there is less chance that stocks that have already quadrupled in value will continue to rise. I suggested Atul Auto in November 2013 for about ₹145 (split adjusted rate). The maker of compact three-wheelers, Atul Auto, has an amazing track record from 2011 to 2013. At that time, the auto industry as a whole was suffering through its worst decade.

I had suggested the same, supported by solid and improving fundamentals and anticipating a comeback in the automotive sector in FY15. But the stock price has already increased from ₹75 to ₹145 between August 2013 and November 2013, yielding a return of nearly 100% in just four months. Following the advice, I had a lot of complaints from our members, some of which were along the lines of "The stock price has already doubled in the last four months." How much farther will it go at this rate? "I want to invest in inexpensive stocks that have the potential to double in the future; I don't want to buy stocks that have already doubled." "Why are you endorsing stocks that have already experienced significant gains?" Atul Auto produced a 170%+ return within ten months of the recommendation, reaching a lifetime high of ₹447 in September 2014. resulting in a threefold return in just ten months! My recommendations are not endorsed by me.

Actually, every stock that is described in the book is just an example; they should never be regarded as advice for investments. Furthermore, past performance does not guarantee future results. The most important thing to realize is that the movement of the stock price is independent of the number of previous multiplicities. Instead, it is dependent upon the company's prospects for the future. As was previously indicated, Atul Auto had demonstrated a strong track record even during the 2011–2013 auto industry recession.

In the same period, the company achieved balance sheet debt-free growth at a pace of over 50% and a return on equity of over 30%. It is evident that these equities receive sufficient support during the economic recovery to increase investors' wealth.

In the case of Atul Auto, the same thing took place. The company positioned itself to become a national player from a regional 3-wheeler maker during the Auto Industry slump. The company found itself in a favorable position as a result of its capacity growth without taking on any external financing and its effective working capital management. Therefore, even if the stock produced a tenfold return during the slowdown period (2011–2013), I still thought it was a good investment during the car industry's comeback. When a company can function effectively in unfavorable macroeconomic circumstances, it is likely to achieve even greater success when the external business climate improves.

Victories occur in difficult circumstances. Past price performance should be the least important factor for investors. The predicted rise in earnings and the forecast for the future directly affect the movement of the stock price in the future. The number of times a stock price has increased in the past is irrelevant. "Earnings growth determines how frequently a stock moves up in the future, not how often it moved in the recent past."

Myth #3: Stocks that decline drastically also have to rise sharply. When a stock is declining as opposed to rising, many investors feel better at ease buying it. In the event that a stock hits its all-time high of ₹1000 and then drops to ₹500, a lot of novice investors seem to believe that it would eventually rise back to ₹1000! The actual situation is entirely different. In January 2008, DLF reached its all-time high of ₹1225. Twelve years later, the stock still wasn't able to hit the 1000 level. But if you pay close attention to the volume of transactions in the stock, you'll see that a lot of new investors entered the market in 2010, mostly in the hopes that it would return to its former glory. The same holds true for other real estate stocks like Unitech. Because of their prior success, a lot of investors started investing in infrastructure and real estate equities in 2010. Refrain from being seduced by the company's previous stock price. The past price action has no bearing on how the stock price moves in the future. The first indication of concern is a steep decline in stock price. A 10%–20% fall in a fundamentally sound stock might not be a reason for alarm. A price adjustment of more than 60%, however, is cause for concern.

Avoid investing in stocks that have experienced a price correction of more than 60% from their previous peak unless you are extremely confident in your investment. "Sharply falling stocks need to move up sharply" This one harmful misunderstanding has been consistently resulting in serious for a very long time losses to individual investors. "Avoid buying stocks that have experienced a correction of 60% or more from their recent peak."

Defending The Portfolio Against A Crisis In The Market

Investors' top objective should be capital protection. In order to maximize the return on our entire portfolio, we invest in equities. Oftentimes, investors experience capital erosion rather than maximizing returns. Protecting their assets is a challenge for investors, particularly during a stock market crisis.

Nonetheless, one can somewhat safeguard their equity investments throughout any market downturn with the appropriate plan and unwavering discipline. We are breaking the stock market meltdown into two segments based on its magnitude: A slight decline in the index (of stocks) by 5% to 30% Huge stock market catastrophe (greater than 50% decline in the index) A tiny crash in the stock market Many instances exist where the market (index) corrected by 5% to 30% in a span of one to two months. Any bull run will include these corrections. For example, in July and August of 2013, the Sensex saw a 14% correction from its previous high (having dropped to approximately 17,800 from a high of over 20,200 in July 2013). How should one respond to a little stock market meltdown? Your portfolio is more likely to be saved by discipline in a moderate stock market catastrophe.

The necessary steps are as follows: Don't sell all of your equity holdings in order to reenter the market at a reduced price. There is no one in the world who can accurately forecast short-term market action. Therefore, it's possible that the market reverses course after your sell-off, making it impossible for you to make investments at a cheaper price. It's possible that you'll sell at a discount and purchase at a premium. Frequent buying and selling also results in higher taxes and transaction costs (brokerage, STT, exchange fees, etc.). In other words, even if you are lucky enough to time the market, the odds are not in your favor. Avoid trying to figure out answers to queries such as "When will the market correct?" You will discover a negative point of view if you watch the business channel, newspaper, or internet during any market correction. If the market begins to rise next week, you can discover a bullish opinion from the same source.

In actuality, it is nearly hard to accurately and consistently forecast short-term market action. Thus, if you're always asking yourself, "How long will the market correct?" Even if you attempt to predict the short-term trajectory of the market, you will discover that it will unexpectedly do a U-turn. Remain calm. Put an end to your daily stock price checks if you are unable to handle volatility. It will be plenty to check the pricing once or twice a week. Recall that there is no actual profit or loss till you sell the stock. Only when the position has been sold should the profit/loss be calculated. Invest in premium equities while the market is correcting. Based on historical data, investing in high-quality stocks during a stock market crisis does not result in losses. For instance, not a single person lost money on investments in October through December 2008, August 2013 or December 2016 will be found.

Here, we'll suppose that the investor has made a pretty good-quality stock investment and will maintain his position for at least the following year. Investors might not have had enough money to reinvest in high-caliber scripts during the stock market meltdown. Another scenario is when you make a significant investment in a market downturn and the market declines even more. An infinite sum of money cannot be used to average out throughout each adjustment. The best and most straightforward course of action in this case is to HOLD your present position. Avoid attempting to determine the lowest possible investment. You can't always sell at the peak and buy at the bottom. Significant Crash in the Stock Market

Following the dot-com bubble burst (in 2000–01), the market saw a significant collapse in January 2008, with the index plunging more than 50%.

First Thought It is nearly hard to make a 20%–30% return during a 50% or more collapse in the equity market. It's easy to understand why. Even the world's greatest swimmer cannot withstand a tsunami. No matter how quickly you can flee or how well you are protected, you cannot save yourself during an atomic bomb blast. Similar to this, no matter how skilled or experienced you are, it is nearly impossible to manage a return of 20% to 30% during a significant stock market crash (index down by 50%+). Your goal during these times should be to produce an annualized return that is at least positive, and there are ways to do so. The Best Equity Hedging Is Gold The price pattern over the last 30 years indicates that stocks and gold typically move in the opposite directions. The return from gold stayed muted during the equities market's bull run, and vice versa.

For instance, Sensex delivered a -1% return between January 2008 and December 2012, whereas Gold created a 15% return during that time. Sensex had a 43% return from January 1988 to December 1992, while Gold had a negative (-7.5%) return over the same time. When comparing the performance across a few years, the situation largely stays the same. Therefore, it may be wise to allocate some of your portfolio to gold during a significant market downturn.

Avoidable Stocks: Stocks to Steer Clear

Companies with High Debt In a bull market, a lot of businesses are expanding incredibly quickly. Such growth can only be financed by raising funds. A business can borrow money or dilute its shares to raise cash. Choosing the second choice is much simpler.

There's nothing to be really concerned about as long as the growth trend keeps going. Once things start to improve, the issue arises. One of the most popular stocks during the bull market of 2006–2008 was Suzlon. The business was involved in wind power, which was regarded as the "next big thing" in renewable energy. Everything was alright. In 2007, stock values doubled. Regrettably, an overwhelming desire for expansion led to a rise in debt. The business made expensive acquisitions that widened its balance sheet. Later, the business was caught in a debt trap. A significant interest expense reduced the earnings. Things began to become worse. Its overall debt increased even more as a result of a rise in working capital requirements and the enormous debt from the REPower acquisition. Debt rose from ₹5,164 crore in FY07 to ₹17,053 crore at the end of FY14.

The business has kept up its narrative of recording losses since 2009. It makes sense that throughout the following four years, the stock price dropped by about 95% from its peak in January 2008! Once the stock market's darling, Suzlon turned out to be one of the biggest wealth destroyers of the decade. Avoid high-debt businesses at all costs. Examining the debt to equity ratio is the simplest method for identifying organizations with a high debt load. An increasing debt-to-equity ratio is problematic. Steer clear of companies with an interest coverage ratio of less than three and a debt to equity ratio greater than one that is also rising annually. We have already seen examples in the previous chapter of how corporations with significant levels of debt in 2014–15 caused enormous losses in the next 4–5 years. Any year's data point might be used; the outcome would be the same. Stocks to Steer Clear of #2: Microcaps and Low Promoter Holdings The owners are the ones that know the company the best.

What does it mean, as an owner, if you are uncomfortable owning the majority of your company? Steer clear of microcap firms in which the promoters do not own a majority stake. In order to guarantee a seamless exit, promoters have listed their company on the stock exchange on multiple occasions. If the stock is a micro-cap or small-cap, the problem gets worse. Generally speaking, steer clear of businesses with promoter ownership of less than 20% and a market value of less than 300 crores. A select few high-quality businesses, such as City Union Bank (CUB) and Larsen and Toubro (L&T), have no promoter ownership. There are no specific owners or promoters for either of the two businesses. These companies are managed by institutions. Less than 20% of the promoters of certain well-known banks are also committed to upholding regulatory standards. Those companies are backed by institutional investors. The aggregate amount of shares held by institutional investors and promoters may be taken into account. If institutional investors' and promoters' total shareholdings are less than 20%, this is a major cause for concern.

Steer clear of microcap or small cap stocks where the promoters own less than 20% of the shares. You won't find a proper research report or trustworthy information in the public domain because our company is small. Investing in stocks where the promoters are unwilling to hold a controlling stake is risky. This might destroy all of your money. Let's examine a few instances.

The accompanying table shows that these stocks did not perform well, even throughout the bull run. In contrast to the 27% return of the Sensex, nearly all of the aforementioned equities had a negative performance over the previous year. Regardless of the state of the market as a whole, these stocks are steadily depleting investors' capital. You can choose any future date as an example, such as 2022 or 2025, although the results won't usually be positive! If you own any such stocks in your portfolio, be informed. Avoid being seduced by transient price fluctuations, as microcap firms with modest promoter holdings have the potential to quickly deplete your hard-earned savings. "Avoid investing in stocks where the promoters own less than 20% of the company and their market capitalization is less than 300 crores."

Avoidable Stock #3: High-Promoter Pledges (and Raises) The promoter's pledge is covered in length in the Management Analysis chapter. Since one of the most frequent causes of wealth destruction is an increase in the promoter's pledged holding, you can review this again. Avoid equities where the promoter's committed position is increasing, regardless of the number of analysts advising against it or how many times the stock price has increased. The pledge problem hurt even elite companies with a competitive edge, such as Zee Entertainment, the proprietor of well-known TV networks. Due only to the pledge issue, the stock price fell by over 50% in 2019. Stocks to Steer Clear of #4: Stocks Nearing New Low Steer clear of companies that keep setting new lows unless you have faith in the company's future prospects. The stock may not rise to its previous peak. Any stock that has dropped more than 50% from its most recent top is a warning indicator.

Avoid catching the falling blade. These stocks have the potential to totally deplete an investor's money. From 2010 to 2014, Suzlon consistently set new 52-week lows. Even during the many years that followed, the downward trajectory persisted. Suzlon is not the only one in this group. Numerous other formerly well-known stocks, such as Unitech, Opto Circuits, Educomp, etc., suffered a similar fate. Numerous instances exist where stocks have disappeared from the market following a persistent decline. However, equities that reach a 52-week high merit further investigation. A positive development must be there if a stock price reaches a new high in spite of the stock market's general downturn. While equities that are approaching their 52-week high should not be bought, they are still worthy of additional investigation. Throughout my investing experience, I have filtered stocks that have reached 52-week highs several times and had excellent returns. "Equities that reach a 52-week high are a far better candidate to start further research for investments, while stocks that frequently reach a 52-week low should be handled carefully."

Recap

While a portfolio of 10 stocks can be well diversified, a portfolio of 80 stocks might not be. A well-diversified portfolio should consist of a small number of stocks that are spread throughout several industries.

A stock's future price movements are determined by its business prospects and profits growth, not by how much it has moved in the past. Steer clear of equities that have corrected more than 60% from their recent peak.

Gold is thought to be the finest equity hedge. You can park a sizable portion of your capital in gold after a significant stock market fall when the index corrects by more than 50%. Steer clear of equities where the promoters own less than 20% of the company and whose market value is less than 300 crores.

Day Trading Forex - Simple Forex Day Trading Strategy Work

Finding the best times to enter and leave a trade in order to maximize earnings is the aim of any successful trader. Technical indicators like oscillators and moving averages, as well as price movement and chart patterns, can produce entry and exit indications. The key to identifying high probability entry/exit signals is to search for patterns or convergence between several indicators. This entails figuring out when several signs all point in the same direction, which increases the signal's probability of being correct.

Here's an illustration of how this could appear: There is an oversold RSI. Furthermore, there was an RSI oversold signal and the price is close to a significant support level. Higher temporal trends are increasing. Three levels of confluence in this example point to a strong likelihood of a market recovery off the support level and a favorable entry point for a long trade. An illustration of price close to a support level with oversold RSI values Your accuracy can be significantly improved and the number of potential false signals can be decreased by merging your entrance and exit signals with those from other confluence levels. Different Indicer Types Traders employ a range of indicators to pinpoint possible signals for entering or leaving the market.

Depending on what they compute or measure, indicators can be divided into several categories. These categories include: relocating averages Volume meters oscillators of momentum indications of volatility. Acceleration Oscillators: Technical indicators that gauge market momentum are called momentum oscillators. To accomplish this, they compute the rate of change, usually over a predetermined duration, between two price points. Both mean reversion/scalping and trend-following techniques can benefit greatly from the use of momentum oscillators. Generally, we want to look for a trend that is gaining or losing momentum as a signal to enter or exit the market when utilizing momentum oscillators in a trend following approach. We want to search for momentum oscillators that are overbought or oversold in a mean reversion technique.

Oversold/overbought signs suggest that a downturn is probably in store if the market has moved too quickly either way. It is crucial to understand that OB/OS signals are unreliable in trending markets and perform best in sideways situations. Among the momentum oscillators that are frequently employed are the following: • Average Convergence Divergence, or MACD • Moving averages for Williams %R: Lagging indicators such as moving averages smooth out price movement and make it easier to spot market patterns. To achieve this, they compute and plot the average price over a predetermined time frame. Since they may be used to determine both the trend's direction and possible entry and exit locations, moving averages are most frequently employed in trend-following methods. Moving averages with longer periods, such as 200 EMA, are more appropriate for longer-term trends, while those with shorter periods, such as 20 EMA, are more appropriate for shorter-term trends.

Finding the market's levels of support and resistance is another application for moving averages. Depending on whether the trend is up or down, price will normally behave as support or resistance when it crosses a long-term moving average. It's crucial to remember that moving averages can be inaccurate in choppy or sideways markets because they frequently provide a lot of false signals and lag price action. Volume Measurement Tools: Traders employ volume indicators to determine the strength of price fluctuations in the market. To achieve this, they gauge the volume entering or leaving a particular market or asset. Volume can be utilized to provide entry/exit signals, identify breakouts, and validate the direction of trends.

Volume indicators mostly come in two varieties: • On-balance volume (OBV): OBV calculates the net quantity of purchases and sales for a specific time frame. When the OBV rises, more money is coming into the asset; when it falls, more money is leaving the asset. • Accumulation/Distribution (A/D): A/D tracks price and volume in relation to one another to determine the net amount of purchasing and selling over time. Buying pressure is indicated by a rising A/D line, and selling pressure is shown by a falling A/D line. It is crucial to remember that although volume is a useful instrument for determining the strength of price changes, it can be erratic in low-volume markets or during times of extreme volatility. Volatility Measures: Technical indicators called volatility indicators gauge how much the price has fluctuated over a specific time frame. The average true range (ATR) of a market or asset over a given time period is computed to achieve this.

The average of the high/low and open/close prices for a specific time period is used to compute the ATR. Markets can be predicted to breakout, stall, or continue trending using volatility indicators. An increasing ATR denotes more volatility, whereas a dropping ATR denotes less volatility. The following are a few often used volatility indicators: Keltner Channels; Bollinger Bands®; Average True Range (ATR); • Supertrend When utilized properly, indicators may be an extremely useful tool for traders. It is crucial to comprehend how each indicator functions and when to utilize it because some indications are more appropriate for various markets and trading techniques.

Enhancing Trading Signals

Using Filters One of the most well-known trading tenets is that it is always preferable to trade in the direction of the general trend. This implies that it is advisable to trade in the direction of a trend if one is present. One technique to make sure you are constantly trading with the direction of the overall trend is to use filters. All a filter is is a tool for bettering entry/exit accuracy by determining market circumstances and trend direction. To ensure that the market is moving horizontally and not trending, we need to apply a filter if we are employing a signal that performs best in a sideways market. On the other hand, we would want to confirm that the market is trending and not consolidating if we were utilizing a signal that is most effective in trending markets. By removing erroneous signals, filters can increase trade accuracy.

Among the often employed filters are: • Moving Averages • ATR • ADX (average directional index) Applying a Trend Direction Filter to the 200 EMA Because they are an excellent tool for determining the trend direction, moving averages are frequently employed as filters in trading. By removing short-term price swings, the 200 EMA (exponential moving average) helps you determine the direction of the longer-term trend. A price above the 200 EMA indicates an overall upward trend, whereas a price below the 200 EMA indicates an overall downward trend. We would only search for long trades if the price is above the 200 EMA and short trades if the price is below the 200 EMA if we were to utilize the 200 EMA as a filter. Indicators of the Trend Strength and Consolidation Filter These two TradingView indicators are excellent for quickly determining if a market is trending or not.

These indicators work well as filters for any trading strategy and are very user-friendly. First Trend/Consolidation Filter: BobRivera990's Trend Type Indicator (TradingView indicator) Open TradingView Type Trend Type Indicator by BobRivera990 in the indicator search box to locate this indicator. According to the screenshot above, BobRivera990 is the indicator's author. How to Use It: This indicator distinguishes between uptrends, downtrends, and sideways markets by combining the ATR and ADX. An uptrend is probably happening if the indicator line is green and in the green zone (above 1). In the event that the indication is gray and the market is moving sideways, The market is in a downtrend if the indicator is red and in the red zone. An illustration of a trend type indicator showing both an upward and downward trend Breakout/Consolidation Filter (TradingView indicator) is the second trend/consolidation filter. Access the TradingView Type Breakout/Consolidation Filter [jammu 12] indicator search box to locate this indicator. According to the screenshot above, jwammo12 is the indicator's author.

How It Operates This indicator, which uses a single line that swings up or down depending on how strong the current trend is, is comparable to the ADX. A period of consolidation is occurring in the price if this indicator is below 50. When this indicator is above 50, the market is trending rather than stabilizing. To aid in observing these signals, this indicator has a yellow line at the 50 level. An illustration of a Breakout/Consolidation Filter below 50, which shows that prices are fluctuating As you can see, this indicator is quite effective in spotting ranges, trends, and consolidation breakouts. When Scalping Using This Indicator: Trade only when the Breakout/Consolidation Filter value is less than 50. This is one of my favorite indicators, and I use it in many of my tactics; later in this book, we will look at some effective scalping strategies employing it.

Momentum Oscillators for Effective Entry/Exit

Signals with High Win Rates Momentum oscillators contain several types of signals. Oversold/Overbought Signals These indications, which indicate that an investment is overbought or oversold, appear when a momentum oscillator hits an extreme level.

Potential entry and departure points into a trend can be determined using this indicator. An overbought signal suggests that the price has climbed too quickly and is likely to regress, whereas an oversold signal suggests that the price has dropped too quickly and is likely to rebound. Signals of Divergence When an asset's price moves in one way while the momentum oscillator moves in a different direction, this is known as a divergence signal. This can suggest that the trend is waning and that a reversal is possible. When the oscillator makes higher lows and the price makes lower lows, this is known as bullish divergence and suggests that there may be an upside reversal. When the oscillator makes lower highs and the price makes higher highs, this is known as bearish divergence and suggests that there may be a potential downside reversal.

Centerline Turnovers When a momentum oscillator crosses its center line, also known as the zero line, signals known as centerline crossovers are produced. When price crosses above or below the center line, a signal is produced that indicates a change in momentum. Potential entry and departure points into a trend can be determined using this indicator. Two Line Dividers When a slower line on the oscillator crosses above or below a quicker line, this happens. This indicates a shift in momentum's direction and can be used to pinpoint possible places of entry and departure for a trend. These two line crossover signals are included in a number of momentum oscillators, such as the MACD and stochastic. However, these signals may be obtained by adding a moving average to almost any momentum oscillator. When utilized properly, momentum oscillators can be a helpful tool for traders. Knowing the many kinds of signals that each indicator produces and how to use them to pinpoint trend entry and exit points is crucial.

We'll also examine some of the top momentum oscillator entry/exit indications to give you a trading advantage. Where to Look for These Signal Indicators These are free indicators that have been designed and coded on TradingView by other traders. These are the greatest indicators I have found and utilized in my scalping methods, while there are many other members' developed indicators available on TradingView. Crucial: These indicators shouldn't be utilized in isolation; rather, they should be part of an entire scalping strategy. Additionally, before utilizing these signals with real money, you should backtest and paper trade them! To utilize TradingView to view these indicators: 1. Create a TradingView account (TradingView.com). If you prefer not to pay, you can register for a free account. 2. In TradingView, open a chart and select the "indicators" icon from the toolbar at the top. 3. Next, just enter the desired indicator into the search field.

The TradingView indicator search field Now that you are aware of where to look for these signs, let's get going! Signal #1 for Oscillator Entry/Exit: TMO with TTM Squeeze Through: ssc charts Type "TMO with TTM Squeeze " into TradingView's indicator search box (by ssk charts) to locate this indicator. Synopsis: Similar in momentum to the stochastic oscillator, the TMO (trend momentum oscillator) has the advantage of generating fewer false signals. To create entry/exit signals, the TMO uses the crossover of two lines, one slow and the other fast. This indicator also uses overbought (above 70) and oversold (below -70) conditions to generate alerts.

This indicator's centerline can be used as a filter to easily identify signals that are moving in the direction of the trend because it alternates between green and red based on the trend.

Long Entry/Short Exit: When the TMO crosses up and falls below 50, the color turns green. The TMO exits the oversold area by crossing upward. The TMO's centerline is green. Using the TMO indicator to create long entry and departure signals Short Entry/Long Exit: The TMO crosses down and is above 50 (the color of the TMO turns red). The TMO exits the overbought area by descending. The TMO's centerline is red. Using the TMO indication, a brief entrance and departure Oscillator Ingress/Regress Signal #2: Divergence in RSI Written by: Shizaru Enter "RSI Divergence" in TradingView's indicator search box to locate this indicator (by Shizaru) Synopsis: To identify divergence, this indicator combines a rapid and slow period RSI. When the indicator line passes over 50 or changes color, a signal is generated.

This leading indicator is incredibly precise and will move in either direction prior to a change in the price. When paired with other indicators, this is a useful indicator for trend tracking or scalping.

Long Entry: Over 50 is where the RSI divergence line crosses. The hue of the RSI divergence line turns green. Long Exit: A red color shift occurs in the RSI divergence line. Below 50, the RSI divergence line crosses. Using the RSI divergence indicator, an example of long entry and exit signals Brief Entry: Below 50, the RSI divergence line crosses. The hue of the RSI divergence line turns red. Short Exit: A green color shift occurs in the RSI divergence line. Above 50, the RSI divergence line crosses. a brief entry signal based on the divergence indicator of the RSI Oscillator Entry/Exit Signal #3: Customized CCI Indicator for the Black Cat Written by: Black Cat 1402 To

To locate this indicator, use TradingView's indicator search box and enter "[blackcat] L1 Blackcat Customized CCI Indicator" (by blackcat1402). Overview: This is an indicator that is a variant of the commodities channel index, or CCI.

Compared to a standard CCI, this variant of the CCI makes signals easier to see by including buy and sell indications on the indicator. When the CCI crosses into the overbought or oversold territory, entry/exit signals happen. When the CCI crosses below -200, it indicates a "Buy" and is a good indicator for scalping. Long Entry/Short Exit Yellow is the color of the CCI histogram, which is excellent for trend trading. Long Entry/Short Exit: If the CCI passes 200, it indicates a "sell" (better suited for scalping). Purple appears on the CCI histogram, which is a better color for trend trading. Zero Lag MACD Enhanced - Version 1.2 is an example of an entry and exit signal using the Blackcat Customized CCI Indicator Oscillator Entry/Exit Signal #4. By: Alberto Callisto Enter "Zero Lag MACD Enhanced - Version 1.2" in TradingView's indicator search field (by albert.callisto) to locate the indicator. Synopsis:

This indicator, known as the moving average convergence divergence, is an enhanced and adjusted version of the widely used MACD. Similar to the standard MACD, this variant generates a buy/sell signal using the signal (slow) line and the MACD (fast) line. Compared to the standard version, this MACD's signals are more accurate and contain less false positives. Another EMA is included in this edition as well, but it is optional and may be disabled in the settings. This indicator may accurately forecast short-term market peaks and bottoms and performs best when price activity is more volatile. A dot will show up on the indicator when a crossover signal happens, which makes signal identification easier.

Indicator Tip: Adjust the following indicator setting to increase signal accuracy: Quick MM time = 12 Delete the "Use EMA" check box. Turn off "Use Glaz algo." Long Entry/Exit Short: A green dot indicates where the MACD line crosses above the signal line. Short Entry/Exit Long: A red dot indicates where the MACD line passes below the signal line. An illustration of entry/exit signals with zero lag MACD improved indicator Oscillator Ingress/Regress Signal #5: Whale Pump Detector with L2 KDJ Written by: Blackcat 1402 Use the TradingView indicator search box and enter "L2 KDJ with Whale Pump Detector" to locate this indicator (by blackcat1402). Synopsis: This signal is a variant of the KDJ indicators, which use a stochastic oscillator-like momentum oscillator. The name KDJ comes from the fact that in addition to using the K and D lines from the stochastic, it also employs the J line.

When all three lines cross over in a specific direction, signals are produced. For entry/exit signals, the KDJ additionally contains overbought (above100) and oversold (below0) zones. In a sideways market, the KDJ's signals will be the most trustworthy. Indicator Tip: Go into the settings and take out the DJ's backdrop colors. Long Entry: You can use any of the following.The KDJ has a green "B" label on it. The KDJ's three lines intersect. Extended Exit: You can use one of the following: The KDJ has a red "S" label on it. Each of the three lines crosses below Overbought, the KDJ crosses above 100. Example of utilizing the L2 KDJ indication for entry and exit signals Short Entry: The KDJ has a red "S " label on it. You can use one of the following. The KDJ's three lines cross downward. Quick Exit: You can utilize any of the following: The KDJ has a green "B" label on it. Each of the three lines below Below 20 is the KDJ crossover (oversold). Oscillator Ingress/Regress Sixth Signal: Williams %R

Written by: Enter "Williams %R" in TradingView's indicator search box to locate this indicator.

This is a variant of the Williams %R indicator, a momentum oscillator that may be used to detect overbought and oversold market circumstances. It resembles the RSI. An EMA is included in this version of the Williams %R, and signals are generated when the Williams %R crosses above or below the EMA. This indicator is excellent for scalping since it responds to price movements quickly. It is recommended to utilize the Williams %R indicator in conjunction with other technical indicators and tools. The Williams %R can assist in providing high probability entry and exit signals when paired with other indicators such as trend lines, MACD, and support/resistance levels. Long Entry: Above the EMA, the Williams %R crosses The oversold zone (-80) is crossed by the Williams percentage return. Extended Exit: When the Williams%R surpasses -20 (overbought), Below the EMA, the Williams %R crosses. An illustration of extended entry and exit signals utilizing the Williams %R indication

Short Entry: The EMA is crossed below by the Williams %R Williams %R exits the overbought zone (-20) by crossing below. Short Exit: Oversold, when the Williams%R crosses below -80. Below the EMA, the Williams %R crosses. Using the Williams %R indicator, create brief entry and exit signals L2 Vitali Apirine Stochastic MACD Oscillator Entry/Exit Signal #7 Written by: Blackcat 1402 Use the TradingView indicator search box and enter "L2 Vitali Apirine Stochastic MACD Oscillator" to locate this indicator (by blackcat1402). Synopsis: This is a variant that combines the stochastic oscillator (SO) and the moving average convergence divergence (MACD) indicator.

Compared to the standard MACD, this variant of the indicator is smoother and generates less whipsaw signs in erratic markets. The addition of overbought/oversold zones, which would have to be done by hand with the normal MACD, is one of the main differences with this MACD. Moreover, the color of this MACD indicator will vary based on whether it is crossed up, down, or in the OB/OS zones. Signals can be quickly identified because of these color shifts. Indicator Tip: When employing crossover signals, you can eliminate the MACD histogram to make the MACD more visible. Long Entry: -The oversold (below -10) MACD -The MACD crosses up, changing its color to green. -The MACD exits the oversold area by crossing upward. -The MACD crosses over 10 (overbought) to indicate a long exit. -The MACD crosses down, changing its color to red. Using the L2 Vitali Apirine Stochastic MACD Oscillator, long entry and exit signals Brief Entry: -The MACD color goes to red (crosses down) -The MACD is over 10 (overbought) -The MACD exits the overbought area by crossing downward. Short Exit: -Oversold, or when the MACD crosses below -10. -The MACD color crosses up, turning green.

L2 Vitali Apirine Stochastic MACD Oscillator Oscillator Entry/Exit Signal #8: Cyclic Smoothed RSI with Divergence Indicator Short entry and exit signals Written by: Dr. Roboto Enter "Cyclic Smoothed RSI with Divergence Indicator" in TradingView's indicator search bar to locate this indicator (by Dr_Roboto). Synopsis: This is a relative strength index (RSI) indicator variant that generates entry/exit signals using a significantly altered RSI. This indicator consists of a weighted moving average (WMA) and bands on the RSI. When this indicator has multiple ways to produce a signal, these are as follows: On the RSI, a red or green dot appears. The bands are crossed by the RSI above or below. Crossing the WMA is the RSI. When the RSI reaches overbought or oversold areas The bands shift in hue from red to green. While some of these indications work better for scalping, others are more appropriate for trend trading.

When the bands shift from red to green, they can be used as a trend filter. Indicator Tip: This indicator's colors can be altered to make signals easier to recognize. Long Entry: RSI displays a green dot (better for scalping). The bottom band is crossed by the RSI. The WMA is crossed by the RSI above. The oversold zone is crossed by the RSI upward. Long Exit: The RSI displays a red dot. After crossing over the upper band, the RSI crosses below it. The WMA is crossed below by the RSI. Above 70, the RSI enters the overbought zone. An illustration of extended entry and exit signals utilizing the Divergence Indicator and Cyclic Smoothed RSI Short Entry: RSI displays a green dot, which is preferable for scalping. The bottom band is crossed by the RSI. The WMA is crossed by the RSI above. The oversold zone is crossed by the RSI upward. Short Exit: The RSI displays a red dot. After crossing over the upper band, the RSI crosses below it. The WMA is crossed below by the RSI. Above 70, the RSI enters the overbought zone. An illustration of brief entry and exit signals utilizing the Divergence Indicator and Cyclic Smoothed RSI Oscillator Ingress/Regress MFI + Moving Average is Signal #9. Cross Include in the chart: Change the MFI (Money Flow Index) length to 21. On the MFI, add a simple moving average of 18. Synopsis: The money flow index (MFI) and moving average crossover are used by this entry/exit signal to determine peaks and bottoms.

The main distinction between the MFI and RSI oscillators is that the MFI uses volume in its computations. Long Entry/Short Exit: When the MFI is below 50 and crosses over the SMA Short Entry/Long Exit: The MFI crosses over 50 and below the SMA. Example of the MFI + 18 SMA cross entry and exit signals

Trend Tracking Entry and Exit Signals of Indicators

Traders employ trend following indicators as tools to determine a trend's direction. When a trend has formed, trend following indicators will notify traders of it and also warn them of possible price breakouts or reversals. The moving average crossover, which generates buy and sell signals using two separate moving averages, is the most basic type of trend following indicator.

A purchase signal is produced when the shorter-term moving average crosses over and above the longer-term one (and vice versa for a sell signal). Another typical trend-following indicator is when the price crosses above or below a moving average. A purchase signal is often shown when the price moves above a predetermined moving average, and a sell signal is typically indicated when it moves below. Additionally, trend followers might search for other kinds of signals, such breakouts or divergences. When the price is setting new highs or lows and the indicator is not supporting the move with new highs or lows of its own, this is known as divergence. This can suggest that the direction of pricing is about to reverse. Prices that surpass a particular level constitute a "breakout" from the established trend line and suggest the possibility of significant momentum in either direction.

It's crucial to keep in mind that trend following indicators, of any kind, shouldn't be employed as a stand-alone trading tactic. To obtain a more comprehensive understanding of the market's direction, traders must integrate them with other types of technical analysis, such as price action or support/resistance levels. When trading with trend following indicators, traders need also make sure they are using good money management strategies. Traders can improve their chances of success in the markets by utilizing excellent risk management tactics together with a variety of analysis approaches. Trend After Entry/Exit Signal No. 1: UT Bot Notifications From: QuantNomad Enter "UT Bot Alerts" in the TradingView indicator search box (created by QuantNomad) to locate this indicator. Synopsis: This trend-following indicator, akin to the supertrend indicator, is based on the average true rate.

Depending on the trend, the color of the candles will alternate between green and red. The "buy" and "sell" labels that show up on the screen when a signal occurs make this indicator useful for quickly spotting changes in trends. When markets are trending, this indicator performs well; but, when prices are sideways, it will give erroneous signals. ATR period = 20 and Key Value = 3 are the settings to use when utilizing the indicator as a trend filter. Long Entry: The color of the candle turns green A candle has a green "buy" label underneath it. Long Exit: Reddish-colored candle A candle has a red "sell" label underneath it. Brief Entry: Reddening of candle color A candle has a red "sell" label underneath it. Quick Exit: Green candle color shift A candle has a green "buy" label underneath it. Trend Following Signal #2 for Entry/Exit: Bjorgum MTF MA

Written by: Bjorgum Enter "Bjorgum MTF MA" in the TradingView indicator search box to locate this indicator (by Bjorgum) Synopsis: This indicator, a moving average, is quite good at spotting trends and trend reversals in their early stages. When price crosses and closes above or below the moving average, it generates signals. A signal also causes the color of the candles to change. With few false signals, this indicator will try to keep you in trends for as long as possible. When utilizing this indicator, an upward trend is indicated by blue candles and a downward trend is indicated by red candles. To better suit your trading strategy, you can adjust the indicator settings to modify the MA type. When markets are horizontal and there is little volatility, this indicator should not be used because there will be more false signals.

The EMA and SMA are better for trading trends, whereas the DEMA and HMA are better for scalping. Long Entry: A candle rises above the MA and then falls. The color of the MA line changes from red to blue. Blue replaces red in a candle. Long Exit: Red instead of blue color changes in the MA A candle goes out beneath the MA. Blue to red candle color shift (less dependable) An example of utilizing the Bjorgum MTF for entry and departure signals MA Brief Entry: A candle crosses below the MA and closes. The MA line turns red from blue. Blue candles turn red with time. Quick Exit: The MA turns blue instead of red. The color of the candle shifts from red to blue (less dependable). Trend Tracking Entry/Exit Signal #3: Line Indicator Follows Angle Attack Through Dreadblitz Type "Angle Attack Follow Line" into TradingView's indicator search box (by Dreadblitz) to locate the indicator.

Overview: The AAFLI is an indicator based on the ATR that additionally generates buy and sell signals by computing from the Bollinger bands.

One of my favorite trend-following indicators, it's quite good at spotting shifts in market trends. The AAFLI is shown at the bottom of the chart as a histogram. Depending on the trend, candles will become blue or red when a signal is detected. The histogram will also have a buy/sell label, which makes it very simple to recognize signals on this indicator. Tip for Indicators: Within the configurations Disable the histogram's backdrop color scheme. Save for the "buy" and "sell" signals, turn off all other signals. Long Entry: Blue hue shifts in the candle There's a "buy" label on the histogram. Long Exit: The color of the candle turns red, and the histogram displays a "sell" indication. Example of utilizing the AAFLI indicator for entrance and exit signals

Brief Entry: Reddening of candle color There's a "buy" label on the histogram. Short Exit: The histogram's "buy" label appears, and the candle's color changes to blue. Using the AAFLI indication, create brief entry and exit signals Trend Following Signal #4 for Entry/Exit: AlphaTrend Written by: Kivanc Ozbilgin In TradingView's indicator search box, enter "AlphaTrend " to discover the indicator (by Kivanc Ozbilgin). Synopsis: This indicator consists of two moving average-like lines that track price based on the average true range, or ATR. These lines will cross to provide buy/sell indications. With few false signals, this indicator is able to predict market fluctuations in price with high accuracy.

The "buy" or "sell" label will show up when the ATR lines cross and a signal occurs, making this indicator incredibly simple to use. Large price swings and more volatility are the ideal conditions for this indicator to function. If the volatility is too low, steer clear of utilizing this indicator as it will generate misleading indications. indication Tip: To make this indication easier to view, you can adjust its colors in the settings. Long Entry: A buy label is displayed and the price is higher than the AlphaTrend. Prolonged Exit: The market ends below the AlphaTrend. There's a sell label. Example of utilizing the AphaTrend indicator for entry and exit signals Short Entry: A sell label emerges and the price is below the AlphaTrend. Short Sale: The market ends above the AlphaTrend. There's a buy label. Trend After Entrance/Exit

Half Trend Indicator (Signal #5) Through: everget Enter "half trend" in TradingView's indicator search box (by everget) to find an indicator. Synopsis: When it comes to correctly identifying market tops and bottoms in the near term, the half trend indicator excels. This is quite easy to use and comprehend because an arrow will show below or above the price when a buy or sell indication happens.

The ideal markets for this indicator to function in are those with greater volatility and wider price swings. This indicator will be less trustworthy and generate more false alerts when volatility is extremely low. Tip for the indicator: Try the following configurations when the market is not very volatile: Amplitude 1 Deviation 1 of Channel Long Entry: A candle has a blue arrow beneath it. Line color variations Long Exit: Select from the options below.- A candle has a red arrow above it. Red line color shifts a snapshot of the half trend indicator's entry/exit signals Brief Entry: A candle has a red arrow above it. The line turns red. Short Exit: Select one of the following: A candle has a blue arrow beneath it. The hue of the lines turns blue. inclination Subsequent Entry/Exit

Kaufman Moving Average Adaptive (KAMA) is the sixth signal. Through HPotter Enter "Kaufman Moving Average Adaptive" in TradingView's indicator search box (by HPotter) to locate this indicator. Synopsis: The KAMA is a moving average that only tracks prices when a trend is evident and is intended to filter out non-trending price changes. This moving average will show up as a flow in a sideways market and will only have a slope when the price is trending. In non-trending markets, this lessens whipsaw signals that arise from using other moving averages. Long Entry: Above the KAMA, a candle crosses and closes. The slope of the KAMA is uphill. Candle closes below the KAMA on a long exit. Using the KAMA, extend arrival and departure signals Brief Entry: Below the KAMA, a candle crosses and closes. The slope of the KAMA is downhill. Short Exit: The KAMA is closed with a candle.

Stock Market Fundamental Analysis

The Value of Information "The market is like a beautiful woman — endlessly fascinating, endlessly complex, always changing, and always mystifying," Mr. Johnson writes in Adam Smith's The Money Game. Since 1924, I have been engrossed and involved, and I am aware that this is not science. It's artistic. Even with computers and a plethora of facts at our disposal, the market remains unchanged and comprehension of it remains challenging. It is human intuition, recognizing behavioral patterns. The market is interesting and seductive, and once you enter it, "it is foolish to think that you can withdraw from the exchange after you have tasted the sweetness of the honey," as De La Vega observed in the seventeenth century. "There is always something unknown, undiscerned." The prospect of enormous fortune is what draws people to the market.

For a number of years, one of the richest individuals on the planet has been Warren Buffett. Forbes estimated his net worth to be $47 billion in 2010. All of the money comes from the market, specifically from running the Hathaway investment firm. He is a supporter of fundamental research and value investment. Investing is driven by the prospect of immense wealth, the desire to emulate individuals such as Warren Buffett and his mentors Benjamin Graham and Bernard Baruch. This bait was seen in India in 1992, early 2000 (the last four months of the year), late 2003 (the end of the second quarter), and more recently in 2006 and 2007, when prices spiked. These speculative urges happen in a similar way and very frequently. This is also not limited to shares. The seventeenth-century Dutch tulip frenzy drove their values skyrocketing.

Ancestral land and family treasures were sold or pawned in 1992 due to the tremendous rush to purchase shares in India due to the overwhelming thirst for riches. Prices increased for a while before the bubble burst. When the price of information technology shares reached incredible heights at the beginning of 2000, this happened once more. Several astute marketers made a fortune in the market by renaming their businesses as "infotech" or adding the term to their names. Their prices dropped significantly in March and April 2000, proving that the law of gravity must be obeyed and that business pricing will eventually stabilize at their actual level. Share prices increased as the masses gained control, leaving no room for reason or common sense.

In his Psychologie des Foules, Gustave Le Bon noted that the masses behave irrationally and with a single-minded goal. Whatever the individuals that make up a crowd, however similar or dissimilar their lifestyle, their occupations, or their intellectual nature, he claims that the most remarkable characteristic of a crowd is that "they have become a collective mind that causes them to feel, think, and act differently from that in which each individual of them would feel, think, and act were he in a state of isolation." Le Bon describes how the logical investor becomes mindless—that is, giving up his ability to think rationally in favor of the prevailing mood of the moment—and how the mob is in a state of captivated curiosity. Everywhere in late 1999 and early 2000, as well as in India in 1992 and once more in 2006 and 2007, the masses behaved impulsively, driven by gossip that was fueled by avarice as well as expectations and optimism.

Like a balloon, the index ballooned up and then exploded. It was required. Regretfully, at periods like these, small investors lose out since they don't constantly monitor the market and lack the resources or connections to understand what is likely to happen to it. Let's look at what has occurred in India over the past 20 years. Investors were purchasing in 1992 for the most tenuous of reasons, thinking the bubble would never stop. I recall someone telling me to purchase stock in a specific company. This company wasn't too well-known at the time. What action did the corporation take, I asked him to tell me? Who served as its directors? What was its past three years' performance like? He didn't know and didn't give a damn. He was sending along a tip he had got that the price would treble. Karnataka Ball Bearings is another share that needs to be brought up; at the time, its share price was in the low 20s. In just ten days, the price of the share increased from Rs. 60 to Rs. 68 to Rs. 180, all due to a rumor that Harshad Mehta was purchasing it. Then, it was learned that the rumor of Harshad Mehta's ownership stake in the share was untrue. In four days, the share price fell to Rs. 50. The initial rumor sprung up. Again, the cost increased to Rs. 120.

The price dropped after the rumor was once more refuted as untrue. I was speaking at the time with someone who was quite close to the business. He informed me that there was no business activity and that the company was unwell. It was actually in danger of closing. The audience, which was made up of otherwise bright, reasonable, and sensible people, behaved irrationally and illogically once the price increased on the most tenuous of justifications. Many people made money on the stock, but the majority lost money because they only knew that Harshad Mehta was purchasing the shares when they acquired it. One could have assumed that one learns. Not at all. History is repeated. Indian shares, particularly those associated with Information Technology (IT), like Wipro, Infosys (fondly termed Infy), and Satyam (Sify), started to be quoted on the NASDAQ in the United States towards the close of the previous century. These shares started to soar along with the NASDAQ, and there was a general consensus that software was the new buzzword and that the stock prices of all IT businesses could only go higher.

This sparked a rising trend that grew stronger every day until prices skyrocketed. As the exit of the wise took hold, prices started to decline. The effect of this was compounding, and before long, prices had dropped by over 50%. Afterwards, during the dotcom boom, shares were valued according to the "stickiness of eyeballs." It is hardly possible to become any more mystical. People started purchasing the shares that Ketan Parekh was allegedly purchasing later in 2000. The question "Will investors never learn? "begs to be answered.The most likely explanation is that human greed knows no bounds. In 2003, price increases started to occur once more. After the Sensex crossed the 5,000 mark, many people forecast that it would hit 6,000 in six months, a year, or very soon. The Sensex saw an unheard-of spike between 2006 and 2007. The Sensex finished at 21,078 on January 8, 2008, marking the culmination of it. It was projected at the time that the Sensex would reach 50,000 in a matter of months. Many people place their trust in the "strength" of these forecasts, which are really hopes, expectations, and forecasts.

Nothing sensible or logical. According to fundamental analysis, no one should buy stock at random. Purchasing shares is a serious endeavor, and every element—no matter how small—must be examined and taken into account. "No one should buy (a share) without knowing as much as possible about the company that issues it," remarked billionaire Jean Paul Getty, who was the richest man in the world until his death. Among the greatest stock pickers of all time was Jim Slater. He developed the Zulu idea, which holds that one needs to be fully informed about the business, the sector, and every other element that can have an impact on the performance of the organization. He maintained that with this knowledge, one could never lose. If there is a chance that the company will do poorly, one can purchase shares at a discount when the price drops and vice versa. Informed investing is the way that successful and experienced investors think. And the key idea of fundamental analysis is this.

There is no alternative for information, in the words of Adam Smith. It's not a roulette wheel, the market.

The only things that are absolutely necessary in the marketplace are competent research and ideas. Fundamental analysis requires—nay, insists—on accurate information about a company. It necessitates closely examining a firm's financial accounts and performance, as well as conducting in-depth analyses of the economy and the sector in which the company works. The fundamentalist then decides whether to purchase or sell based on his analysis, experience, and investment maturity, as well as how he interprets the information he has been given. All information is significant and falls into one of the following categories: economic information. information on taxes, levies, duties, and other aspects of government policy. Details regarding the sector in which the business works. Details about the business, such as its sales, management, performance, and goods, as well as how it stacks up against other businesses of a similar nature. information regarding the expenditures, trends, and views of consumers.

We are fortunate in India that there is a growing awareness of the need for knowledge today more than ever before, and that the media, scholars, and qualified investment consultants are addressing this demand. Internet: The internet is a fantastic informational resource. It can provide you with a wealth of information, including biographies, corporate results, and the state of the economy. One can now instantaneously purchase and sell shares via the internet. Media The economy, industry, and specific companies are covered in a number of investment and business-focused periodicals, newspapers, and directories that are now available. These include excellent articles that provide a detailed analysis of many industries and businesses. They also provide informative articles about money, investing methods, taxation, and related topics. I would strongly suggest that a serious investor read two magazines a month in addition to at least one excellent financial publication each day. This should keep him up to date.

Investment Newsletters: A number of knowledgeable and experienced professionals handle and publish investments. They are frequently quite current and feature information that investors would not typically have access to, which makes them incredibly helpful. Insiders are those who work for a corporation or have close relationships with it and have knowledge of or access to information that is not widely known. This could include details on the company's success, impending bonus or rights difficulties, or other pertinent news. Since not everyone is aware of the knowledge, the investor needs to move quickly if he wants to profit handsomely. Within its declared norms, the Securities Exchange Board of India (SEBI) forbids insider trading. Aside from the fact that insider trading violates SEBI regulations and the law, I would also advise against it due to the numerous hazards involved. Excellent seminars and lectures by investment experts are being held throughout the nation. Edwin Leferre cautioned against it in his book Reminiscences of a Stockbroker, writing, "Wall Street professionals know that acting on inside tips will break a man more quickly than famine, pestilence, crop failure, political readjustments or what may be called normal accidents." These lectures are given by distinguished people, and attending them will provide you with a wealth of knowledge. These could be about the state of the industry, their perception of it, or something similar. Even new people can be thought of as thought partners.

This may lead to the formation of opinions. Taking these ideas to action could be beneficial. Stockbrokers: Stockbrokers typically keep track of a company's performance as well as other factors that influence a share's price because they are in constant communication with them. But keep in mind this: Stockbrokers typically have a short-term perspective on companies. A broker will often provide information based on tips and rumors, many of which may be false and unsupported. Stockbrokers occasionally give positive company descriptions based on rumors; this could be deceptive. Brokers could also provide you with information to force you to purchase the shares they're trying to sell. These are the principal information sources. You have to practice listening and taking in new information. To choose the most advantageous Book of action, you should evaluate and comprehend the data. The primary tenet of fundamental analysis is to take action only after gathering and evaluating facts. Additionally, it is crucial to move quickly upon receiving knowledge because, more often than not, the first person to do so will stand to gain the most from it. Rothschild acted in this manner. On June 18, 1815, the Duke of Wellington matched his 75,000 English soldiers against Napoleon's 100,000 forces in what will go down in history as one of the most important battles in European history.

The outcome of the battle would determine the fate of Europe and its colonies around the world, making it a crucial battle. London's investors were nervous and alarmed. There was fear that England might lose the fight because, at the start of the conflict, Marshal Von Blucher's German army had not joined forces with its English partner. Trade between China and India for the British East India Company was in jeopardy. There was concern that England's friends may turn on it. There was a stake in the destiny of the English Empire. The market anticipated news. Leading merchant banker Nathan Rothschild of the House of Rothschild made a substantial investment to create a private intelligence organization because he understood the value of knowledge. This was widely recognized. Furthermore, it was widely recognized that Rothschild had made significant bets on an English triumph. Rothschild's operatives sent carrier pigeons bearing the war's outcome in code to him as soon as it ended. Rothschild started selling everything he owned as soon as they got there, even before the official dispatches.

Investors panicked, thinking the English had lost, and started selling. The market fell apart. Rothschild intervened in the down market and continued to buy along with his agents. The market boomed within hours of Wellington's triumph being announced. Rothschild said, "The best time to buy is when blood is running in the streets," after using this maneuver to gain a million pounds—a huge sum of money at the time.

Essential Evaluation

Every share has a certain intrinsic value at a given point in time, according to the fundamental analysis known as the Search for Intrinsic Value. This inherent worth fluctuates throughout time due to a variety of internal and external influences. According to the fundamental analysis hypothesis, a share should be bought when it is priced below its intrinsic worth and sold when it is higher. A share is undervalued when its market value is less than its intrinsic worth, and it is overvalued when its market value is greater than its intrinsic value. Thus, the goal of fundamentalists is to buy cheap shares and sell expensive ones. They contend that while there may be short-term fluctuations between the market price and intrinsic value, ultimately the market price will match the intrinsic value.

What is Intrinsic Value: How much is a share worth on its own? How is it ascertained? According to fundamental analysis, the intrinsic value of a share must be determined by the advantages that investors receive from it. Strict fundamental analysis determines that the intrinsic value of a company is the present value of future dividends discounted based on perceived safety or risk, since the return to shareholders takes the form of dividends.

Because a dividend is what a shareholder or investor receives from a corporation, rather than the earnings per share of the company, the intrinsic value of a dividend is based on it. This is a crucial distinction. Intrinsic Value Calculation So how does one figure out a share's intrinsic value? Assume for the moment that someone is looking for a 20% annual return on their investment after three years. Assume for the moment that the corporation will pay dividends on its Rs. 10 share of 20%, 25%, and 30%. Thus, a share would yield a dividend of Rs. 2.00 in the first year, Rs. 2.50 in the second, and Rs. 3.00 in the third year. Let's also assume that after three years, the share can be sold for Rs. 200. The reasoning is to discount the dividend that has been paid and is projected to be received in the future, as well as the predicted price at a later period with the expected return or yield, to determine the intrinsic value of the share. This approach to determining intrinsic value is regarded as the most equitable and balanced since it takes into account both the price at that future period and the potential for capital appreciation.

If the share's market price is less than Rs. 120.88, it is still well worth buying because it is below its intrinsic value. The share should be sold if, however, the market price is greater as this is a sell signal. Considerations It is important to remember that various people will value a share differently when it comes to its intrinsic value. The intrinsic value (assuming the dividends and the sale value at the end of three years will remain the same) will be as follows if, with regard to the aforementioned investment, another individual (Kumar) expects a return of 16% and a third individual (Nair) expects a return of 25%. Specifically, if the market price is Rs. 120.88, the first individual (let's call him Siddharth) will hold onto the share, whereas Nair would sell the share and Kumar would buy it. To put it briefly, each person's intrinsic value for a share will be different and will depend on their willingness to take on risk as well as their expectations for return. It makes sense to eliminate this anomaly. The projected return should be the same as what would be expected from a different, somewhat safe investment in that market.

Given that riskier investments yield higher returns, this rate ought to be supported by a risk component. A blue chip investment, which is extremely safe, will have a risk rate of 0. The risk rate of an established near-blue chip share will be 1. A business in growth will have a risk rating of two. A new, risky business will get a risk rating of three. Given the following assumptions: the intrinsic value of a share of the company will depend on its financial strength and stage of growth, but it will always be higher the safer the share. For example, if one assumes that the return on a reasonably safe investment (say, an investment with the Unit Trust of India) is 16%, and the dividend is expected to be Rs. 2 in the first year, Rs. 2.5 in the second year, and Rs. 3 in the third year, and the anticipated sale price is expected to be Rs. 200. One aspect is projected or presumed to exist, nevertheless, and that is the final cost after three years. I think that basing the price on an earnings multiple is the most acceptable approach, despite the fact that this is debatable.

A share's market price divided by its earnings per share is known as its price-earnings multiple, or P/E. In the event that a company's earnings per share (EPS) increase by 20% to Rs. 7 in the current year, and assuming a conservative 15% annual growth rate, the EPS at the end of the first year will be Rs. 7.70, and at the end of the second year it will be Rs. 8.47, and at the end of the third year it will be Rs. 9.32. In that industry, a good price-to-earnings ratio for a company of that size would be 15, therefore after three years, the market price would be 9.32 × 15 = Rs. 139.80. Now let's examine a real-world case. A company's shares were priced at Rs. 465 on May 31, 2010.

For the fiscal year that concluded on March 31, 2010, the corporation announced earnings per share of Rs. 13.1 and a dividend of 65%. Given a continuous dividend and a respectable P/E ratio of 20, the intrinsic value of the company's shares is estimated to be Rs. 266. Based on a 20% annual growth rate in earnings, the projected earnings per share (EPS) after three years would be Rs. 22,98 (13.3 x 1.20 x 1.20 x 1.20). Assuming such, the price after three years would be 459.60 rupees (EPS x P/E of 20). The intrinsic value today, assuming a 20% projected return, is as follows: The company's share price at Rs. 465 was, therefore, approximately 67% above its intrinsic value, and this suggestion suggests that the shares be sold.

On May 31, 2010, a 100% export-oriented unit cost 160. Up to March 31, 2010, its profit had increased by 60% to Rs. 17.88 crore. With earnings per share of Rs. 10.26, it saw a 23% increase. The EPS at the end of the two years would be Rs. 14.77 if we estimate that its EPs will grow by 20% over the next two years.

After two years, at a P/E of 15, its market value would be Rs. 221.55. The business distributed a 25% dividend in 2010. Based on the supposition that the dividend of 25% would be upheld in 2011 and will increase to 30% in 2005, the following represents its intrinsic worth with a 20% projected return: At Rs. 158.02, its intrinsic value was extremely near to the Rs. 160 market value. Since the export-oriented unit is a relatively young business, one could expect a 25% return, in which case the intrinsic value would be as follows: At a 25% expected return, the share should be sold because its market value of Rs. 160 exceeded its intrinsic value of Rs. 145.71. The subjective presumptions used to calculate the intrinsic value lead to variations in each individual's intrinsic value for a share. In the preceding example, the intrinsic value of the firm share would be Rs. 158.02 for an investor anticipating a 20% return, but for an individual expecting a 25% return, it would be Rs. 145.71. The other assumptions, such as the projected price at the conclusion of the period and the projected dividends during the time, are also purely subjective. That being said, this approach makes perfect sense. It takes into account the anticipated capital growth as well as the dividends that will be paid. Efficient Market idea: Fundamental analysts frequently utilize this idea to ascertain a share's fundamental value.

According to this hypothesis, in an efficient market, information is promptly available to all investors, is comprehended and evaluated by all parties involved, and is immediately reflected in market pricing. Thus, the most recent position is always represented by the market price at all times. According to efficient market theory, it is impossible to turn a profit by examining historical data or past price change trends. It makes the assumption that the present market price has already factored in all anticipated developments. Thus, fundamentalists invest time and energy in determining the impact of numerous events—both past and present—on the company's profitability and its expected outcomes in order to calculate the likely future price at a later date and identify the share's present intrinsic worth. This needs to cover the potential for the business to offer rights shares or issue bonus shares. Because of this, fundamental analysis is divided into three distinct parts: the economy, the industry the company operates in, and the company itself. Information about the economy, the industry, and the company itself is the most important factor in fundamental analysis.

Any information that can affect the growth and profitability of the company is considered significant. The intrinsic worth of the share must be ascertained by interpreting and analyzing the data. An investment decision can only be made after comparing this intrinsic worth to what the fundamentalists claim is the market value.

Political-Economic Interpretation

As a result, imports are far less expensive, which has an impact on numerous businesses. It is crucial to assess a company's sensitivity to regulatory policies and restrictive practices. Foreign Debt and the Trade Balance: A country's economy may be severely burdened by foreign debt, particularly if it is very substantial. India pays interest and principal repayments of about $5 billion annually. This is a substantial amount. Due to a negative balance of payments and significantly more imports than exports, this is the price the nation has had to pay. The nation had no other option when it decided to borrow money. During the 1991 devaluation, India's foreign exchange reserves could barely cover a few weeks' worth of imports.

The government borrowed money from the World Bank in order to reverse this and depreciate the currency. Only when there is a greater influx of foreign cash than outflow will a permanent solution be reached; for this reason, the travel, export, and exchange-earning/saving businesses are promoted. Inflation The economy is greatly impacted by inflation. It reduces purchasing power domestically. Demand declines as a result. The cost of production in the nation from which a corporation imports will inevitably increase if that nation has a high rate of inflation. This could make the finished product less cost-competitive to manufacture. On the other hand, if the nation to which one exports has a high rate of inflation, the products become more appealing and sales rise. Inflation rates in the USA and Europe are quite modest, at roughly 5%.

Inflation in India has been gradually declining recently. As of right now, estimates range from 2.5% to 3%. It was once more than 1000% in South America. There, money was worthless. Ironically, roaring inflation and the ensuing depreciation of their currency make South

American exports appealing because their goods are now more affordable on global marketplaces. A stable nation is one with low inflation, and during these periods, local businesses and industries thrive. The Danger of Nationalization: The worry that a business might be taken over by the government is a genuine concern in many nations. Nationalized businesses have often been less efficient than their private sector equivalents, with relatively few exceptions. If one depends on a business for specific goods, nationalization may cause those supplies to become unpredictable. Furthermore, private investment is stifled by the fear of nationalization, and there may be a capital flight abroad. Interest Rates: Industry and investment are encouraged by low interest rates.

On the other hand, high interest rates raise manufacturing costs and reduce consumption. The competitiveness of a corporation declines when costs are high. The Indian government has started pushing for lower interest rates. This works well. Many companies save a large amount of money on interest. Taxation A nation's economy is directly impacted by the amount of taxes levied there. Individuals with low tax rates have more disposable money. They also have an incentive to put in more effort and make more money. as well as a reason to invest. The economy will benefit from this. It's noteworthy to observe that the highest tax collection occurs between 35 and 55 percent of GDP in every economy. Tax rates may rise, while revenue collection will decrease. For this reason, some have claimed that rates in India ought to be cut. Government Policy The economy is directly impacted by government policy. Investment will come to a government that is seen as pro-industry. The developed world was enthralled with the Narsimha Rao government's liberalization measures, and international businesses became eager to invest in India and grow their current interests in their Indian projects. Rekindled interest is being generated by the BJP government's efforts to construct and enhance infrastructure.

Domestic Savings and Their Use: If domestic savings are put to good use, they help quicken economic expansion. India boasts one of the highest savings rates (22%). It is as high as 23% in Japan, but barely 2% in the USA. Japan's growth can be attributed to its successful and efficient use of its domestic savings. India has a large amount of savings, however these funds have not been allocated effectively or sensibly. As such, there hasn't been much development. Always keep in mind that savings are the foundation of every investment. Investment money that was borrowed must be reimbursed. Savings investments result in higher future consumption. The government has acknowledged this. The 1992 Finance Act stated that an individual's productive assets (such as shares, debentures, etc.) would not be subject to wealth tax in an effort to redirect savings to industry. The Infrastructure An economy's ability to grow is reliant on its infrastructure.

Roads are needed to move products, and industry needs electricity to manufacture. Inadequate infrastructure results in waste, delays, low production, and inefficiencies. This may be the cause of the 1993 budget's heavy emphasis on and generous incentives to the infrastructure sectors, including transportation and electricity. There has been more of an emphasis in recent years. There are now flyovers, improved and wider national highways, and amazing advancements in communications. Budgetary Deficit: When government spending surpasses revenue, a budgetary deficit is created. Spending boosts demand and creates jobs, which both benefit the economy. But inflation and deficit financing are both possible outcomes of this. If left unchecked, both of these can lead to price spirals. In order to reduce and manage deficits, governments typically reduce their spending. Additionally, this would cause the money supply to decline, which would lower demand and control inflation. As governments spend to create roads, power plants, and other infrastructure improvements, all emerging economies experience budget deficits.

India is not an anomaly. There have been large budget deficits. In order to combat inflation, the government has deliberately lowered spending, which has dropped from a peak of almost 15% a few years ago to 6% to 7% currently. Monsoons: Because India's economy is based primarily on agriculture, the monsoon season is crucial to it. In late March and early April, economic activity usually grinds to a complete halt as people wait to see if the monsoon will be favorable or not. Employment To have a healthy growth in the national GDP, high employment is necessary. The rate of unemployment is rising as population expansion outpaces economic growth. The economy will not benefit from this.

The Economic Cycle

Every nation experiences an economic or business cycle, and the stage of the cycle that a nation is in directly affects industry and specific businesses. It influences demand, employment, investment decisions, and business profitability. The business cycle has a significant impact on certain industries, including shipping and consumer durable goods, but not on others, like the food or health sectors. This is due to the fact that consumers can delay making decisions about some things while they cannot with others. An economic cycle has four stages: depression, recovery, boom, and recession. Depression: Demand is low and declining during a depression. Both interest rates and inflation are frequently high. Companies are obliged to reduce production, close down operations established during periods of increased demand, and fire employees as a result of high financing costs and declining revenues.

The late 1970s saw a slump in the United States. The 1980s were a golden year as the economy rebounded. The late 1980s and early 1990s saw another decline, particularly in the wake of the Gulf War. In 1993, the economies of the US and the rest of Western Europe started to revive once more. Later, around the turn of the 2000, the US had another depressive phase. India experienced a challenging time as well, and in 2002 it started to recover. Recovery The economy starts to improve during this stage. Demand increases and fresh investment is made. Businesses start to report their profits. Spending with conspicuousness starts once again.

At a higher proportionate pace, profits start to grow once the recovery stage fully takes hold. To keep up with the economy's growing demand, a rising number of new businesses are being launched. 2003 might be considered a year of recovery in India. The economy exhibits every characteristic of a recovery. Boom: During this stage, demand is at its highest point ever. Additionally, investment is high. There are low interest rates. Over time, supply eventually starts to outpace demand. After increasing, prices now start to decline. A rise in inflation is observed. Recession: A gradual decline in the economy. Demand begins to decline. Both inflation and interest rates start to rise. Businesses begin to struggle to sell their products. The economy starts to deteriorate gradually. Demand begins to decline. Both inflation and interest rates start to rise. Businesses begin to struggle to sell their products. Beginning in 1996, India had a severe recession for four years. The Investment Decision: Investors ought to try to ascertain whatever phase of the nation's economic cycle it is in. When the economy starts to recover at the end of a depression and at the conclusion of a recession, that is when they should invest.

Investors should sell their holdings as soon as the boom starts, continues, or, in the worst case scenario, ends. Investors that make these kinds of decisions will profit the most from their investments and withdrawals. It is important to remember, though, that there is no set length of time for a boom to last or a certain number of years for a recession to last. As a result, estimating the duration of a current cycle should not be done using the length of past cycles. It is essential for investors to consider the effects of political and governmental decisions on the economy before making a final investment decision because they have the power to undo progress made in the past due to events or government policies. "Cycles are not, like tonsils, separable things that might be treated by themselves; rather, like the beat of the heart, they are of the essence of the organism that displays them," stated Joseph Schumpeter once.

Understanding Asset Bubbles and Protecting Yourself

When they Burst: An asset bubble arises when an excess of demand drives up asset values beyond reasonable limits. It happens when the money supply is large, interest rates are low, credit is readily available, and the jobless rate is low. It happens during a period of great economic optimism. A variety of assets, such as stocks, real estate, and commodities, are susceptible to asset bubbles. There is typically happiness and a general feeling of enthusiasm during a bubble. Price increases are warranted by logic and the anticipation of future price increases.

Following a period of economic expansion, prices started to climb following several years of a down market. The Indian stock markets saw an unrelenting increase in prices throughout 2006 and 2007. On January 8, 2008, the Bombay Stock Exchange Sensitivity Index (Sensex) reached a record high of 21,078. The excitement was so intense at the time that forecasters said the Sensex would reach 50,000 by June 2008. In tandem, real estate values also increased. Getting credit was simple. There were comparatively low interest rates. The atmosphere was one of celebration. Bubbles broke. There will inevitably be a crash when the euphoria becomes unsustainable. There were significant declines in the Sensex during the third week of January 2008. January 21, 2008, saw a 1,408-point decline in the Sensex. Later, it entered a wild decline, dropping steadily month after month until closing at less than 9,000 in November 2008.

When demand dwindled amid an economic downturn, other assets also experienced a corresponding decline. Following the Harshad Mehta scam, there was a comparable asset bubble burst in 1992–1993 and 2001–2002. An asset bubble in the stock market is a protracted period of severe overvaluation. When there is excessive speculation, bubbles form. Speculators examine a share's resale value rather than its intrinsic value, which is determined by basic study. When purchasing an asset, one hopes that it will double or triple in a short period of time. Rumors spread. There are cited cases of investors who generated enormous profits. Greed replaces rational cognition and economic data. Herd mentality sets in, and everyone follows the bull as the leader without question or reason. It doesn't matter whether the price is absurdly high in bubbles.

All that matters is that it may be sold later for an even more absurd amount. Bubbles terminate in severe drops where most of the speculative gains are soon wiped away, as was the case with the Sensex. The issue is that bubbles are difficult to spot until they burst. Intervention by central or other regulatory authorities results in a free fall, which is precisely what their purpose was to prevent. Two varieties of bubbles exist. The first kind of asset bubble is the result of brokerage firms or banks. They inflate an asset's value. Shares, money, or other financial instruments might be considered assets. The promise of unbelievable returns and interest payments entices greedy and gullible investors into investment scams in the second kind of bubble. Many initial public offers (IPOs) of investment and other enterprises occurred in India in the late 1980s and early 1990s, all luring unsuspecting investors with promises of enormous returns.

Numerous commentators, experts, and educational institutions attempt to defend bubbles while they persist. I remember commentators defending the Harshad Mehta-led bubble by saying Indian stocks were incredibly cheap and had only higher ground to go. The mantra throughout the 2006–2007 boom was that Indian companies had inconceivable potential and that their economy will develop even faster. India is the shining star of the world economy. Some even claimed that "old rules and archaic modes of thinking" did not apply to the thriving, new economy. They argued that productivity had increased and produced a trend line that was steeper but still stable. I recall a dispute in the early 1990s concerning ACC's valuation. The gurus maintained that the cost to establish a comparable business should be used to determine the company's value rather than its core competencies. The problem is that individual investors believe these knowledgeable people because they sound authoritative and self-assured.

You should be cautious of these "This time it's different" claims as a fundamental investor. It might be prudent to sell your assets if you are unable to see the rationale behind the increase in stock prices, if the growth is speculative, and if everyone, even your maids and cab drivers, is discussing shares. When a buddy asked when the boom would end in late 2007, I recall another acquaintance telling me it wouldn't happen for a while. He expressed it with such conviction that a few others acquired shares after asking him for advice. Within six months, their shares plunged by 300%, much to their despair. Furthermore, you shouldn't let newspaper articles and television interviews get to you. Keep in mind that these authorities are typically just as ignorant as you are. Would they be imparting their wisdom to you if they could truly see so clearly into the future?

They would be out there purchasing or selling shares and making a tidy sum of money. They are not altruistic people who wish for you to become wealthy with them. Before the Great Depression, the United States was engulfed in an illogical exuberance that was captured by writer Claud Cockburn, who wrote from New York for the Times of London. "A person with my European background felt alarmingly lonely at times, but the atmosphere of the great boom was savagely exciting," he wrote. The greatest analysts with the most impeccable credentials and track records failed to predict the crash and the unprecedented economic depression that followed.

He would have preferred to believe, as these people believed, in the endless upswing of the big bull market or else to meet just one person with whom he might discuss some general doubts without being regarded as an imbecile or a person of deliberately evil intent — some kind of anarchist, perhaps. Even newspapers deceived readers. Nearer home, even our media continues to make remarks like this. The New York Times wrote, "Rally at close cheers brokers, bankers optimistic," on Black Monday (October 24, 1929), when the market collapsed. In their paper "Bull and Bear Markets in the Twentieth Century," Bradford De Long and Robert Barsky stated that "major swings of this century were plausibly caused by shifts in assessments of fundamentals; investors had little knowledge of crucial factors, in particular the long run dividend growth rate and their changing expectations of average growth." I agree with their assessment. Hearsay-based investments are doomed from the outset, unlike those based on fundamental study.

Purchasing a share at Rs. 250 with the hope that it will increase to Rs. 500 in a year at a time when its intrinsic value is Rs. 30 is a naive assumption. It is best to buy it at its intrinsic, core value. Purchase it if the market price is less than Rs. 30, but do not pay more. In 2008, one bubble burst. The next bubble might appear soon. There's always a chance of this happening.

Evaluation of the Industry

The Indian investor is now more aware than ever of the value of industry analysis. In the past, investors bought company shares without giving the industry the company ran in any thought. And thirty years ago, they could get away with it. This occurred because, at the time, India was a sellers' market, meaning that goods created there would almost certainly be sold—often for a premium. Those carefree times are gone. There is fierce competition right now. Nowadays, consumers are price, quality, and fashion conscious. Indian goods must contend with the readily available foreign goods. Significant technical advancements cause "state of the art" equipment to become outdated in a matter of years. if not several months. During the late 1970s and early 1980s, projectors and movie cameras were highly valued. They were rendered obsolete in the mid-1980s with the introduction of the video camera. Laptop computers were the "in" thing in 1988.

Everyone was ecstatic about the creation and the way that technology could fit such a large computer into a tiny box. These early variants have two fixed disk drives instead of a hard disk. Hard drives were added a few months later; at first, they held 20 megabytes of storage. After that, the memory was expanded to 40 megabytes. The invention of the notebook in 18 months rendered the laptop obsolete. Even with their capacities reaching up to 120 megabytes, these notebooks are still far from the pinnacle of compressed computing. Now, the palm tops are here. These days, mobile phones are capable of computing. Sincerely, one has no idea what will come next. I've used these instances to show how a highly esteemed product becomes outdated due to technology advancements. Technological developments in one field can also have an impact on another.

When less expensive alternatives to jute were being utilized as packaging materials, the jute sector began to collapse. The Western world's predilection for cotton clothing had an impact on the man-made (synthetic) textile sector. As a result, an investor needs to research the industry a company works in, as this can have a significant impact on both its performance and continued existence. A corporation may have excellent management, a solid balance sheet, and an amazing reputation. But the business might not have diversified, and the sector in which it works might be going through a downturn. This may cause a sharp drop in sales and possibly jeopardize the company's survival. Cycle Identifying the industry's cycle and maturity level is the first step in doing an industry study. The following stages are seen in all industries' evolution: the entrepreneurial, dawn or fledgling, expansion or growth, stabilization, stagnation or maturity, and decline or sunset stages.

An inverted "S" curve, as seen above, can be used to depict the life cycle of an industry. The Entrepreneurial or Nascent Stage: During this initial phase, the industry is still developing and may require some time to fully establish itself. It can even lose money in these early stages. There could not be many businesses in the sector right now as well. It is important to remember that the first five to ten years are the most crucial. Businesses have the highest risk of failing right now. Establishing businesses and developing new items takes time. Losses could occur, and significant cash infusions might be required. A business or an industry may fail if it is not supported or nourished at this point. I know of a good journalist who started a business magazine. His goal was to launch a magazine run entirely by journalists, free from political or business interests. The magazine was really easy to read. But, it was forced to fail because it lacked the funding necessary to survive those crucial early years. It might have persisted and prospered if it had had the necessary funding at the time. In summary, investors accept a significant risk at this point in the hopes of receiving a large payout should the product be successful.

The Expansion or Growth Stage: Following its establishment, an industry moves into a growth stage. A large number of new businesses enter the market as it expands. As demand now exceeds supply, investors can benefit from high profit at little risk at this point. An excellent example in 2000 was the software sector in India. The BPO sector was arguably in its boom stage in 2003. With more recent models and new players, the mobile phone market is likewise expanding. Businesses who have made it through the first stage also upgrade their products throughout the expansion stage. Indeed, these businesses frequently manage to reduce their costs even further. Now that companies have proven they can survive, investors are more eager to make investments. The Maturity or Stabilization Stage: An industry reaches maturity and stability following its golden days of expansion. Both the risk and the rewards are low. Growth is not very fast. Sales may rise, but they do so more slowly than they did previously. There are many competitors, and products are less inventive and more homogenized. India's refrigerator market is a developed one. Growth is not rapid. As of right now, everything appears safe.

For comfort and mediocre returns, investors might put their money into these sectors. They must understand, however, that growth and profits may be adversely affected in the event of an economic downturn and a decline in consumer demand. The Sunset or downturn Stage At last, the industry experiences a downturn. When its products lose their appeal, this happens. This could be the result of a number of things, including shifting societal norms (cable and satellite television, for instance, has hurt the film and video business), legislative changes, and price increases. Right now, there is a lot of danger, but there are also few, if any, positive returns. The different phases can be compared to the four phases of a person's life cycle: childhood, adulthood, middle age, and old age. When an industry is nearing the end of its entrepreneurial or fledgling stage and is growing, investors should start buying shares; when it reaches its mature stage, they should start selling their shares. The Industry in Relation to the Economy: Investors need to know how a sector responds to shifts in the overall economy. Certain industries perform poorly in recessions, while others show less elasticity in booms. However, certain industries remain untouched throughout a boom or a slump. Which are the main categories?

The evergreen industries are those that are typically untouched by shifts in the economy. Then there are the erratic cyclical industries, which perform terribly during a recession and remarkably well during a prosperous economic period. These are the sectors that create commodities that people need, such as the food or agro-based industries (dairy products, etc.). Durable commodities, consumer goods like textiles, and shipping are the best examples. People wait till better times to buy consumer items when things are tough. The industries that are impacted by interest rates are known as interest-sensitive industries. Banking and real estate are two sectors that suffer when interest rates are high. Industry growth refers to the expansion of an industry at a faster rate than other industries, even in the face of economic downturns. How should investors proceed? Investors should ascertain how shifts in interest rates and the state of the economy impact a given industry. Investors should sell their cyclical industry holdings and move into growth or evergreen industries if the economy is headed into a recession.

Investors might think about making real estate or construction company investments if they anticipate a decline in interest rates. Conversely, investments in the consumer and durable goods sectors are probably going to be beneficial if the economy is expanding.

Competition The degree of rivalry between different businesses in an industry is another important consideration. Initially, industry competition fosters efficiency, innovation, and better products. As competition intensifies further, fierce price wars start to emerge, which lower margins, reduce earnings, and eventually cause some businesses to start losing money. Even the more inefficient businesses go out of business. In order to fully comprehend this phenomenon, one must recognize that new investors will enter the market if the returns are high, resulting in an influx of capital. Companies that already exist might also expand. On the other hand, the opposite will happen if the returns are poor or less than those that may be found elsewhere. There will be an outflow of funds and no investment of them. To put it briefly, competition is drawn to high returns and vice versa. However, just because the profits are substantial does not cause competition in the form of new businesses to bacterially multiply.

The level of capital intake, the rate of return on investment, and the capacity of businesses to maintain these returns are all influenced by competitive pressures. These competitive factors include rivalry between rivals, bargaining power of suppliers and buyers, threat of substitution, and entrance obstacles. Obstacles to Entry: Newcomers boost an industry's capacity and cash inflow. How simple it is to break into an industry is the question that comes up. Entry-level obstacles include economies of scale, which make it impractical to establish small capacities in several businesses. This is particularly true if there are now quite large units producing a large quantity. These well-established giants' products will be noticeably less expensive. Product Differentiation: A business that offers unique items is more likely to survive. Product differences could stem from the brand name or the caliber of the company's offerings, such as Mercedes Benz automobiles, National VCRs, or Reebok footwear. Consumers are willing to pay more for things, thus they are sold at a premium. Investing in these companies is generally safe because there will always be a need.

Capital Requirement: Low capital and technological know-how are prerequisites for easy entry sectors. This leads to low margins, high expenses, fierce competition, and a large number of competitors. Conversely, because entry is challenging, industries that require a significant initial investment and have a high fixed cost structure have few rivals. One of the best examples of such an industry is the car sector. Its high fixed expenses must be paid for, and a decline in sales may cause profits to fall more than proportionately. Entry hurdles will include substantial capital bases and investments. Cost of Switching: The expense of moving from one supplier's product to another could be another barrier to entrance. This might cover things like equipment costs and employee retraining expenses. For a buyer to switch if switching costs are high, new competitors must provide a significant improvement. Computers are a prime example.

A honeywell computer could be in use by a firm. It would need to replace all of the terminals, the unit, and even the software if it wanted to switch to an IBM computer. Obtaining Distribution Channel Access can be a challenge for new businesses, particularly if established companies already have robust and well-established channels. Cost Disadvantages Independent of Scale: This type of barrier arises when more established businesses have advantages that are difficult for newcomers to match. These consist of long learning curves, government subsidies, favorable access to raw materials, and proprietary product technology. Coca-Cola is one of the best examples. The business uses exclusive product technology. While there are competitors, it is difficult for them to match the availability of similar cold drinks. Government Policy: By generally refusing to grant licenses, government policy might prevent newcomers from entering a market. Two automakers held a monopoly in the Indian motor automobile business until the mid-1980s. Others applied for licenses, but these were denied. Anticipated Retaliation: If current rivals make a concerted effort to keep newcomers out, the anticipation of retaliation from them may serve as a deterrent for prospective newcomers.

Cost of Capacity Additions: Fewer rivals will enter the market if capacity additions are expensive. multinational Cartels: It's possible that certain multinational cartels prevent new competitors from making a profit. The Risk of Substitution: New products are always being invented, and older ones are being replaced by better ones. Generally, one should exercise caution when investing in an industry if substitutes are either threatening to replace it or can already be found elsewhere. The packaging sector is one where this happens frequently: bottles are swapped out for cans, cans for plastic bottles, and so on. Businesses frequently have to invest significant financial resources in advertising and promotion to combat the possibility of substitution. The sectors that are most at risk are those where the replacements are either better or cheaper, or are made by very profitable industries. It should be mentioned that substitutes restrict a company's prospective returns. purchasers' Bargaining Power: In a buyer-controlled industry, or "buyer's market," purchasers are continuously driving down prices and putting up demands for better products or services, which frequently reduces profitability. It is important to determine whether: A specific customer makes the majority of the purchases (high purchase volumes).

Such consumers have the power to ruin an industry if they stop buying from them. They may also compel price reductions. Customers can negotiate lower rates by pitting one business against another. Additionally, one should be mindful that: The buyer's power increases when sellers suffer high switching costs.

This is particularly valid in cases where purchasers have minimal switching costs. Sellers run the risk of being fully integrated if buyers have attained partial backward integration. Buyers who are well-informed about specifics and trends have an advantage over sellers since they can make sure they don't spend more than is necessary. Buyers would aggressively try to lower prices if a product accounted for a sizable amount of their expenses. A conventional, undifferentiated product gives the customer more negotiating leverage. The buyer will attempt to lower prices as much as feasible if their earnings are minimal. To put it briefly, an industry that is controlled by consumers is typically fragile and constantly in danger of losing money. Suppliers' Bargaining Power: An industry that is unduly dominated by its suppliers is likewise in danger. This happens when there are few suppliers or when the suppliers have a monopoly. Suppliers are in charge of a necessary item.

Product demand outpaces supply. The supplier provides goods to different businesses. There are significant switching costs. There is no equivalent product for the supplier's offering. The product of the provider is a crucial component of the buyer's enterprise. The supplier does not value the buyer. The item from the supplier is distinct. Competition between Rivals Competition between rivals has the potential to seriously damage an industry. Price reductions, aggressive marketing, extra expensive services or deals, and similar tactics are the main ways that this happens. When there are more competitors than there is demand, a rivalry like this one usually arises. In an effort to draw consumers to their products, businesses decrease prices and increase their advertising. The industry is growing slowly, and businesses are vying with one another for a larger portion of the market. In an attempt to boost demand during the recession, businesses lower the price of their goods and provide better customer service.

The products of different companies are not distinguishable from one another. In these situations, the buyer chooses based on the product or service. Economies of scale in some industries will require a company to increase significantly to its current capacity. Production growth may lead to overcapacity and price reductions. Rivals may employ radically different approaches to marketing their products, and they may always strive to outperform one another by lowering prices or providing better services. When there are large stakes (earnings), competition intensifies. If there are significant exit costs—such as paying a gratuity, an unpaid provident fund, pension liabilities, and so forth—then businesses will fiercely compete with one another. Companies would choose to stay in operation in such a scenario, even if margins are thin and little to no profit is generated. Businesses also frequently continue to operate at low profit margins when there are strategic alliances between them and other members of the group, when government regulations prevent them from closing, or when management refuses to let the business close out of pride or loyalty to the workforce. High exit barriers make it impossible for businesses to shut down surplus capacity, which reduces their competitive advantage and erodes profitability. A high level of exit barriers results in a low yet dangerous return. The return is small but steady if there are few exit barriers.

Conversely, in an environment with minimal entry barriers, returns are large but steady. Risky returns are associated with high entry barriers. Choosing an Industry It would be wise for the investor to consider or ascertain the following information when making their industry choice: Invest in a sector that is still experiencing growth. It is preferable for an industry or firm to grow more quickly. At the beginning of the new century, the Indian software business, for instance, was expanding at a rate of more than 50% annually. Investing in globally competitive industries free from government regulation is a safer bet. Unless investing at a period of economic prosperity, one should steer clear of cyclical sectors. Government support and a number of incentives have put export-oriented industries in a favorable position right now. However, because import tariffs have been lowered and other restrictions have been relaxed, import substitution businesses are currently struggling. It's critical to determine if a sector is a good fit for investment at a given moment. There are industries for sunrises and sunsets. Industries can be classified as labor- or capital-intensive. Every industry has its life cycle. Prior to a decline starting, investments should be made during an industry's growth stage and disbursed throughout its maturity or stagnation stage.

Section Three: Company Analysis The investor analyzes the company at the conclusion of the fundamental analysis process. The two main focuses of this analysis are how the company has done in contrast to other comparable companies and how it has done in terms of past performance. Before analyzing a firm, it is essential to finish the political-economic study and the industry analysis because the company's success throughout time is mostly reflective of the political climate, the economy, and the industry. What aspects of a corporation are examined during an analysis? Nothing is too little, in my opinion, to be disregarded. Everything counts. One of the wealthiest and most successful stock market investors of all time, billionaire Jean Paul Getty, once said, "Do not buy a stock until you know all about it." There are a number of aspects of a company that need to be looked at, including: The Management The Company The Annual Report Ratios Cash flow.

The Administrative

The management of a firm is the most crucial aspect to take into account when making an investment, yet it is also one that is frequently overlooked. A company's future is dependent on the caliber, skill, and vision of its management. A strong, capable management team can propel a business forward, whereas a poor, ineffective management team can bankrupt a successful one. Company history is replete with such tales. In the early 1980s, Chrysler was a beleaguered behemoth. Iacocca used strong, capable management to turn the company around. IBM, the big blue, fired Chief Executive Officer Akers in the first quarter of 1993 because he was held accountable for the company's poor performance.

Lou Gerstner, the former president of American Express, subsequently assumed leadership of R. IBM extended an invitation to J. R. Nabisco to become its CEO. Previously, Mr. Gerstner had been able to successfully and dramatically reduce the liabilities resulting from the leveraged buyout of R. Nabisco, J. R. His achievement played a crucial role in securing him the top position at IBM. Similar to this, Stuart Saunders, the railroad's chief, was a lawyer with limited experience managing a vast network of railroads, which is mostly blamed for Penn Central's demise in the 1970s, the largest railroad in the United States. Such instances abound in the corporate history of India as well. The most reputable and well-known brand was Metal Box—the bluest of blue chips.

The business was forced to shut down all of its plants as a result of a string of unfortunate events, including an unsuccessful diversification. In Western India, one of the most reputable names was Killick Nixon. Not anymore. However, there are also many examples of wealth that have arisen as a result of management's vision and foresight. Welcomgroup, the hotel chain that Haksar expanded ITC into, was replaced by agro-based enterprises. These have shown to be effective. Venugopal Dhoot is largely responsible for Videocon's success, Rahul Bajaj is responsible for Bajaj Auto's expansion and profitability, and Dhirubhai Ambani is solely responsible for the Reliance Empire. There are a number of others, including Deepak Parekh, HDFC, Narayanamurthy, Wipro, and Azim Premji. There are two main categories of management in India: family management and professional management. Family Management: Businesses run by members of the governing family are known as family-managed businesses.

Members of the "ruling" family typically hold the positions of Chairman and Chief Executive Officer, and the members of the Board of Directors are either "rubber stamps" or other family associates. This isn't always a terrible thing. Simply put, the controlling family sets all of the policies, and some of them might not always be in the best interests of the shareholders. Kirloskar Pneumatics was quoted at Rs. 36 per share a few years ago, as I recall. Kirloskar Tractors was struggling at the time. After the merging of the two businesses by the ruling family, Kirloskar Pneumatic's valuations dropped to about Rs. 10. The merger was devastating for the shareholders of Kirloskar Pneumatics, but it was probably beneficial for the family and the shareholders of Kirloskar Tractors. In summary, even top managers are frequently considered as hired family servants, and decisions are frequently made with the family's best interests in mind. For example, I am aware of one company where the HR Manager purchases the vegetables in addition to hiring houseboys and maids for his chairman's residence. Every morning at seven in the morning, the New Delhi manager is expected to be at the corporate house, whenever his "Seth" travels to that city. The moment the Chairman gets up, he is only allowed to leave his master's company when he goes to bed. Many years ago, I witnessed an incident at the airport in Bombay.

The leader of a major corporation was leaving on a trip. The heads of his several businesses had gathered to bid him farewell. These gentlemen were well-known, respected for their accomplishments, and titans of industry in their own right. When their boss departed, these leaders—three of them were actually older than their master—bent double and touched his feet. If these people hadn't degraded themselves with this act of obeisance, I wonder what may have happened. Perhaps this was done as a token of respect, similar to a pupil caressing their teacher's feet. I want to make it clear that devotion to the family is valued even more than skill in many family-run businesses, where employees are expected to be subordinate to them. And this devotion is frequently paid off. When a retainer becomes ill, the family pays for all of his medical bills and ensures that he receives excellent care. He receives a sizable pension upon retirement. I recall a time when a senior employee passed away. His widow received the corporate apartment, her children received an education, and she was even offered employment.

Multinational corporations or those with skilled management seldom would. In his memoir, To Challenge and to Change, Mr. T. Thomas, a former Chairman of Hindustan Lever Ltd., writes about the family company organization in the most poetic way. In his description, an Indian family business is represented by a core consisting of the founder and his brothers or sons, from which a number of concentric circles radiate. Those from the same caste or religion follow the extended family of cousins and relatives in the following circle. Individuals from the same linguistic group make up the fourth circle, while those from the same area make up the outermost circle. According to Mr. Thomas, going above this would have been "like going out of orbit—unthinkably risky." The management of family-owned firms has undergone certain changes. These were initially frequently conventional, authoritarian, conservative, inflexible, and resistant to change. This is no longer accurate. The founding fathers' sons and grandsons received their education from top business colleges in India and other countries, where they were exposed to contemporary practices.

As a result, even though the head of many family-run businesses is a descendant of the company, his staff members are professional managers who have graduated from business schools. This sort of mixes the finest aspects of both worlds, and a lot of these companies have great success. In these kinds of businesses, the professional manager feels frustrated since he is aware that he will never, ever be the company's CEO; that honor will always belong to a family member. Employers who manage their own businesses are said to be practicing professional management. The chief executive officer of these businesses frequently has no financial interest in the business. Thanks to his skill and expertise, he is in charge of things. As a career employee, the professional manager holds the position of authority as long as he achieves his goals. As a result, he is always focused on results, and his short-term goal is often to achieve the annual budget. Loyalty to the organization does not always have an impact on him. As a professional, he often seeks to introduce the most recent developments in management philosophy.

He strives for more production and efficiency by managing his business like a lean, mean machine. Professionally run businesses are therefore typically well-run, focused on expansion, and high achievers. Regular dividends and bonus payments are made to investors. Immediately, ITC, Infosys, HDFC, and Hindustan Lever spring to mind. Nonetheless, there is frequently a lack of loyalty and perhaps a lack of long-term commitment. This is due to the fact that the professional manager must eventually retire and step aside, meaning he cannot live to always enjoy the fruits of his labor. Nor will his sons succeed him, despite the efforts of a few to make this happen. Not to be overlooked is the fact that a professional manager is a hired gun. He offers his services to the highest bidder, and as a result, those who purchase his services are typically not seen as loyal. Employers now use stock options as a means of encouraging or fostering commitment. These are awarded to staff members based on their performance and become theirs after a predetermined amount of service. As a result, the worker shares ownership of the company and is impacted by its success. Furthermore, because these things become apparent to the employee after a while, he usually stays until they do.

Given that these choices are granted, frequently once a year, the employee stays with the organization for a considerable amount of time. It is a mutually beneficial arrangement. A skilled and devoted employee is hired by the organization. The worker increases his wealth. Corporate politics and infighting are also common in many professionally run companies. This is a result of managers' persistent efforts to move up the corporate ladder and their belief that the goal should always take precedence over the methods. As a result, it frequently happens that the best player wins the top position rather than the best individual. In family-run businesses, this isn't always the case because it's understood that the son or daughter of the household will always hold the position of leadership. What to Look for It would be incorrect to say that investing should only be done in family-run businesses or professionally managed firms. Both categories contain profitable, well-run businesses. In all groups, there exist organizations with poor management as well. So what are the things that one should search for? The integrity of the management stands out as the most crucial factor. This has to be beyond reasonable doubt. It is frequently said that even with strong systems and controls, a determined employee can commit fraud.

In a similar vein, management has the power to manipulate statistics and inflict significant harm and financial loss on a firm (for their own personal gain). So, if you have any doubts about the honesty of a company's management, I would advise you to leave it alone. Mr. C. S. Patel, the former CEO of Unit Trust of India, was someone I once had the honor to hear speak.

I have rarely heard more wise counsel than the one he received from his mentor, Mr. A. D. Shroff, the former Chairman of the New India Assurance: "If you have the slightest doubt of management, do not touch the company with a pair of tongs." When a company's management is referred to informally as "chor (thief) management" in a discussion about the company, it is a warning to stay far away from that business. In this situation, it would be wise to find out who the company's primary shareholders are. Certain managers have a track record of influencing stock prices. I was told a story of a scion of a family-run business who was questioned by a non-Indian journalist how he could guarantee that the price of his company's shares would never drop below Rs. 230. The honorable one retorted, "We will not allow it to." Stocks in these companies are speculative and are purposefully held at a premium price.

They have to be stayed away from. Proven competency, or the management's track record, is an additional factor to take into account. How has the company's management handled its business in the past few years? Has the business expanded? Has it started to make more money? Has it expanded more spectacularly than other companies in the same sector?

New enterprises and new management should always be approached with caution because of their high mortality rate. Hold off until the business begins to prosper and the management demonstrates its skill. How well-regarded is the management among its contemporaries in the same field? This is a crucial indicator. Competitors are aware of almost all of a management's advantages and disadvantages, thus if they respect the management, it is genuinely deserving of respect. It is important to keep in mind that the industry generally views a company's management as impartial, just, and accurate. Everyone succeeds when things are good.

In difficult circumstances, a management team's resilience is put to the test. Furthermore, it's critical to evaluate the management's performance during a recession or depression. Has it made its operations more efficient? Did its factories close down? Did it fire staff, if it could have done so? Was it successful in selling its goods? Was the business able to outperform its rivals? What was the sales situation? Generally speaking, a management team that can guide the business through challenging times will succeed. The level of expertise possessed by the management on its goods, markets, and industry is critical as it can significantly impact the company's success. When a corporation enjoys a dominant position, its management tends to assume that it will remain thus for eternity. By doing this, it becomes disconnected from its markets, consumers, and rivals. It's not until it's too late that the reality sets in. The management needs to be up to date on the newest methods and technologies and stay in constant communication with the customers and industry. It cannot advance and maintain its lead until then.

Finding out the market share of the company's products and if they are increasing or at the very least staying the same is an easy way to verify this. The management needs to have a plan, be creative, and be transparent. It needs to be ready to adapt as needed. It basically needs to know where it's going and have a route planned to get there. It needs to be lively and open to new ideas. A top-heavy, multi-layered organization is typically exceedingly bureaucratic and sluggish. "Many chiefs and few braves" are present. They frequently obstruct change because they oppose it. They typically use a personal approach to try and hang onto their careers. Investing in a firm that has not yet reached a professional level is not something I would advise doing, as choices are made at the whim of the CEO rather than with the company's best interests in mind. The most capable employees in these organizations do not hold positions of authority. Nepotism could exist if the chief executive's nephews, nieces, cousins, and other relatives hold jobs not because of demonstrated ability but rather because of blood ties.

Additionally, it would be prudent to steer clear of family-run businesses when there is internal strife, as these businesses suffer and the investor or shareholder may end up losing out the most. Numerous family-owned businesses have split up in recent years; the Birlas, Goenkas, and Mafatlals are just a few examples. The most turbulent periods are those that preceded and immediately followed the separation. That's the time to avoid doing business with such companies. One can decide whether or not to invest once the new management sets in. Many major enterprises in India are run by families, although professional managers oversee their daily operations. There are also a number of businesses with professional management. Which is better cannot be generalized, nor would it be fair. An investor needs to determine whether he is comfortable with a company's management before risking his money. This is ultimately what will decide the security and outcome of the money you invest.

The Organization

The company is one element that isn't always looked at in a fundamentals study. This is due to the fact that a company's perception—which is based on subjective data—may not always be substantiated by objective facts and statistics. Even when a company has lost money consistently for two years or longer and you may not want to touch its shares, it might still be an excellent business that is worthwhile investing in. There are a number of things to consider. The perception of a company by its rivals is one of the most important things to find out. Is it regarded highly? The Oscar is the most coveted honor among stars in Hollywood and is considered the greatest. Why? The reason for this is that it signifies an actor or actress being acknowledged by their colleagues.

A business that is derided by a rival is not one that is worth investigating. However, one who is in awe of something has to think about it more than once. Its goods might be much better. It might be more structured. Its management is reputed for having aggression, vision, maturity, and competence. The investor needs to find out why, and then assess if it will persist for the foreseeable future. Finding out if the company leads its industry in terms of products or segments is another important consideration. Investing in market leaders carries a lower risk. Market leaders' shares do not decline as quickly as those of other businesses. People would choose to purchase their stuff above others because of the enchantment associated with their name. Let's use an actual case study. The production of consumer products virtually skyrocketed in the 1980s. Manufacturers of televisions were numerous. Their televisions were comparable since nearly every component was imported. But after ten years, only the market leaders remained in business. The others had perished. Normally, if given the option to choose an article, one would choose the better one. This is typical human conduct, and it also occurs in the marketplace.

As a result, market leaders' prices decline more slowly than those of their competitors in the same sector. The policies that a business adheres to are also crucial. What expansion ambitions does it have? What does it hope to achieve? Each business has an existence. It will mature to a certain point, level out, and eventually perish if given a regular existence. It has to be given fresh vitality because it is about to level out. This may provide it with new vitality and a fresh start. ITC Ltd. is a prime example that immediately comes to mind. Under Haksar, this tobacco empire expanded into hotels, and under Sapru, it entered the agricultural sector. At first, Reliance Industries was a textile company. After that, it ventured into petroleum, petrochemicals, and refining goods after seeing an opportunity. In 2003, it started to appear in cell phones. Blue Star operates an air conditioning business. It had a software branch that was separated into a different business. Both of these businesses have expanded since then. Labor relations are of utmost importance. A corporation with a hardworking, motivated workforce experiences very little work disturbance and excellent production. Conversely, a business with poor labor relations will slow down and lose hundreds of man-days as a result of strikes.

The enormous shoe business Bata had terrible performance in the year ending March 31, 1993, largely because it was closed for over four months in 1992 due to strikes. Most people agree that the militant unions led by the late Datta Samant were the reason Mumbai's textile industry collapsed. Many firms became hesitant to invest in states like Kerala and West Bengal due to the labor force's militancy. Finding out the location of the company's factories and plants as well as its history of labor relations is crucial. The company's location and the locations of its plants must also be taken into account. The company may face severe issues if the infrastructure is poor and there is insufficient water or energy. Due to power outages, numerous businesses in Madhya Pradesh are in serious financial trouble. Many people are unable to purchase captive power. Another problem is transportation. This has been acknowledged by the government, and within the next ten years, plans are underway to build superhighways throughout the nation. These are the primary considerations that one should have when evaluating a firm.

The Annual Report

An organization's annual report is the main and most significant source of information about it. This is required by law to be compiled annually and given to the shareholders. Annual reports are often presented in an excellent manner. A vast amount of information is provided regarding a company's performance over time. Pie and bar charts in various colors are used to show and explain how the business has grown and how its earnings have been put to use. Pictures of the factories, recently purchased machinery, the Chairman cutting a ribbon, and the Board of Directors seeming accountable are all included. The typical stockholder doesn't look much farther. He is usually satisfied with the thought that the company is in excellent hands if the Annual Report is spectacular, if the company has turned a profit, and if a respectable dividend has been paid.

This cannot be the standard by which a business is evaluated. An astute investor would thoroughly examine the annual report, looking above the surface level information and uncovering the real story. Only then can he make an informed assessment of the company's performance. The Directors' Report, the Auditor's Report, the Financial Statements, and the Schedules and Notes to the Accounts are the distinct sections that make up the Annual Report. Every one of these components serves a purpose and tells a story. The story needs to be told. The directors' report is a document that informs shareholders of how the firm is doing under their direction and is given by the directors of a corporation. These reports should be taken with a grain of salt because they essentially serve as their justification for continuing to exist. Ultimately, when a team of people is required to give a performance assessment of themselves, they will inevitably emphasize their successes and downplay their shortcomings. It makes sense. That's just how people are.

As a result, the writing in each of these reports is excellent. Every word, every statement is examined with the sharpest of eyes. All significant events are listed and emphasized to persuade a casual reader that the business is in capable hands. Furthermore, there's a propensity to rationalize unpleasant events. Still, the Directors' Report offers an investor useful information: it expresses the directors' assessment of the company's position in relation to the political and economic environments. explains the company's performance and financial outcomes during the period under examination. This is a critical component. Investors may typically ascertain the causes behind the excellent or bad performance of each individual division by looking at the particular results and activities of the numerous divisions. The company's aims for expansion, diversification, and modernization are outlined in the Directors' Report. A business will stagnate and eventually fail without these. talks about the directors' recommended dividend and the profit made during the time under consideration. The directors will always contend that the performance was adequate, thus it is often best to read this paragraph with reasonable skepticism.

If revenues have increased, it is almost certainly due to excellent marketing and diligent effort despite fierce competition. If so, unfavorable economic circumstances are typically to blame. explains in more detail the directors' assessment of the company's future prospects. talks about intentions for further investments and acquisitions. An investor needs to assess the topics brought up in a directors' report with intelligence. While diversity is beneficial, is it always a good idea? It is necessary to take into account the state of the industry and the management's commercial acumen. Burroughs Wellcome's recent foray into the sporting goods industry, specifically Nike Sportswear, was a disastrous diversification. The expansion of Metal Box into ball bearings and Spartek's purchase of Neycer Ceramics were also successful. My aim is to convey that while diversity is necessary for companies to mitigate the effects of industry downturns, not all diversifications are appropriate for every organization. Analyses of the other topics mentioned in the Directors' Report are also necessary. Did the business execute on par with other players in the same field? Is the money being raised in the most sensible and advantageous way for the business?

The investor must look below the surface of the directors' report to get the answers to these queries. To put it briefly, a well-executed read of a directors' report can provide investors with a solid understanding of a company's operations, challenges it faces, the path it plans to take, and its prospects for the future. The Auditor's Report: As the representative of the shareholders, the auditor has an obligation to inform both the public and the shareholders on the directors' stewardship of the firm. It is mandatory for auditors to report on whether the financial statements they have given accurately depict the company's state. Investors need to keep in mind that the auditors are their legal representatives and have an obligation to disclose any irregularities in the financial statements. Additionally, they must disclose any changes that have an impact on profitability, such as adjustments to accounting rules or omission of fees.

Since the auditor's report is the only unbiased report that shareholders or investors get, this fact alone should encourage careful examination of the document. Unfortunately, it is not read the majority of the time. Contradictions that are fascinating can exist. "As at the year end 31st March 2010, the accumulated losses exceed the net worth of the Company and the Company has suffered cash losses in the financial year ended 31st March 2010 as well as in the immediately preceding financial year," according to the Auditor's Report of ABC Ltd for the year 2009–2010. Thus, in our view, the Company qualifies as a sick industrial company for purposes of Sick Industrial Companies (Special Provisions) Act 1985, clause (O) of Section 3(1).

"The financial year under review has not been a favorable year for the Company as the Computer Industry in general continued to be in the grip of recession," the directors' report said, nonetheless. Operations were hindered by high input costs and resource limitations. It is necessary to evaluate your company's success in light of these considerations. To ensure cost effectiveness, production operations were reduced throughout the year. ......Your directors are optimistic that this year will see improved outcomes from the initiatives to boost company volumes and control costs. The board expressed optimism that things would improve in the future, but the auditors believed the company was sick! Being directors, I guess they couldn't say otherwise. It's possible that you won't notice the impact of their certification when reading an Auditor's Report.

In the Royston Electronics Limited Auditor's Report for 2009–2010, it was stated that the said accounts, subject to Note No. 3 regarding doubtful debts, No. 4 regarding balance confirmations, No. 5 on custom liability and interests thereon, No. 11 on product development expenses, No. 14 on gratuity, and Notes No. 8, 16 (C) and 16(F) regarding stocks, give a true and fair view and the information is presented in a manner required by the Companies Act 1956. Now let's examine the particular notes in this instance: Note 3 indicated that no allowance had been made for questionable loans. Note 4 mentioned that loans and advances, as well as balance confirmation of various creditors and debtors, had not been acquired. At Note 5, it was mentioned that as of 31.3.2010, the imported raw materials at the ICF / Bonded godown were not accompanied by a customs responsibility or interest payment of Rs. 3,14,30,073.

Note 11 highlighted that from 2009 to 2010, product development costs totaling Rs. 17,44,049 were being written down over a ten-year period. Under this heading, Rs. 2,16,51,023 had been capitalized for the development of CT142, Digital TV, Cooler, and CFBT; this amount will be written down over a ten-year period starting in 2010–11. As of March 31, 2010, the company's portion of prior gratuity liabilities had not been determined or covered, with the exception of the amount of premiums paid against a LIC group gratuity insurance that the trust had purchased (Note 14). Note 16C mentioned that the auditors had not verified the management's estimate of the amount of raw material used. A little more than Rs. 1 crore was profit for the company. The profit would have become a loss if the costs associated with product development, customer duty and interest, and bad debt provision had been made in accordance with widely accepted accounting rules. It's important to keep in mind that, occasionally, businesses will alter their accounting principles or turn to imaginative and inventive accounting techniques in an effort to produce better results. Sometimes the notes to the accounts don't go into depth on the impact of these adjustments. The reader will always be made aware of these modifications and how they affect the financial statements by the Auditor's Report. This is the reason an investor should not only be required, but also required to carefully study the Auditor's Report.

Financial Statements: The Balance Sheet, which shows the company's financial situation at the end of the accounting period, and the Income Statement, or Profit and Loss Account, which summarizes the company's activities for the accounting period, are the publicly available financial statements of a company that are included in an Annual Report. Basic Ltd. Balance Sheet: A balance sheet logically arranges a firm's assets (items it owns) and liabilities (items it owes) under specified headings to show the financial status of the company as of a given date. The financial situation on a given day is detailed in the balance sheet, however it should be emphasized that on that day or the day after, the status may alter considerably. As an illustration, on December 1, 2009, Vasanth Limited obtained a loan of Rs. 200 lakh, which became due on April 1, 2010. It would be OK for an investor examining the balance sheets to come to two somewhat different conclusions.

Vasanth Limited would have been regarded as a highly leveraged, debt-financed business as of March 31, 2010. However, as of April 1, 2010, it would be determined that the business was severely undercapitalized and extremely cautious, which would have restricted its ability to grow. Sources of Funds: In order to finance its operations, buy fixed assets, and obtain working capital, a firm needs to raise money. The funds must be less expensive for the business to create a profit than for it to receive payment for their deployment. Where does a business raise money? Which sources are they? Companies borrow money and receive funding from their stockholders. Funds from Shareholders: A business raises money from its investors by issuing new shares or by reinvesting its profits. The money held by shareholders represents their investment and part of the business. Share Capital: Share capital consists of the publically issued shares.

The following methods are used to issue this: Private Placement: This involves making shares available to particular people or organizations. Shares are available for purchase by the general public. A prospectus contains all the information about the offer, including the rationale behind the funding raise, and it is crucial that investors read it. Public offerings were very popular up until the 1992 hoax because investors would frequently receive shares at a price far below their true value. They were frequently oversubscribed as a result. This is no longer accurate. Since the office of the controller of capital issues was eliminated and corporations are now free to price their issues anyway they see fit, they usually set the price of their shares at what the market will bear. As a result, investors are now selectively applying for new shares rather than submitting applications without due diligence. Rights Issues: Businesses may also grant their shareholders shares as a matter of right, commensurate with their ownership stake.

In many cases, this was done for less than the product's market worth, which greatly benefited the shareholders. Due to the increased flexibility regarding share pricing, businesses are starting to price their shares closer to their inherent value. As a result, investors have not found these issues to be especially appealing, and several have not been completely subscribed. Bonus Shares: By capitalizing reserves, bonus shares are shares that are given away for free to shareholders. In reality, no money is obtained from shareholders. However, it can be claimed that shareholders are actually contributing capital if these shares are issued by capitalization distributable reserves, or profits that are not paid out as dividends. Profits or gains that are held in reserve rather than being distributed are known as reserves. Businesses have two types of reserves: capital reserves and revenue reserves. Gains from a growth in asset value result in capital reserves, which are not freely distributed to shareholders. The capital revaluation reserve, which represents an unrealized gain on the value of assets, and the share premium account, which results from the issuance of shares at a premium, are the two most frequent types of capital reserves.

Revenue Reserves: These are operating profits that are reinvested in the business rather than being paid out as dividends to shareholders. It is crucial that not all of the earnings are distributed since businesses need the money for working capital, expansion, and the acquisition of new assets to replace their current ones. Loan Funds Borrowings are an additional source of funding available to a business. Companies frequently favor borrowing since it is quicker, easier overall, and requires less rules to be followed. Companies either take out secured loans, wherein they pledge some of their assets as collateral, or they take out floating charges on some or all of their assets. Term loans and debentures are the typical secured loans held by a business. Unsecured Loans: When businesses take out unsecured loans, they do not put up any collateral. Typically, a lender finds solace solely in the company's reputation and creditworthiness. Short-term loans and fixed deposits are two of a company's most popular unsecured loans.

Unsecured lenders are often reimbursed after secured lenders are satisfied in the event that a firm dissolves. Credits or borrowings for working capital that are subject to fluctuations, such as trade creditors and bank overdrafts, are typically categorized as current liabilities rather than loan funds. Fixed Assets: These are the resources that a firm owns and uses to run its operations and manufacture items; these are usually pieces of machinery. They include land, buildings (such as offices, warehouses, and factories), automobiles, machinery, furniture, equipment, and the like; they are not for resale. Although the type and quantity of fixed assets differ from business to business, every company has some. The main fixed assets of a maritime firm are its ships, while the main fixed assets of a manufacturing company would be its plant and machinery.

The balance sheet presents fixed assets at cost minus accrued depreciation. The extremely reasonable idea that an object has a useful life and eventually wears down after years of usage is the foundation of depreciation. In order to ensure that the asset has no value at the end of its useful life, it seeks to measure wear and tear and reduce the asset's value correspondingly. Since depreciation is a charge against earnings, at the end of the asset's useful life, the business would have deducted from profits the same amount as the asset's initial cost, which might be used to buy another asset. This is insufficient, though, given the current inflationary climate, so some businesses establish a reserve to make sure there is enough money to replace the worn-out asset. The Straight Line Method, which writes off an asset's cost evenly over time, is one of the common techniques for depreciation. As a result, the cost and cumulative depreciation will match at the end of the asset's useful life. Depreciation is computed on the written-down value, or cost-less depreciation, under the reducing balance technique.

As a result, depreciation starts off greater and gets reduced over time. Because depreciation is perpetually computed on a decreasing amount, an asset is never entirely written off. Others: Although they are not frequently employed, there are a few more, like the interest technique and the rate of 72. The only fixed asset that is never depreciated since its value usually increases is land. Factory construction and other capital work-in-progress is not written off until the asset is completely operational. Investments: To generate income or make profitable use of cash surpluses, many businesses buy investments in the form of shares or debentures. The typical investments held by a business include: Trade: Trade investments consist of shares or debentures of rival companies, which a business holds to gain access to data on their expansion, profitability, and other aspects that would not be readily available otherwise. Shares owned in subsidiary or associate corporations are referred to as subsidiary and associate companies. Through cross-holdings in associate and subsidiary companies, the big business houses possess a majority stake in many enterprises. Others: Businesses frequently keep shares or debentures of other businesses in order to invest money or stash extra cash. Large earnings from share trading were the reason for many corporations' windfall profits in the year ending March 31, 2003.

Additionally, there are two types of investments: quoted and unquoted. Quoted investments are debentures and shares that are freely traded and quoted on a recognized stock exchange. A stock exchange does not list or quote unquoted investments. As a result, they are tough to discard and are not very liquid. To be cautious and make sure that losses are sufficiently covered, investments are evaluated and recorded on the balance sheet at the lower of the purchase cost and market value. Current Assets: These are the assets that a business owns and uses in the regular Book of its operations. Examples of these assets include cash, completed stock, and debt collection. As a general rule, a current asset is one that can be converted into cash within a year. Essentially, there are three types of current assets: Converting Assets: These are assets like debtors and completed items that are created or developed during regular business operations.

Constant assets are assets that are acquired and sold without any modifications or additions. An example of a constant asset would be alcohol that a liquor store purchases directly from a manufacturer. Assets that take the form of cash or cash equivalents are referred to as cash equivalents. They can be applied toward other asset purchases or debt repayment. The most popular cash equivalent assets include bank accounts and physical cash, as well as loans. The following are a firm's current assets: stocks or inventories. A corporation gets its earnings from the selling of its stocks, making these assets possibly the most significant current assets. Conversely, stocks are made up of the following: Raw Materials: These are the main items that a firm buys in order to make its products. Goods that are still in the manufacturing process are referred to as work in progress. Finished Goods: The company's completed goods that are prepared for retail sales. Stock Valuation: Stocks are evaluated at net realizable value, which is the lower of cost. This is to guarantee that there won't be any loss because it will have been covered at the time of sale.

FIFO, or First in First Out, is a popular technique for valuing stocks. It makes the assumption that stocks that arrive first will be sold first, and stocks that arrive last would be sold last. Last in, Last Out, or LIFO: This approach is predicated on the opposite idea of FIFO. The last-arrived stocks are supposed to be the first to be sold. Customers favor newer materials or products, so the logic goes. Finding out the method of valuation and the accounting principles used is crucial since it is easy to manipulate stock values by altering the method of valuation. Trade Debtors: Most businesses sell their items on credit rather than for cash, and customers are expected to pay for the goods they purchase within a predetermined window of time, usually 30 or 60 days. The length of credit varies from client to client and from business to business and is determined by the client's creditworthiness, the state of the market, and level of competition.

Customer payment outside of the prearranged credit period is common. This can be the result of careless credit management or unpaid consumers. As a result, debts fall into two categories: those that are older than six months and others. These are further separated into two categories: debts that are deemed good and debts that are deemed bad or dubious. Debts that are expected to be problematic must be covered or written off. In the event that this isn't done, assets will be overvalued to reflect the bad debt. Only when there is no chance of recovery is a write-off made. If not, a clause is included. Provisions might be either general or specific. The term "specific" refers to a provision that is made for a specified percentage of all debts, while "general" refers to a provision that is made for amounts on specific identified debts.

Prepaid Expenses: No payment is made past the deadline. A number of payments, including rent, insurance premiums, and service fees, are made ahead of time for periods of three, six, or even a year. On the balance sheet, the fraction of these costs that pertains to the upcoming accounting period is displayed as prepaid expenses. Cash and Bank Balances The balances in bank accounts as well as cash on hand in safes, tills, and petty cash boxes are displayed under this section of the balance sheet. Loans and Advances: These are sums of money that have been extended to individuals, businesses, and staff members with the need that they be repaid within a specific time frame.

The ratios that are most frequently used are: net profit to sales, gross profit to sales, selling expenditures to sales, and sales to cost of goods sold. Balance Sheet Ratios: These relate the various relationships seen in the balance sheet, including debt to assets, current assets to current liabilities, shareholders' equity to borrowed funds, and liabilities to net value. Ratios between the balance sheet and the profit and loss account connect some items, like earnings to shareholders' funds, net income to assets used, sales to stock, sales to debtors, and cost of products sold to creditors. Financial Statements and Market Ratios: Market value to earnings and book value to market value are examples of financial statements that are related to market prices and are commonly referred to as market ratios. Ratios have been organized into eight categories in this book to make it simple for investors to assess a company's strengths and flaws.

Profitability, Market Value, Leverage, Debt Service Capacity, Asset Management, and Efficiency Margins. Naturally, it's important to make sure the ratios being measured are reliable and constant. The durations of the eras under comparison must be comparable. When computing ratios for earnings or profitability, large non-recurring income or expenses should be excluded; otherwise, the results will be inaccurate. Ratios don't give solutions. They offer potential solutions. To reach a reasonable conclusion and take appropriate action based on that conclusion, investors must consider these options in addition to other general aspects that could impact the company, such as its management, management policy, government policy, the status of the economy, and the industry. Ratios are a great tool for analyzing financial statements, but how they are interpreted logically and intelligently determines how effective they are. Market Value In the end, what counts to an investor is a share's market value. If an investor thought a share had potential for growth and was reasonably priced, he would buy it.

Conversely, an investor might wish to sell a share if it is overpriced. The maxim "buy cheap, sell dear" or, as Baron Rothschild is attributed with saying, "Buy sheep and sell deer" is after all the golden rule of share investing. Moreover, the market value of a share is a reflection of the respect that investors and the general public accord the company. An investor can also ascertain how long it would take to repay their investment by using market value ratios. Price-Earnings Ratio: This ratio, often known as the P/E ratio, is likely the one that is quoted the most. This ratio is cited by analysts, advisors, and investors to bolster their arguments. Its appeal stems from the fact that it simplifies the relationship between market price and earnings per share to an arithmetical figure. This makes it possible to assess whether a share is overpriced or underpriced and to calculate how long it would take to recoup one's investment. Furthermore, it expresses what the investing public believes about the company, including whether it is expanding or contracting and whether the price is expected to increase, decrease, or stay the same.

The market price of a business's shares is divided by its earnings per share, or profit after taxes and preferential dividends divided by the total number of shares the firm has issued, to get the P/E ratio. One company that makes electric bulbs and tube lights is Samudra Lamps Ltd. After taxes and preferential dividends, the company's profit for that year was Rs. 400 lakh. On March 31, the share's market value was Rs. 112. This indicates that it would take the investor 14 years to get his money back via earnings. Moreover, a yield of 7.14% (100/14 years) is obtained from this. Stronger companies have lower P/E ratios because they are riskier investments, but well-established and financially stable corporations have higher P/E ratios since their returns are higher. As long as investors believe that a firm can grow, provide a return, or see its share price rise, the P/E ratio will be high. It will drop as soon as there is less faith in the company's ability to turn a profit. This explains why during boom times, prices soar. They collapse during depressive episodes.

An investor's purchase price for a share is determined by the company's projected earnings and future prospects. Therefore, when the current market price is divided by the previous earnings per share, the P/E ratio is flawed. The market price at the moment ought to be divided by the expected earnings per share at that moment. However, obtaining that figure is challenging. The company's reputation, managerial caliber, and investors' faith in the company's earnings potential are all reflected in the P/E ratio. An investor can wonder what a firm's P/E ratio ought to be and how much it costs to buy a share of the company. The P/E of a number of companies, including Hindustan Lever Ltd. and ITC Ltd., exceeded 100 during the peak of the 1992 fraud in India! Companies listed on the Bombay Stock Exchange had an average P/E ratio of 80. The average P/E was still approximately 37 even a year after the hoax. This was among the commonly stated explanations for why international investors did not pour money into the Indian stock markets in large quantities. The average price to earnings ratio (P/E) of developed economies, such as the US, was allegedly approximately 20 at the time. This provided a 5% yield, which was around 2% higher than the inflation rate. Based on this, the P/E of the shares one wanted to buy should be 8, assuming that the rate of inflation in India is approximately 10%.

With this, the yield would be 12.5%, 2.5% higher than the rate of inflation. The P/E will increase and the yield will decrease as inflation declines. Interest rates in nations such as India have started to decline sharply. What the current P/E should be. At this point, I'd like to present a school of thinking supported by those who I refer to as proponents of the emerging economy. They contend that developing economies, or South East Asian nations, have an average P/E ratio of 45. They contend that since companies are expanding and high P/Es represent this expansion, P/Es must be greater in developing economies. P/E ratios will decrease and earnings will stabilize as companies get older. That might be the case. However, I believe that it would be safer for investors in India to purchase stock in companies with a P/E ratio between 11 and 13.

Buying a share with a higher P/E ratio should be considered carefully. Having stated that, the multiple that various investors would be willing to accept as appropriate would rely on: The firm and their assessment of its management, expansion, and future prospects; The market for the company's shares. Some businesses, like Reliance, ITC, and others, have done well for their investors throughout the years, and their shares are valued at higher P/E ratios. a company's earnings and profitability. the intended returns for various investors. To put it briefly, the P/E that meets each investor's unique investment return requirements will be the one that they deem reasonable. With relation to IT shares, the P/E valuation of shares became meaningless in 1999. One's estimate or pricing in this case was accurate as everyone else's.

Market to Book Ratio: This measure contrasts a company's book value with its market value for its assets. When a share's market value triples or quadruples its book value, investors are very confident in the company's growth prospects. It could also imply that the assets are not valued fairly. Conversely, if the book value exceeds the market value, it could indicate that the business is losing money and that investors are losing faith in it. By dividing the market price per share by the book value per share, one can find the market to book ratio. For instance, Mithawala Chemicals Ltd.'s market to book ratio is $105/48 = 2.1875$ if the share price is Rs. 105 and the book value is Rs. 48. More than twice the book value of Mithawala Chemicals' shares is represented by their market value. This implies that investors think the company will increase in revenue, value, and profitability, or that the company's assets are undervalued and that its prospects are promising. Generally speaking, a share that is priced greater than three times its book value shouldn't be bought because there is a large discrepancy and it isn't supported by physical assets.

Consequently, the price may drop significantly. I'll use a few companies to demonstrate how market and book values differ (See Table 9.1). The market value and the book value diverge significantly. In conclusion, the market value ratios are crucial since they influence investment choices. Market ratios take on another dimension when one recalls that the market price of a share considers profitability, earnings, prospects, and all other aspects of a company, as technical analysts would attest. These ratios are the only ones that assess the price of a share to help an investor decide whether it is underpriced or overpriced.

Profits

The final criterion used to evaluate businesses is earnings, or more specifically, the return on investment made by investors. The fair market value of an investment and the price of a share are frequently ascertained using the earnings ratios. These are therefore the most crucial ratios for investors, and it is critical to recognize and comprehend them. Earnings per Share: The ratio of earnings to shares (EPS) shows how much a common share makes in a given year. With the use of this ratio, investors can ascertain whether a share is properly priced and really measure the income made by it. To calculate the ratio, divide the income that is attributable to common shareholders by the weighted average of common shares. For example, Range View Tea Estates's earnings after taxes in 2003 were Rs. 5,00,000. The firm had 200,000 outstanding shares at a price of Rs. 10 each as of June 30, 2010. The company issued an extra 100,000 shares on July 1st, 2010.

Range View's earnings per share would be: Investors look up a company's fully diluted earnings per share in nations like India where employees are granted stock options. This represents a company's earnings per share following the exchange of all outstanding warrants, share options, and convertible securities for shares at the conclusion of the accounting period. A share's worth to many investors is also based on its multiple of the company's earnings. The share is valued at Rs. 50 if the earning per share is Rs. 5 and a yield of 10% is thought to be appropriate. Cash Earnings per Share: It is sometimes maintained that because depreciation, taxes, and financing costs differ from firm to company, earnings per share is not a reliable indicator of a company's profitability. The dispute continues that the earnings before tax, interest, and depreciation should be used to determine the genuine earnings. By dividing earnings before depreciation, interest, and tax (EDBIT) by the weighted average number of shares issued, one can get the cash earning per share. There is no way that the cash earnings per share will ever equal the earnings per share. Dividend per Share: Investors sometimes use the dividend per share to calculate a share's true value. This school of thought's proponents contend that the only people who truly benefit from earnings per share are those who have the power to decide on a company's policies. An investor's dividends are his source of income.

As a result, it is proposed that a share's value should be greater than the dividend that is paid on it. What is the value of a share? The pricing would rely on the anticipated capital appreciation if one assumes that an investor would make gains in the form of dividend income per share and a rise in the share price. It would be fair to tolerate a low dividend return if the share had consistently increased in value by 30% annually. Example: Over the past three years, the average percentage increase in the market value of Divya Jeans Ltd.'s shares, which are valued at Rs. 40, has been 25. A 5 percent dividend would suffice if an investor was targeting a 30 percent yield. In this case, Divya Jeans' market value based on dividend per share would be as follows (assuming 15% dividend on face value = 5% on market value) if the company has paid a 15% dividend. Based on this, the shares of Divya Jeans are expensive. On the other hand, a high dividend yield would be anticipated if a share does not increase in value by more than 5% and a 30% return is needed. The real value of the share would be 30% dividend, which would be interpreted as a 23% yield, if PDP's shares have been appreciating at a rate of 7% annually and the company declares a dividend of 30%, or Rs. 3 per share. It should be noted that this method of valuation is so fraught with assumptions (annual appreciation and expected return) that it is rarely used.

Dividend Payout Ratio: This ratio calculates the total amount of dividends that are paid out of earnings. With the use of this ratio, an investor can ascertain what portion of the company's annual earnings is reinvested in the business for long-term growth, and what portion is distributed as a dividend to shareholders. This ratio is crucial for evaluating a firm's future because, in the event that all of its income were dispersed, the company would not be able to generate enough capital internally to fund expansion or counteract the effects of inflation; instead, it would have to take on debt in order to meet these goals. Divide the dividend by net income after taxes to find this ratio. Typically, young, fast-growing businesses have low dividend payout ratios because they reinvest their profits back into the business. Conversely, mature businesses offer large payments. This is concerning since they might not be holding onto capital to expand or renew assets. In order to avoid depleting the funds set aside for asset replacement, growth, and expansion, investors must also make sure that the dividend is being paid from current income rather than retained earnings. For example, Excel Railings Ltd. made Rs. 68 lakh after taxes in the most recent fiscal year. It distributed a dividend of Rs. 28 lakh out of this.

The ratio of dividend payout would be 28/68, or 0.412. 41.2% of the company's net income was paid out as dividends, with 58.8% being retained for the company's expansion. Recap: It's critical to keep in mind that profitability is not indicated by earnings ratios. They offer guidance to investors regarding a company's dividend policy, earnings per share, and the amount of income reinvested in the business for growth, expansion, and asset replacement. Investors must carefully review these figures, paying particular attention to the dividend payout and earnings per share. Determining if the market price of a share is appropriate might be aided by looking at the earnings per share. Investors should be wary if the dividend payout ratios are extremely high, since this may suggest that the company's management is not especially focused on the company's long-term growth and prospects.

Advisability

A company's profitability is a key consideration for investors. A company cannot expand, pay dividends, see a growth in value, or endure over the long term if it is not profitable. With the help of profitability ratios, an investor can assess a company's performance both in comparison to other businesses in the same industry and to its own past results.

Utilizing these statistics, an investor can assess the efficacy of management based on the profits realized from investments and sales. Investors should keep the following in mind when assessing a company's profitability: ratios should, to the greatest extent feasible, be computed using average assets and liabilities rather than assets and liabilities as of a certain date. Throughout the year, these numbers may vary significantly, which could dramatically skew the results. Additionally, businesses have been known to manipulate their balance sheets by adding or subtracting assets or liabilities. Furthermore, as profits are produced over the Book of a year rather than on a certain date, ratios based on average assets and liabilities would provide a more accurate picture of the outcomes attained by a business. The cost of capital and borrowings, along with the rate of inflation, should be considered by the investor. An investor should think about if they could have made a higher return elsewhere when analyzing a profitability ratio.

Additionally, if the return has increased at the same rate as inflation. In conclusion, ratios ought to be seen as a signpost or a recommendation for further advancement. Return on Total Assets: This is the first ratio that needs to be examined. This is a crucial measure since it would enable the investor to assess if the business has received a fair return on its sales. Whether the company's resources have been employed profitably and efficiently, as well as whether the interest rate on its debt is excessive. This ratio should be used to evaluate a company's performance against prior years as well as against other businesses in the same sector. Return on Equity (ROE): The return on equity (ROE) is a commonly used metric to assess profitability. This ratio is used to assess if the return obtained is comparable to that of other accessible options. Income, or the net profit after taxes, is expressed as a percentage of shareholders' equity to compute this return. It should be emphasized that including extraordinary, uncommon, or non-recurring items in the income figure can distort the conclusions drawn. Additionally, dividends on preference shares should not be included in the net income used to compute this percentage. The portion of a firm that common shareholders own, comprising reserves and retained earnings, is known as shareholders' equity. It is important to keep in mind that low profitability indicates that there are alternative investments available that have lower risks and generate a larger return. Considering the investment's dangers, the ROE ought to be contrasted with other options. Generally speaking, the risk increases with the return.

Pre-interest Return on Assets: This ratio is frequently cited as a more accurate indicator of profitability than post-tax performance since it is challenging to compare businesses' post-tax results due to tax and interest implications. This is due to the fact that interest rates differ amongst businesses and are reliant on their borrowing arrangements. In a similar vein, a company's tax liability varies and is determined by how it has budgeted its taxes. By dividing earnings before interest and taxes by the average total assets, this ratio indicates that operational income should be the basis for the return. To assess if a company's return is high or low, an investor needs to compare it to that of other businesses, ideally in the same industry. Pre-interest After Tax Return of Assets This ratio is calculated to assess how well management uses assets without needing funding. Since tax is subtracted before earnings are calculated, it is included in the computation. However, as interest is a payment for capital or funds and varies from firm to company, it is not taken into account. By expressing net return after taxes, but excluding interest, as a percentage of average total assets, the ratio is calculated.

Return on Total Invested Capital: This ratio is used to assess how well a company has used its capital. An investor can use this ratio to see if he could have made more money somewhere else. As such, it provides him with the chance to evaluate returns from other companies. Debentures, share capital, loans, and other obligations with related costs are all included in the term "invested capital" in this ratio. A company's earnings before interest and tax divided by the average amount of capital invested yields the ratio. For example, Bombay Pistons Ltd.'s earnings before interest and tax for the current year were Rs. 18.50 crore. Investors need to make sure that the return on capital exceeds both the weighted average cost of borrowings and the current interest rate. The return on capital should be deemed insufficient if the interest rate is higher. In summary, profitability ratios are undoubtedly the most crucial statistics for investors since they show if a business is viable and how it compares to others in its industry. Nonetheless, these ratios shouldn't be seen in a vacuum. It's important to keep in mind that a lower ratio is not always undesirable. In volume-driven businesses, companies may provide goods at a reduced price in an effort to boost sales and profits. These ratios should be viewed as indicators, just like all ratios are.

Availability

One of the main components of any investment is liquidity. Liquid investments are crucial because they make it simple to turn them into cash when you need them to pay bills. Comparably, a business needs to be liquid to be able to pay its maturing debt and to have enough cash on hand to cover its operational needs. In the event that a business is unable to accomplish this, it can be compelled to liquidate and/or sell its more valuable assets at a loss.

Many mutual funds were compelled to sell their blue chip shares in order to create liquidity following the 1992 securities scam since they were unable to sell their sizable holdings of securities from public sector undertakings (PSUs). When information technology share values fell precipitously in the first quarter of 2000, mutual funds sold shares to cover unit redemptions, raising fears that prices might fall even further. Following his appointment as UTI's CEO, Mr. Damodaran arranged for the sale of the more tradable securities in order to book gains and have enough cash on hand to satisfy redemption requests. Current Ratio: The most widely utilized ratio for calculating liquidity is the current ratio. Its goal is to determine if a company's present assets are sufficient to cover its short-term debt—that is, debt that will mature within a year.

Divide current assets by current liabilities to get the ratio. For example, as of March 31, Spear Canisters Ltd. has current assets of Rs. 400 crore and current liabilities of Rs. 125 crore. Consequently, its current ratio is 16:5, or 3.2. To put it briefly, Spear Canisters Ltd. has no trouble covering its present debts. It only needs to sell 31.25% of its present assets to achieve this. The current ratio is often in the range of one to slightly less than one. This is not horrible on its own. These days, just-in-time (JIT) inventory control, the opportunity cost of tying up money inefficiently, and the cost of capital are all known to all businesses. As a result, efforts are made to maintain modest levels of current assets, including cash, debts, and shares. Thus, the current ratio is frequently much lower than 1. This may just indicate that the business is making efficient use of its assets, not that it is illiquid per se. Fast or Acid Test: Creditors and investors like the acid test. This ratio is used to determine if a business has sufficient cash on hand or in cash equivalents to cover its current liabilities. The fundamental reasoning is that paying debts with cash or cash equivalents typically results in no conversion costs. If sold during a distressed period, other assets like stocks and inventory might not realize their full book value.

To put it another way, in an emergency, the corporation might lose money converting them to cash. By dividing cash, marketable investments, and debtors by current obligations, one can get this ratio. It should be mentioned that investments are considered to calculate this ratio even though they aren't technically speaking current assets. Net Working Investments Networking investments, also known as net current assets, are calculated by subtracting current liabilities from current working assets (trade assets). Clearly, this is not a ratio. It is helpful for rapidly determining if a business has enough current assets to cover its current liabilities. In actuality, a company's working capital is its net current assets. As a result, this number can be used to compute a number of derivatives, including those related to capital, income, and sales. One can also use net current assets as a starting point to calculate the amount of working capital needed to sustain a particular level of sales. A 20% ratio would imply that net current assets would have to rise correspondingly in order for sales to rise by 20%. A low ratio is preferable in this situation since less working capital will be required to increase. This allows the business to expand very quickly.

Samudra Fisheries provided an example where net current assets were Rs. 450 lakh and sales were Rs. 2000 lakh. Its net current assets to sales would be as follows: Samudra Fisheries had a sales turnover of Rs. 2,000 lakh in its most recent financial year. Accordingly, for every 1% growth in sales, working capital needs to rise by 21.25%. Therefore, working capital would have to rise by Rs. 21.25 lakh if sales were to increase by Rs. 1 crore. Net Trade Cycle: It's critical to ascertain how long it takes a business to realize sales proceeds following payment for the acquisition of raw materials. This is a very helpful tool for figuring out how liquid a company is. It is calculated by taking the days from the debtor turnover to the stock turnover and subtracting the days from the creditors turnover. An improvement in the ratio's value would suggest better net current working asset management. Naturally, it may also mean that the business is having trouble making its debt payments to creditors. Therefore, in order to ascertain the causes of a shift in the net trade cycle, one needs to look beyond the numbers. It is important to keep in mind that the longer the cycle, the more funding is required. Therefore, it is important to reduce the net trade cycle as much as possible. Lowering the number of debtors and stock levels will help achieve this.

Investors should examine each component separately in addition to determining whether the cycle is improving. A rise in the turnover of creditors may potentially indicate a problem with the company's ability to make payments. A decrease in debtors may indicate a decline in credit sales or better debt collection. The cause has to be investigated. Defensive Interval: This ratio shows how many days a business can operate without taking on new funding or clients. It is comparable to a strike by employees. How many days can he live off of his assets before going bankrupt? By dividing a company's typical daily cash operating expenses by its most liquid assets, one can compute the defensive interval ratio. It's crucial to remember that this ratio is only computed using the assets that are the most liquid, like cash and cash equivalents. Since they are not cash equivalents, debtors and stocks should not be taken into consideration.

Example General Balls Ltd.'s cash and cash equivalents. Current Liability Coverage: By analyzing the link between cash inflows from operations and current liabilities, investors can ascertain whether the company will be able to satisfy its maturing obligations with funds generated domestically or through external sources. This ratio is crucial in the face of creative accounting and financial constraints. For example, Bharat Bolts Ltd. reported net income before taxes of Rs. 750 lakh in its most recent year, which concluded on March 31. The amount depreciated was 25 lakh. As of March 31 of last year, current liabilities were Rs. 2,350 lakh, but as of March 31 of this year, they were Rs. 1,450 lakh. To put it another way, cash flow from activities only accounted for 41% of current obligations. This is the current liability coverage. It would take 2.44 years to pay off existing liabilities with money generated domestically. In summary, the importance of liquidity to businesses is growing, and this issue alone has caused businesses to become ill due to a lack of capital to support operations.

Investors must assess a company's liquidity and determine if it is increasing or decreasing. Companies start to put off and delay paying their debts when they start to experience financial difficulties. Current obligations start to accumulate. The accumulation of current liabilities makes suppliers less and less willing to offer products. This has a domino effect, affecting sales and production first. Investors should therefore be concerned if a company's liquidity ratios are declining. Negative liquidity ratios, however, are not always a bad thing. Strong businesses often maintain minimal current assets and can obtain extended credit from suppliers, particularly those who run extremely thin margins. In the past, before a crash, corporations had outstanding liquidity ratios. This happens as a result of the sale of stocks and fixed assets and their conversion to cash.

As debts are settled, current liabilities decline. Thus, having good liquidity isn't always a good thing. An investor ought to consistently assess the caliber of a business's present assets. Finding out if they are at their present realizable worth is also important. Furthermore, since deferred revenue expenses like advertising do not have an encashable value, they should not be included in current assets. Lastly, it is important to keep in mind that balance sheets can have window dressing. As a result, the numbers need to be carefully examined. The ideal level of liquidity needed differs depending on the business and the sector. It is dependent on both the state of the market and a company's level of recognition.

Investors should review liquidity ratios to determine whether a firm has sufficient liquidity and whether its liquidity condition has improved or worsened. Selling the company's stock should be taken into consideration if it has gotten worse and there doesn't seem to be any chance of it getting better very soon.

Make Use of

The amount that a business depends on borrowed money to support its operations is indicated by its leverage. These loans could come in the form of bank overdrafts, term loans, short-term loans, or debentures. Highly leveraged companies allow their owners to govern the business with a relatively small stake and very little capital. Lenders bear the majority of the risk. These enterprises, especially those with high margins, generate significant profits during prosperous times. Recessions, on the other hand, bring about the opposite. Exorbitant interest rates and significant losses might result from the huge gains realized during economic booms. Table 9.2 provides an illustration of the impact on profitability. Company B has borrowed 20% of its entire finances, Company C is cash wealthy and does not borrow at all, and Company A is severely leveraged.

In an exceptional year, Company A generates an astounding 170% of its return before taxes, whereas Company C only generates a very meager 50%. It should be mentioned that a highly leveraged corporation will generate outstanding profits as long as the return or the earnings rate is higher than the cost of borrowing. Profits will decline when this rate declines. Even in a normal year, heavily leveraged businesses would make more money than non-borrowing businesses.

In years of depression or recession, the tide shifts because debt needs to be paid back. During these periods, borrowing costs frequently outweigh earnings, resulting in losses; the firm with no borrowings is the one with the biggest profits. Therefore, it is safe to say that highly leveraged companies are dangerous and can have negative earnings in a downturn, whereas organizations with very little or no borrowing are safer and can be relied upon for some returns in both good and bad years. On the other hand, heavily leveraged organizations can have extremely good outcomes during prosperous times. obligations to Assets Ratio: This ratio shows how much money the corporation has borrowed overall and how much of that money has come from external obligations. In this sense, both present and long-term liabilities are considered liabilities. A company's contingent liabilities, such as guarantees and lawsuits, should also be carefully reviewed by investors. Assets are all assets, excluding intangibles such deferred revenue expenditure (preliminary expenses, goodwill, deferred advertising expenditure and the like). The ratio would alter significantly if these were significant and likely to crystallize.

Debt to Assets Ratio: This ratio is more precise than the others. It assesses how much debt or borrowed money is covered by assets and calculates the amount that assets can lose value while still making good on their debt obligations. Overdrafts from banks are considered debts since they are regarded as borrowed money. Intangibles like goodwill and deferred assets are not considered assets. Debt to Net Worth Ratio: This measure reveals how much of a company's funds come from outside sources, indicating how reliant it is on borrowing to support its operations. It is calculated by dividing the debt of an organization by its net worth. The formula for calculating net value is shareholders' equity minus intangible assets. For example, as of March 31, Nikhila Ltd. owed Rs. 385 lakh. Equity held by shareholders was Rs. 105 lakh. Intangible assets were absent. To put it another way, the debt to net worth ratio was 3.67 times the shareholders' equity.

For each Re. 1 was contributed by stockholders, while 3.67 was borrowed. This indicates that the business is well-geared. Liabilities to Net Worth: This metric, which is bigger than the debt-to-net-worth ratio, aims to assess how reliant on liabilities a company has on funding its operations. It is computed by dividing an organization's total liabilities by its net worth. Incremental Gearing: The incremental gearing ratio looks at how much more borrowing is needed to support expansion. This ratio and the net working investments ratio are comparable in certain ways. To calculate the ratio, divide the net increase in debt by the net income rise after taxes but before dividends. Here's an example using Raman Tea Ltd.'s financial statements. Other Ratios: Although there are a few other gearing ratios, they are not frequently utilized.

The long-term debt ratio, for example, establishes the relative importance of borrowings to overall long-term obligations and shareholders' equity. The issue of liability to equity is another ratio. In this computation, liabilities comprise both shareholders' equity and total liabilities. Synopsis: The gearing ratios show how reliant a business is on outside funding and how much of the business is financed by liabilities. Investors should take these figures into serious consideration when assessing a company.

Ability to Pay Debt

One kind of funding that has grown in popularity recently is debt. Few businesses issued or provided convertible and non-convertible debentures fifteen years ago. Currently, debentures of all kinds are provided in greater quantities than equity. In this case, the investor needs to determine if a business can pay off its debt using money that is created internally. Can it use its revenues to cover the principal and interest payments? Naturally, this is predicated on the idea that the business can continue to make money and that debt won't be paid off by taking on more loans, acquiring rights, or issuing shares to the general public. Debt Coverage: Using income or internally generated money, this ratio is used to calculate how long a company would need to pay off its short- and long-term debt. This is important if the debt cannot be paid off by selling assets or by issuing new debt or cash.

Internally produced funds are defined as income after taxes plus non-cash expenses like depreciation and non-operating income and expenses for the purpose of calculating this ratio. Term loans, debentures, and bank overdrafts would all be considered debt. To calculate the ratio, divide the amount of funds generated internally by the company by the average amount of debt. Here is an example taken from Pear Ltd.'s financial statements. Liability Coverage Ratio: This ratio builds upon the debt coverage ratio. It is employed to determine if a business can use internal generation to pay off all of its debts. This ratio is computed by dividing a firm's internally generated cash by the average total liabilities of the company. For example, Tongues and Tongs Ltd. generated Rs. 500 lakh internally in its most recent year, which concluded on March 31. At the end of the most recent year, its total liabilities were Rs. 4,500 lakh, and at the end of the previous year, they were Rs. 3,500 lakh. This indicates that just

25% of the average total liabilities of the corporation were funded internally. At this rate, the loan can be settled in full in four years.

The reasoning is that what needs to be taken into account is the amount of time it would take to repay the entire obligations at a specific moment, hence it is also viable to calculate this ratio using the liabilities figure at the date of the balance sheet. Interest Cover: Whether a company's profits are sufficient to cover its interest obligations is a crucial question for investors to answer. If not, the company's reserves, new capital issues, or extra borrowings will have to be used to pay the interest, all of which are indicative of severe financial distress. A company's earnings before interest and tax is divided by its interest expense to get the interest cover ratio. Always have a ratio greater than 1, and the higher the better. Even a slight decline in profit would require the business to use capital or retained earnings to cover interest if it is less than 1. For instance, in its most recent fiscal year, Bombay Green Ltd. made Rs. 450 crore before interest and taxes.

A total of Rs. 200 crore was spent on interest. The company's interest expense is more than doubled by its earnings before interest. a cozy setting. Fixed Charge Cover Several finance and leasing businesses were established in India throughout the 1980s. Instead of buying equipment, these businesses provide the option to lease it. Leasing has the advantage that all rent payments are fully tax deductible. Second, money does not have to be invested in order to buy assets. This type of financing is referred to as "off balance sheet financing," since neither the asset's true cost nor its liability are shown on the balance sheet. The fixed charge cover examines whether a business generates enough revenue to satisfy its interest and rental obligations in addition to taking into account off-balance sheet obligations like rental charges. There are arguments made occasionally that since the dividend payable on preferred shares is a fixed expense that must be paid, it should also be taken into consideration when determining this ratio.

The fixed fee cover is then computed in two steps. This ratio is superior to the interest cover ratio because it accounts for all of a company's fixed expenses and determines whether earnings are adequate to cover them. First, the fixed charge cover is calculated as previously mentioned, and after that, the preferred dividends paid are considered. Cash Flow Surplus: This ratio is predicated on the going concern theory, which holds that businesses will typically expand and need to invest in capital projects, which will raise their net working capital. Therefore, it is only appropriate to assess a company's debt-paying capacity after accounting for changes in net working capital and capital expenditures. Net income plus non-cash charges, such as depreciation and other expenses, less capital expenditures and growth in net working investments, equals cash flow.

The cash flow excess is divided by the total amount of debt to get the ratio. Example Culture Ltd.'s average debt in its most recent fiscal year was Rs. 400 crore. It made forty crores of rupees internally. The company had spent Rs. 20 crore on capital projects, and its net working investments had gone up by Rs. 10 crore. If the corporation used its excess cash flow for debt repayment, it would take 40 years. Frequently, this ratio is negative. This is due to the fact that when a business expands quickly, it acquires capital assets and increases its net working investments, which typically exceeds domestically generated money. Typically, loans or short-term bank facilities are used to finance this.

Debt service ratios are a crucial factor for investors to take into account, as they aid in assessing a company's ability to meet its financial obligations and settle its debts. This is especially important during recessions and periods of excessive inflation, as a company's inability to pay its debts might force it into bankruptcy.

Effectiveness and Asset Management

Businesses generate a profit because of their adept asset management. Investors must therefore assess if a company's assets are sufficient to meet its needs and whether the returns are appropriate. It is important to keep in mind that assets are obtained through either capital or borrowing. If the corporation has more assets than it needs, it is either stowing away money that it could have used more profitably or, on the other hand, it is paying interest that is not essential. The business's operations would not be utilizing its resources as efficiently and profitably if there were fewer assets than what was needed. Investors can ascertain whether a company has sufficient assets and is making effective use of them by using asset management ratios.

It is expected that asset utilization has an impact on sales volumes. Asset ratios are used to evaluate usage patterns and track the effectiveness of asset allocation. It is possible to compare one year to the next, as well as between companies within the same industry and outside of it. Additionally, these ratios are quite helpful for creating budgets and forecasts. However, it is important to keep in mind that asset management ratios are also indicators, just like other ratios. A high asset turnover rate may indicate insufficient asset retention, which can have a long-term negative impact on a company's profitability, rather than exceptional efficiency or a good return on investment. For this reason, investors should never limit their search to the signs. It's critical to remember that declining asset ratios are an indication of decline and should be taken seriously.

Stock utilization Ratios are used to calculate the effective usage of a company's stocks. Managers must maintain low stock levels at all times due to the high cost of borrowing. These ratios are constantly closely examined and assessed in the age of the just-in-time concept. Two ratios can be used to measure stock utilization: stock holding ratio, which calculates the number of days a company has stocks (relative to sales) and stock turnover ratio, which shows how frequently stocks (inventory) are turned over in a year by dividing the cost of goods sold by the average number of stocks held. This is a crucial efficiency metric for businesses who aim to maintain the least amount of inventory.

The computation involves quantifying the stock held in terms of the days of cost of goods sold: Example Nandan Switchgears Ltd.'s average inventory was Rs. 150 crore in the prior year and Rs. 160 crore in the most recent fiscal year. The cost of items sold during this time was 1,200 crore and 1,050 crore, respectively. The following ratios show how Nandan Switchgears Ltd. has successfully lowered inventory levels by 3.47 production days and increased stock turnover by 0.5 times. Usually, this is beneficial. It is imperative for investors to determine the cause of the recent increase in stocks. Specifically, could it be attributed to dealer-dumped inventory, supply chain challenges, or a manufacturing plant strike? Stock levels decline as businesses close. Existing stock is sold and no new stock is purchased. Therefore, it is necessary to determine the causes of the improvement in this ratio. Furthermore, it is imperative for an investor to determine if the current stock price is sufficient to sustain the company's sales volume.

Average Collection Time: Most businesses offer credit to their clients. They must either limit their own internal money or turn to bank financing in order to finance these sales. Because of this, the cost of financing is typically included in the sale price, and businesses give consumers who pay with cash at the time of sale or shortly after a cash discount. By dividing average trade debtors by average daily sales, one may find the average collection ratio. For example, in PDN

Ltd.'s most recent year, sales increased by 15% to Rs. 400 crore from Rs. 348 crore. In the preceding and current years, its average trade debtors were Rs. 49 crore and Rs. 59 crore, respectively.

Consequently, the average collection period was: The credit term grew over the prior year. PDN Ltd may be having trouble getting its customers to pay on time, it may be extending extended credit lengths, or the management may not be efficiently controlling credit, if the company's regular credit terms are only 30 days and consumers are taking 51 to 54 days to pay. Controlling this can increase efficiency and lower borrowing, which will save interest. An increasing average collection period ratio is a warning sign of significant bad debts and financial illness. However, a declining ratio is not always fantastic. Companies start collecting on their debts and selling their products for cash right before they fail. A decreasing average collection period ratio is the outcome. Average Payment Period: The ratio of average payment periods, also known as creditor ratios, shows how long it takes a business to pay its trade creditors, or how many days of credit it has. True Steel Ltd. is a sizable Pondicherry-based firm.

The ratio is computed by dividing trade creditors by the average daily cost of items sold. According to its financial statements, its average trade creditors were Rs. 29 crore in the prior year and Rs. 34 crore in the most recent one. Its cost of goods sold was 425 crore this year compared to Rs. 410 crore the year before. Its average payment period would be: Although it has increased from the prior year, the average payment period ratio in this example is still low. The investor ought to ascertain whether the company is utilizing all available credit. The business is having trouble getting credit. The business is struggling to make its debt payments to creditors.

The company may be able to secure longer credit terms if it is in a strong and dominant position. This is advantageous since the business can finance its working capital through creditors in an efficient manner, lowering financing costs to some level. Ratio of Net Working Investments: Trade debtors, stocks, and trade creditors are examples of assets that have a direct impact on sales. Net working assets are divided by sales to get the ratio.

Tamara Ltd.'s average stocks, debtors, and creditors were Rs. 38 crore, Rs. 45 crore, and Rs. 30 crore in the most recent fiscal year. It made 500 crores in sales that year. 8.6% of the company's sales were made up of net working investments. If this is the ideal level, net operating investments would have to increase by Rs. 8.6 lakh for every Rs. 100 lakh in sales. For this reason, this ratio is quite helpful in determining working capital needs. To put it briefly, this ratio illustrates a company's working capital needs and assists an investor in assessing how effectively the working capital of the business is managed. Total Asset Utilisation To find out if a business is making sales commensurate with its asset investment, the total asset utilization ratio is computed. It is a very helpful ratio for creating forecasts since it shows how well resources are being used.

By dividing the sales by the average total assets, the ratio is computed. As an example, Divya Tyres Ltd. was able to boost revenues from Rs. 495 crore to Rs. 630 crore in the most recent financial year. Its average asset value increased to Rs. 90 crore, or 10%. Its overall asset utilization ratios during the Book of the two years were as follows: Clearly, the ratio has increased. Additionally, this indicates that fewer assets are needed to support a rise in sales, which may indicate that assets are being used more effectively. Fixed Asset Utilization: A company's ability to make effective use of its fixed assets is gauged by this ratio. Investors can assess a company's efficiency in using its fixed assets by contrasting this with the utilization of other businesses in the same sector. It's important to keep in mind that this ratio must be computed on net fixed assets, or cost less cumulative depreciation. Sales are divided by the average net fixed assets to arrive at this figure. The net fixed asset utilization grew by 31% despite a mere 6% increase in sales.

This implies that the business may be growing, even while the net fixed asset utilization hasn't yet shown the benefits or results of this growth. A rising net fixed asset utilization ratio may indicate a decline in sales and a decline in the effectiveness of managing net fixed assets. Keep in mind that when comparing organizations, fixed asset costs can vary, making this ratio not a true indicator of success. A newly established business with recently purchased fixed assets will have a lower ratio than one with older assets. It would be unjust to call the older company inefficient in this situation.

By calculating summary asset management ratios, one can evaluate the effectiveness and competency of management by evaluating the degree of efficiency with which assets have been managed. It also shows how well the credit policy has been implemented and whether a business is utilizing all of the credit that its suppliers are willing to give it. It can also reveal whether a business is having problems.

Margin

The phrase "although sales have increased by 24 percent in the year, profits have fallen due to increases in the cost of production causing margins to erode" appears frequently in annual reports. Margin is a measure of a business's profit on sales, or its markup on the price of the goods it produces or trades in. The profit per item sold increases with a higher markup and vice versa. Margin plays such a crucial role in determining whether a corporation succeeds or fails. Furthermore, the seller's markup or margin is typically determined by what he feels the market will bear or what will encourage sales. Low volume companies typically have significant profit margins since their products must frequently be kept for a while. Others, including supermarkets and brokers, operate with extremely thin margins due to their large volume.

Margin helps identify a company's cost structure, i.e., whether it is high or low cost, and whether it is a high volume, low margin firm. This is significant since it will show how reliant on margins the business is. When a business has narrow profit margins, even a slight increase in expenses can lead to significant losses. Margin can also be used to compare the performance of companies within a group or an industry. Assume for the purposes of this analysis, Hindustan York's gross margin is 20% whereas the industry average is 18%. In this case, one may say that Hindustan York is more productive and that its goods are more expensive. Margin can also be used to evaluate management trends. Strong and effective management will strive to increase margins or at the very least keep them stable. An investor can use margins to assess the extent to which cost increases—whether due to inflation or governmental levies—have been partially or fully passed on to customers.

The corporation will pass on the full cost rise to customers if there is a high demand for its product. However, if there is little demand for the company's products, it frequently absorbs a portion of the cost rise out of concern that the consumer won't buy the product. The TV sector is a prime illustration of declining margins. Because there is fierce competition and a wide range of brands available to consumers, manufacturers have had to absorb some cost increases and, in certain cases, lower their prices in order to remain competitive. The mix of products influences margins.

A business might sell a variety of goods, each with a distinct price. Products may have low margins for some and high margins for others. The corporation would earn a higher margin if more high-margin products were sold. On the other hand, the average margin on sales will decrease if more low-margin products are offered. It's important to keep in mind that low profit companies might be beneficial. Businesses with low margins, high turnover rates, and remarkable returns on capital utilized are among the most prosperous in the world. Gross Margin: The amount of surplus available to cover the business's costs is known as the gross margin. It is computed as a percentage of sales by dividing the difference between sales and the cost of goods sold. Hindustan York saw a 25% growth in sales to Rs. 500 crore in Year 2, and a 20% increase in gross profit of Rs. 25 crore. In these trying times, these two are advantageous. But its gross margin decreased by 1.25 percent. Several factors could be to blame for this, including: heightened competition: in an effort to increase sales, the corporation lowered its margins.

The business made the deliberate choice to lower its profits in an effort to boost sales. a decline in the composition of products. Cost increases were too great for the corporation to pass on to its customers. When an investor notices a growth or decline in the gross margin, they shouldn't draw conclusions too quickly. He needs to look beyond the numbers to determine what caused the shift. A decline in the margin could be from the company's failure to pass on inflationary cost rises to customers or from a deliberate effort to raise sales. An increase in the margin could simply be the result of raising prices. Operating Margin: This measures a company's profitability before deducting interest charges, taxes, and other incidental income. By subtracting selling, general, and administrative costs from gross profit and expressing the result as a percentage of sales, one can get the operating margin: Illustration The pertinent data from Patel Nair Ltd.'s results. The operating margin experienced a 1.17% increase.

The fact that operating costs did not rise as quickly as sales could be one of the causes of this. Operating expenses increased by 25% while sales and gross profit both increased by 33%. While not the only explanation, this might be one of them. In a different scenario, the operating margin may decline even while sales are increasing due to a decline in the gross margin and an increase in costs. Since costs typically increase at a different rate than revenues, the operating margin should typically increase with sales. The opposite may be true during an inflationary period or a recession. It's possible for costs to rise more quickly than revenues, and gross margins to decline as well. An investor should constantly look at the operating margin ratio since it shows the probable causes of a company's profitability improvement or decline, and one needs to determine the real reasons behind this. Breakeven Margin In the event that there are no sales, every organization must still pay for overhead such as selling, administration, and other incidental costs.

The number of units that a business needs to sell to cover these costs is indicated by the breakeven margin. If a business produces and sells half of its capacity, it would be in a no-profit, no-loss situation if its breakeven point is at 50% of its capacity. Profits would be made on any units sold in excess of this, and vice versa. The expenses, including financing costs, are divided by the gross income per unit to determine the breakeven margin ratio. Profits that are uncommon or nonrecurring must be subtracted from the total. Although 1000 units were sold in total, Kumar Wheels Ltd. needs to sell 675 units at current prices to cover its costs. It would earn by Rs. 2 if it sold 676 units. If the company only sold 674 units, it would lose Rs. 2. Some investors would rather determine the breakeven margin by taking the gross profit and subtracting the selling costs to get the gross profit per unit.

This is carried out because selling expenses are linked to sales, and without sales, selling costs would not be spent. If selling expenditures in the aforementioned Kumar Wheels Ltd. example were 400, the breakeven margin would be computed as follows: This is arguably a more accurate measurement. The breakeven margin is a crucial metric since it shows the precise number of units that a business must sell in order to turn a profit. When making decisions and weighing options, this management ratio is also crucial. Pre-Financing Margin: This is the percentage of profit made before financing expenses are deducted. The rationale behind the exclusion of finance costs is their variation across different organizations. These also differ based on how they are financed. Therefore, to calculate the pre-financing margin, divide earnings before interest and tax by sales, then represent the result as a percentage. Illustration It would be more reasonable to compute the pre-financing margin in the previous Kumar Wheels Ltd. example after deducting non-recurring income and expenses. In that instance, the profit on the sale of a factory should be subtracted to get the following margin: This is a useful metric for evaluating the profitability of different businesses. Pre-tax Margin: This represents the percentage of profit on sales before taxes and after financing costs have been deducted.

To put it briefly, this is determined using income before taxes and reported as a percentage of sales. Non-recurring revenue or expenses should be excluded from the computation since they would skew comparisons, as was previously indicated. The margin would drop to 8.125% if the Rs. 50 lakh in non-recurring income were removed, as shown below: Pre-tax margin is not a reliable indicator of profitability or comparison because funding methods, or financing expenses, differ between businesses. Nonetheless, it might be useful when comparing a company's success across a number of years. Net Profit Margin: This represents a company's earnings on sales after deducting taxes. It shows the percentage of sales that can be appropriated if all costs and obligations have been satisfied. Non-recurring revenue and expenses should be subtracted from the computation in order to make comparison easier and provide a more accurate image.

Pre-tax income of Kumar Wheels Ltd. was Rs. 700 lakh. Pre-tax income would be Rs. 350 lakh if taxes were Rs. 350 lakh. The one-time revenue was fifty lakh rupees. Hence, the net profit margin was: 3.75% was the sales return to shareholders after taxes. A shareholder can also ascertain the increased earnings that will be at their disposal due to increases in sales by using the net profit margin. Thus, summary margins are useful for both analyzing a company's cost structure and performance assessment. It's crucial to keep in mind that neither high nor low margins are always desirable. To attain volumes, a corporation may choose to operate on extremely low margins. Conversely, a business with large profit margins can experience a decline in product demand. Investors should always investigate the causes of changes, and the many measurements discussed in this chapter will help the investor identify potential causes.

Flow of Cash

In the era of creative accounting, firms are changing generally accepted accounting principles, creating new provisions or reversing existing ones, and generally accepting accounting rules in order to display profits. When shareholders view the reported earnings in a company's financial accounts, they are unaware of this. Therefore, it is unexpected when a consistently profitable business abruptly closes and enters liquidation. When a business can't get financing or pay its debtors, this happens. There are numerous instances of this throughout history, thus investors should constantly inquire about the company's cash earnings. In what way is the business funded? What is the business doing with its finances? Making a declaration of the sources and uses of finances will help you find the answers to the questions above.

Its significance has been acknowledged in the US and other European nations where publishing an annual report that includes a summary of changes in financial statements—basically, a cash flow statement—is required of companies. The profit for the year is the starting point for a statement of sources and uses, to which increases in liability accounts (sources) are added and increases in asset accounts (uses) are subtracted. The net result reveals the amount of excess or shortfall in finances as well as how it was paid for. For instance, Fundamental & Company Limited (Fundamental) declared a profit before tax of Rs. 108.12 lakh, as Table 10.2 illustrates. However, this also includes Rs. 247.74 lakh in other revenue, Rs. 112.88 lakh in profit from the sale of fixed assets, and Rs. 38.56 lakh taken out of a revaluation reserve. When these are subtracted, the profit becomes a Rs. 291.06 lakh loss. Table 10.1 provides an overview of the changes to Fundamental's Balance Sheet, while Table 10.2 provides specifics on its Sources and Uses of Funds (S & U) for the most recent year that concluded on March 31.

According to the S&U statement, the company's most recent year had a cash flow deficit, necessitating a loan of Rs. 1,927.92 lakh to cover its current asset costs. The corporation paid its preference share dividend from reserves rather than current profits since it had lost money. Furthermore, it is possible that the business was unable to get rid of its excess stock as inventories and other current assets rose. Table 10.3: Steel and Iron Dynamic Company, Ltd. Despite generating a cash profit of Rs. 429.44 crore, the Dynamic Iron and Steel Company Ltd. (DISCO) (see Tables 10.3 and 10.4) also experienced a cash flow deficit. The dividend of Rs. 80.55 lakh was again financed by loans, if it is assumed that this was utilized to finance the growth in inventories and partially finance assets. Investors need to look closely at a company's cash flow since it shows them exactly where the money came from and was spent. If a business is funding its inventory or paying dividends from borrowings without seeing actual growth, investors should be concerned as that indicates a decline. To put it briefly, financial statements lose their creative accounting due to the cash flow or sources and uses of funds statement.

What Next

According to fundamental analysis, no investment choice should be taken before thoroughly reviewing and evaluating all available data. Its power is not in guesswork or gut feelings, but in the fact that the data it analyzes is factual. However, whereas fundamental analysis deals with concrete facts, it tends to overlook the reality that people act irrationally sometimes. There are instances when market prices diverge from fundamentals. A number of factors, including speculation, rumor, insider trading, and others, can cause prices to rise or fall. Gerald Loeb, author of The Battle for Investment Survival, put it succinctly when he said, "There is no such thing as a final answer to security values." Twelve specialists will reach twelve distinct judgments.

It frequently occurs that, if given the opportunity to think again due to a changed circumstance, each would change his decision a short while later. Only a small portion of balance sheets and income statements, as well as human aspirations and fears, avarice, ambition, divine intervention, creativity, financial stress and strain, weather, discovery, fashion, and countless other factors that are too numerous to mention all together, determine market values. This is somewhat accurate, however the advantage of fundamental analysis is that it makes investment decisions based on information analysis and reasoned conclusions and assumptions. And this is the point at which numbers can diverge since different analysts would have made different assumptions. Their thinking will be grounded in their knowledge, experience, maturity, and intuition about the market.

Furthermore, fundamental analysis makes sure that shares are not bought or sold rashly, especially when it comes to buying. A share would only be purchased if its book value was less than its intrinsic worth. Since a share whose market value exceeds its inherent value would be sold, this also shields the seller from potential losses. Therefore, prudent investing is supported and encouraged by fundamental analysis. There is no perfect system. There has never been a system that regularly beats the market. No system exists that does not require human opinion and input.

Every system demands some consideration and presumptions. However, fundamental analysis is the most logical and significant of all the systems I have worked with and tested, so it is the one with which I am most at ease. And as an investor, this is the system that I strongly recommend you look into. Happy making purchases!

Basic Analysis: Method by Method

First Step: Political-Economic Evaluation An industry and a nation are impacted by political and economic considerations. A stable political climate is essential for consistent, well-balanced growth. Events on a global scale affect businesses and industries. To fulfill obligations, cover import costs, and pay off international debt, nations require reserves of foreign currency. There is a genuine danger that one's money could depreciate or appreciate in value. By entering into forward contracts, one can hedge this. Companies and industries may be impacted by trade restrictions or national cartels. Investors need to ascertain a company's sensitivity to regulatory and restrictive regulations. A significant load like foreign debt might have a negative impact on a company's performance. Purchasing power is diminished by inflation.

Low inflation is a sign of stability, and businesses thrive in these environments. Low tax and interest rates encourage business and investment. Economic growth can be accelerated by domestic savings. A nation's infrastructure determines its level of development. Excessive government spending leads to budgetary deficits, which boost the economy. Additionally, it results in rising inflation and demand. Financial Cycle Industry and individual businesses are directly impacted by business or economic cycles. Demand, employment, investment decisions, and profitability are all impacted. The economic cycle has four stages: boom, recession, recovery, and depression. Prior to making an investment, investors should ascertain the economic cycle's stage. Investors ought to sell their holdings right before or during a boom.

Step 2: Study of the Industry The industry's significance cannot be overstated. The performance of a corporation will be impacted by the industry. The cycle must be determined. These stages are the stages of entrepreneurship or sunrise, development or expansion, maturity or stabilization, and decline or sunset. When investing, it is best to buy during the initial two stages and sell when an asset reaches maturity. Investing in evergreen businesses is preferable. Cycle-related enterprises have erratic results. Competition is something that investors should take into account because higher competition means lesser profitability.

Investing in sectors of the economy free from governmental regulation is safer. industries focused on exports are currently supported by the government. Step 3: Evaluation of the Company Company analysis is the last phase of fundamental analysis. Examine the following areas: cash flow, ratios, performance, and the company. Supervisory The most crucial element to take into account in a business is the management. The quality of it determines the company's destiny. There are two primary forms of management in India: familial and professional. Investors need to investigate the managers' honesty, demonstrated skill, peer rating, resilience in the face of difficulty, breadth of experience, creativity, and professionalism. The Business Verifying if a company is the market leader for its products or in its area and how its rivals view it are crucial. Investors need to ascertain the company's growth strategies and philosophy. Workplace relations are crucial. The yearly summary The main and most significant source of information about a firm is its annual report. To ascertain the current status of the company under consideration, an investor needs to go beyond the surface of an annual report.

The financial statements, schedules, directors' report, and auditor's report are the separate sections of the annual report. The Report of the Directors Investors can learn more about the business from this report. It expresses the directors' opinions regarding the political, business, and economic environments. It provides an explanation of the company's performance as well as its expansion, modernization, and diversification goals. It outlines the suggested dividends and talks about the earnings made. If the report is carefully read, it might help the investor understand how the business operates. In their capacity as the firm's representative, the auditor updates shareholders on the directors' management and determines whether the financial statements accurately portray the company. Any modifications to accounting standards and their impact on the outcomes will be discussed by the auditors.

Auditors will also offer their opinions on any accounting procedure or activity that they disagree with. Investors should carefully review the auditor's report since any changes made in response to the observations or suggestions included within could significantly alter the outcomes. Statements of Finance A company's profit and loss account and balance sheet are the financial statements that are included in its annual report. These include specifics about the company's performance and financial standing. All of a company's assets and liabilities as of a specific date are listed on the balance sheet. The things that the business possesses are called assets. These include current assets (stocks, debts, and cash), investments, and fixed assets (buildings, cars, etc.). Liabilities include debts owed by the business to third parties (loans, trade creditors, etc.) as well as investments made by shareholders in the business (share capital and reserves).

The company's actions during the accounting period and their outcome (profit or loss) are shown numerically in the profit and loss statement. Liabilities that are contingent are also described. These are obligations that might develop in the event of an unlikely circumstance (guarantees, discounted bills). Liability becomes apparent as soon as the event occurs. The proposed and actual dividends are also included in the profit and loss statement. Timetables and Accounts Receivable Notes An annual report's schedules and account notes are located after the financial statements. The schedules include important details about the items in the profit and loss account and balance sheet. The notes are much more significant because they provide critical information on the company's accounting practices, potential liabilities, and other matters. To get a better idea of the company's financial situation, it is essential to study the schedules and notes to the accounts. Ratios Without first reviewing a company's financial accounts and contrasting its current performance with past performance, no investment should be made.

Ratios provide an easily interpretable mathematical expression of the relationship between performance metrics and/or assets/liabilities. The whole tale cannot be told by a single ratio. Four major categories can be used to group ratios: (a) profit and loss ratios; (b) balance sheet ratios. Financial Statements to Market Ratios; (c) Balance Sheet and Profit and Loss Ratios. In order to make it easier for investors to assess the company's strengths and flaws, ratios can also be categorized. A share's market value and the time it would take an investor to recoup his investment are both reflected in market value ratios. The market to book ratio and the price/earnings ratio are prominent indicators. Earnings ratios are used to assess investments and establish the fair market value of shares.

Earnings per share, cash earnings per share, dividend per share, and dividend payout ratio are the ratios that are computed. Profitability is the most important factor, and these ratios—return on equity, return on total assets, pre-interest return on assets, pre-interest after tax return on assets, and return on total invested capital—help investors assess a company's performance both in comparison to other businesses in the same industry and to its own past performance. The company's liquidity ratios show us how liquid its assets are and how easy it can pay its debts. The current ratio, defensive interval, quick or asset test, net current assets, and current obligation coverage are the ratios that are computed. The degree to which a business depends on borrowings in the form of bank overdrafts, debentures, and short- and long-term loans is shown by leverage ratios. Liabilities to assets ratio, debt to assets ratio, liabilities to net worth ratio, and incremental gearing are the ratios that are computed to indicate leverage.

Ratios for debt service capability show if a business can pay off its debts. The ones that are frequently calculated include cash flow surplus, interest cover, fixed charge cover, debt coverage, and liability coverage. Ratios for asset management are used to assess how well an organization is managing its assets. The stock utilization ratios, average payment and collection periods, net working investments ratio, total asset utilization, and fixed asset utilization are the more significant factors. The profits a business makes from its sales are shown by its margins.

The gross margin, operational margin, breakeven margin, pre-financing margin, pretax margin, and net profit margin are the margins that are calculated. Cash Movement An investor can ascertain the company's cash profits, financing method, and usage of obtained financing by examining the cash flow statements. The cash on hand at the start of the period is the first item in the statement. After then, it goes into detail on the sources, amounts, and uses of the funds received, culminating in the actual cash on hand. Its primary function is to remove creative accounting from the accounting statements.

Essential Analysis: Concise Overview

Examine the state of politics. Is it secure? Do any issues exist? Is it possible for the government to fall and if so, will there be problems? What do the economic indicators show? Is the rate of growth appropriate? Have exports increased? How secure is the position of the balance of payments? Examine the industry or industries that the business works in. Which phase of the cycle is the company currently in?

Who are its rivals? How simple is it to get into or out of the company? Next, investigate the business. Its management and annual report are the things to consider. It is necessary to examine the cash flow and analyze the ratios. Lastly, determine the intrinsic worth of a share before buying or selling it. This should be completed before making a decision.

Value Investing Strategies for Stock Market Investing

teach you the same investment method that the world's top investors employ. Checklist for investments Everything you need to know about value investing is covered in this book, from the basics to the most complex ideas. You may easily become a value investing expert and feel confident enough to manage your own portfolio with lifetime access to this value investing book.

Concerning

This book was recently published by a renowned research analyst. With the advent of discount brokerage firms and the increase in retail investor engagement in options and market delivery, the days of investors purchasing huge quantities of a stock and holding it for a 15–20 percent return have long passed. Because of this, the outdated stock market techniques are essentially worthless right now.

The bulk of retail investors are currently either trading intraday, profiting from a call option with a seven-day short expiry or on a single day, or collecting a little profit from a swing trade that results in more small range market fluctuations. The current book's author, who wrote it in this context, is the only one of its kind to purposefully employ swing, option, and intraday trading to provide a wealth of information in a short quantity of words. Would you like to know the "Investment Secrets" that the greatest investors of all time have learned?

People who are interested in learning about investing are drowned out by the constant barrage of financial news and schemes to become rich quickly, leaving them ignorant of what works and what doesn't. Usually, they lose money because they can't focus. Do you ever feel that there is too much information available? Have you ever been perplexed by the intricate jargon and strategies employed in the financial industry? Then maybe you might benefit from this Book! Value investing is a powerful strategy that has helped the most successful investors of our time, like Warren Buffett and Seth Klarman, generate billions of dollars in the stock market.

This book will teach you how to do it. Ideas are presented gradually so that even a non-expert may follow along and gain confidence in investing quickly. Enroll immediately to receive a copy of the original

Value Investing Bootcamp Book. It took me months to distill the ten years of content mastery into this book, which is an incredible value!

If the Book helps you buy only one good stock or avoid one bad one, you will have already made your money back. If you're serious about investing your hard-earned money, enroll today because the value of your assets will decrease owing to inflation every day you wait. So click "Take This Book" to join them and START GROWING YOUR WEALTH NOW!

Be Sure To Create A Plan Before Trading

You know that the design of a magnificent structure would have been sketched out on paper prior to construction even starting? Or do you think that the building would have been constructed in that manner if some masons had simply turned there and started creating the structure out of bricks and mortar at random right away? Before a building is constructed, its design must be created.

For the sake of argument, let's say that you are an army captain. How would you respond in a situation if you had to win a fight? Would you urge the guys to fight now while you think of a strategy later, or would you first create a strategy before engaging in combat? You might have heard this story before. There was once a tremendously successful businessman. He had four sons. When he was older, he gave each of them one rupee and told them to use it to launch a company and earn money. I will give control of my company to the first individual to profit two rupees out of this one.

The businessman tried to find out which of his sons actually had business acumen because most people are gamblers rather than businesspeople and do not even comprehend the basic rule of trade, which indicates that trading requires some kind of strategy. A gambler doesn't think about making a plan; they just start playing. Thus, be sure to have a plan in place before dealing in the stock market. The kind or form of strategy would be explained in forthcoming trading advice, nevertheless.

Grow from a Small Plant to a Giant Banyan Tree

Ever notice a plant sprouting? Are there any banyan trees or seeds that you have seen? The banyan seed is as little as a mustard seed. Can this be completed in a single day and reach its full potential? Of course not! The banyan seed first sprouts into a cute small plant. The same increases marginally the next day. Two leaves eventually grow from that delicate little bud. These little reddish-purple leaves are very pretty.

Nature is trying to teach you commerce through the same. That is, however, a different story if you are truly eager to learn from the same! The natural environment is not the place for hurrying. That banyan tree continues to grow slowly. In a few years, this will develop the ability to house birds. After a few more years of growth, this can provide shade for travelers. And this grows into a huge banyan tree very rapidly. Which would you prefer—your trading company expanding like a banyan tree, or a trading method that works something like this?

Alternatively, would you rather make a tidy profit from one to seven exhilarating transactions and then give up the stock market, swearing to yourself that it will never let you lose again when you do? You have to know by now what my second piece of advice is for the day. Just like with a banyan seed, you should make a small initial expenditure. As you continue to turn a profit, you should progressively raise your trading volume. Permit me to elaborate on this. Assume you have $5 lakh in liquid assets. That money is what you plan to invest in the stock market with the hope of making a substantial profit that will yield a monthly income of approximately 40,000 to 50,000 rupees. Then, all you have to do is begin trading with a sum of $10,000.

Consider a goal: "If I am able to turn this investment of 10,000 into 12,000, or if I am able to make a profit of 2,000 with this investment, I will increase my working capital used for trading to 20,000, just like a banyan tree." After I turned a £4,000 profit, the working capital would increase to £30,000. When I turn a $6,000 profit, I'd raise the same to $40,000. As a result, for every 2,000 in profit, the working capital may rise by 10,000. "What if I can't turn a profit?" one may wonder. Therefore, if you go through this book from cover to cover, I don't think you'll lose money trading.

Of course, you can make money. When you trade with discipline, making money in the stock market is also not that difficult. On the other hand, trading is a simpler way to make money than investing because it provides opportunities for profit in both bull and bear markets. It's possible that investing opportunities are limited to bull markets. Nevertheless, you are not required to invest 10,000 rupees in a single stock. Since you are reading a book published, there is no way for my readers to lose. I never advise you to invest all of your funds in a single transaction. Ten smaller pieces of the total would be traded.

Ultimately, the banyan seed is minuscule before it develops into a plant. We would have to start trading in smaller amounts and increase our capital to $20,000 as soon as we realized a net profit of $2,000 from our deals, much like a banyan tree grows. Then, with $2,000 from our gains and $20,000 from our initial cash, we would have $22,000 accessible for trading. I shall use the term "net profit" in this context since a business usually makes both profit and loss.

A business may not always suffer from losses. In actuality, an endeavor cannot be called a business if it involves no possibility of loss. A businessman is also considered successful if his profits exceed his losses. In this context, "net profit" means the amount that remains after subtracting all losses from all profits.

You only need to raise capital if your net profit is $2,000 or higher. To help your trading business grow like a banyan tree, the second trading tip of the day is to start each deal with 1/50th of your total capital and add 1/50th of initial capital to your working capital each time you make a 20% "net profit".

Take Part In Little Transactions Only

If you simultaneously buy at a margin and sell with the appropriate "stop loss," your broker will assume that your loss is limited by your "stop loss." Generally, your broker allows you to trade intraday with very little leverage. Consequently, he gives you the opportunity to buy and sell stocks for amounts between 50,000 and one lakh rupees with a meager 1,000 rupee margin. 'Margin plus' or comparable terminology is employed to depict this. The bulk of novice traders simply lose money for this reason.

Why is it the case? Have you ever experienced a traffic jam? You would have seen that smaller vehicles, like motorbikes and bicycles, cannot get past the traffic jams, but heavier vehicles, like trucks, can. Similar to that truck, you would likewise become detained in traffic if you made deals of that magnitude in the market. This happens because this is a market. A "buy" trade for that quantity of stock could only be completed by a seller who is available and has the matching quantity of the stock. A "sell" trade for a stock would only be executed when a buyer was available for the equivalent quantity of the stock, just as a "buy" trade.

Look at the picture down below. I'm just showing you the depth of the TCS stock market as it shows up on the NSE website. The stock's current market price is $2,362.35, as you may have noticed. A glance at the order book reveals that someone is willing to pay $2,362.15 for five stocks. On the other hand, nine stocks are available for $2,362.35 apiece. When trading intraday, think about putting in an order with a big margin to buy 100 stocks. Although you would think that you are paying $2,362.35 for your purchase, in actuality, you would receive 48 stocks at $2,362.60—the price that was set for the seller who came after you—and 9 stocks at that price.

A further ten equities would be bought at $2,362.65. Thus, the stock price would rise on your order alone, and the stock price would fall on your selling order alone when you sold this quantity. This is just an example utilizing the likewise liquid large-cap stock TCS. The stock price fluctuates between 40 and 50 pesos as a result of your order. If you place a single buy order of two to three lakh rupees, a low-volume stock may hit its upper circuit; when you sell the same lot, the stock price would rapidly decline. The sight of it all may surprise you.

Receiving stocks at prices higher than the ones at which you had placed the "buy" order and having them sold at prices lower than the ones at which you had placed the "sell" order resulted in a substantial loss for you. It is possible that you believed that a "limit" order was used instead of a "market" order. Your order might not be filled, though, if no seller or buyer could be located who was selling or buying at the "limit" rate you quoted. Because of this, you should avoid using your broker's minimum brokerage costs to purchase or sell stocks on leverage for more than 40,000 to 50,000 rupees at a time. Make sure to investigate the market depth of a stock before deciding to trade it.

To ensure that there are always buyers or sellers to fulfill your "buy" and "sell" orders, you should select a large volume stock. If not, you run the danger of purchasing stocks at prices that are near to the upper circuit and selling them at prices that are near the lower circuit. In this case, even "stop loss" is useless because, in a low-volume stock, there are usually either buyers or sellers at the price you have set for "stop loss."

My final piece of advice is to make little trades in order to achieve small profits. You have to fill a pitcher one small drop at a time. If you profit 200 to 500 rupees in a single trade and 7 out of 10 trades in a day are profitable, you might finish up with a profit of 2,000 to 2,500 rupees. However, you should only make little trades.

You Should Always Aim For A Little Profit And Set An Even Smaller Stop-Loss

As I mentioned earlier, you should begin your intraday trading business with 10,000 in cash and gradually increase it. Imagine a situation where you make 2% monthly profit and don't increase your capital. That means that after a month of intraday trading, you only make $200. You make an additional 2% profit, or $204, the following month on the same $10,200, bringing your capital to $10,404. If you continue to add your profits to your capital as previously mentioned and maintain a 2% monthly profit, how much capital would you have after thirty years?

You could have a heart attack when you hear the reply. Therefore, you should stop reading right now if you have a weak heart! If you produced just the 2% profit each month as described above, your capital of 10,000 would increase to 1,24,75,611 (Rupees one crore twenty four lakh seventy five thousand six hundred and eleven only) in thirty years! A copy of the excel file containing this computation can be found in Appendix A at the conclusion of the book for those who disagree. Is making $200 a month on a $10,000 investment really such a ridiculous goal? There are roughly twenty trade sessions every month. That implies that you just need to turn a $10 profit per day!

Is it feasible for a business owner to invest $10,000 and not make $10? A vegetable vendor usually has more intelligence than a novice stock trader because, unlike the latter, who even with a target of 10 rupees loses 200 to 300 rupees of capital by the end of the day, the vegetable vendor regularly brings vegetables worth 10,000 rupees and sells them for 200 to 300 rupees profit. My proverb, "A person who cannot sell stocks, cannot sell tomatoes," has this justification. The two are very similar to one other.

Tomatoes run the risk of becoming bad if they are not sold immediately. If the tomatoes are not sold, even at a small loss, the entire batch runs the risk of going bad. The tomato trader is aware of this knowledge. For him, fresh tomatoes generate a sizable profit. He starts to lower his profit target as dusk approaches, and he even incurs a loss in order to sell the tomatoes before they go bad.

A novice stock trader, on the other hand, waits for the stocks to drop while maintaining concentration on a predefined objective. Finally, he only departs after experiencing a severe setback. Even though a novice stock trader loses even pennies in hopes of making a five to twenty percent profit on an intraday trade, their stocks end up losing money. A tomato vendor sells his produce while making a meager profit of just one rupee. Therefore, the recommendation in tip number four is to avoid setting an intraday trading profit target larger than 1%. Even if your daily earning target was only $10, you might make a profit of 1%, or $100, if you purchase a stock for $10,000 intraday and only pay a $1,000 to $2,000 margin.

For ten days, you will have achieved your aim if you receive 100 rupees. If things continue this way, your 10,000 rupee initial investment might become 1,24,75,540 rupees in 3 years instead of 30. The main problem here, though, is that you neglected to record your $100 profit and to apply a stop-loss. Because of this, you lose this profit and, instead of making 100 rupees, you end up losing 200 to 300 rupees from the trade. After that, you start trading to offset your losses and cease considering profits. This makes me think of some advice I once received from a spiritual guide. "Even Lord Brahma would not be able to impart supreme knowledge to you if you do not stop making mistakes," he says.

Errors must be eliminated in order to obtain ultimate knowledge. To profit from trades, it is therefore imperative to keep a small goal of 1% for profits and an even more modest target of 1/2% for stop-loss. If your trade has already lost fifty rupees and your profit aim is one hundred, that means your tomatoes are beginning to rot. The day may end up profitable even if you just accept a loss of fifty rupees to save your capital. This problem would be explicitly addressed by the following tip.

A 2:1 Profit-To-Loss Ratio Is Required

Let's restate the last line of the earlier guidance. Your transaction is showing a loss of '50, meaning that your stocks—your tomatoes—are withering, and your goal is to make '100. You may safeguard your funds and still close the day with a profit rather than a loss by simply documenting this $50 loss. However, how might the recorded loss of fifty rupees turn into a profit? In the end, stocks need to make money if the profit-to-loss ratio stays at 2:1. You understand that no strategy, no matter how meticulously you select your stocks, can guarantee a transaction will be successful at all times.

It is possible for your transactions to lose money, and this happens. Let's say you trade ten times a day with this firm, maintaining a 2:1 profit to loss ratio. You can trade 10,000 with a 1,000–2,000 margin, as you are aware. This means that you can do four to six trades at once with your $10,000 capital. You can use those margins again to complete other deals when they are available later, after specific trades have produced a profit or loss. I would say that if you have $10,000 in margin, you could close ten deals at $10,000 apiece in a single day. Using a stop-loss of 1/2%, assume that 6 out of 10 trades result in losses and just 4 result in profits. You each lost $50 in 6 transactions for a total of $300 and made $100 in 4 trades for a total of $400 as a consequence. You are still making a profit of $100. That suggests that even if only four out of ten trades turn a profit, you still gain money.

You are still left with '10 even after deducting brokerage and other expenses from that profit; ultimately, you are generating money as opposed to losing it. However, the fear and greed instincts overwhelm a rookie trader. He does not report a loss in line with the stop-loss even after his transaction has dropped by 5%. Because he thinks his stock will rise, he even forgets to set a stop-loss, which leads to an eventual increase in his loss to 4% to 5%. In a similar vein, his greed makes him hold off on declaring a profit when the stock price rises by 1% in order to wait for even larger returns of 4% to 5%. Because of his indiscipline, he would have lost 2,500 to 3,000 rupees in the other 3 trades, even though he would have made 2,000 rupees from the other 7 impulsive trades.

Despite all of this, even if 7 of his 10 trades are positive, he still makes a net loss. As a result, he eventually loses 500–1,000 rupees of capital. The next day, he tries to make up for this loss and ends up losing much more, which feeds his greed even more. For this reason, if you want to make money, you must always keep your profit target and stop-loss ratio at a 2:1 ratio. This theory has been followed by successful traders all around the world. If you think that 1% profit and 1/2% stop-loss is too low, you can increase them to a maximum of 2% profit and 1% stop-loss. But if you start trading after carefully examining the charts and selecting stocks with strong moves, I believe it is rather easy and quick to make profits of 1% instead of 2%.

This also facilitates the discharge of margin that may be used for future transactions. A 2:1 ratio between the profit target and stop-loss must always be maintained in order for stock trading to be lucrative. When it comes to trading, swing trades are preferable than intraday transactions when stop-loss orders are not desired. In the following chapters of this book, the steps involved in swing trading have been explained in detail. Swing trading might help you profit from your capital by 2% to 5% per month without taking any losses.

Engage solely in high volume stocks

The stocks that are trading at high volumes and are especially active during the current session are listed on the NSE website. Shuffle in unison with the group. Large volume traders will either witness a sharp rise in price or a sharp decrease in value for their stocks. Trading in these stocks could be beneficial for you since there will be a lot of buyers and sellers, which lowers the chance that your stop-loss will be triggered and prevents the price of your stock from experiencing substantial volatility. Furthermore, brokers usually have less stringent margin requirements when trading these equities, which are commonly known as liquid stocks. Your broker might block 3,000–4,000 rupees for a 10,000 trade in a midcap stock with minimal activity, but you might start a 10,000 trade with as low as 800–1,600 in margin in a large-cap stock with high turnover.

The margins are not all the same size. This is selected based on the stock's liquidity. Consequently, the only stocks that ought to be traded are those with large volumes. To improve your chances of success, I would advise selecting your stocks from the high-volume stocks from the previous trading day. You can select equities from the list of stocks with the greatest volumes for that day by obtaining an Excel file of the previous day's rates from the NSE website. There is still another approach to accomplish the same goal. On the NSE website, you select the 'Most Active Securities' option from the 'Live Market' link. That displays the stocks that have seen the highest trading activity this session. You can select your stocks from that list. For your convenience, I have included a screenshot of the pertinent page below.

Please carefully examine the links to identify which one you need to click. However, how can you predict which stock's value will rise and which will fall? We'll talk about this subject later in the book. The trading tip of the day is to trade the stocks whose volume was highest the day before. Stocks that were bought yesterday with the expectation of profits might be sold today, which would lower the price, and you could earn by short selling. Furthermore, a stock's price may rise higher if it was bought the day before on the basis of an assumption that is still true today, providing you with the chance to profit by starting a long position.

All Investments Are Either Losses Or Winners; There Are No Good Or Bad Stocks

You have learnt from the previous six suggestions that you can start trading in the stock market even with a modest capital because there is no ideal technique that can forecast the outcome of a trade with 100% accuracy. You will need to make money by trading often and keeping your profit to loss ratio in check. Even though seven of the twelve trades result in losses and five in wins, you can still earn a profit if you maintain your profit-to-stop-loss ratio at 2:1. For example, if you had a $100 profit target and a $50 stop-loss target for trades of $10,000 each, you would lose $350 overall on 7 losing trades and make $500 on the remaining 5 trades, leaving you with a $150 net profit.

You are an experienced trader, thus it is also quite unlikely that 7 out of 12 trades will end in failure. But in reality, the exact reverse takes place. It is typical for 6–8 of the 12 deals to be profitable, with the remaining 5–6 trades possibly losing money. This happens with big traders as well, which is why stop-loss was created. I had read a book called "How I Made $2,000,000 in the Stock Market" published by Nicolas Darvas. He just made one thing very clear: there is no such thing as a good or terrible stock. The market consists of two types of stocks: increasing stocks and declining stocks. Thus, all you need to do is identify them. If you did that, you could trade more profitably.

As a result, there are currently a number of tools and methods available to help you differentiate between businesses that are increasing in value and those that are decreasing. There are many indicators available for this purpose, such as the R.S.I. on Candlestick Charts; but, before we get into these techniques in detail, I'd like to share with you the approach I use for the following recommendations.

Avoid Combining Different Trade Sections

There are five main trading and investment categories on the stock market. Novice traders often find it difficult to discern between the five divisions and consequently view them as a single area. This is why they don't succeed in trading and investing. Below is a list of these five sections: 1. Trading with a margin call or on day 2. BTST (Buy Today, Sell Tomorrow) or swing trading 3. Trading futures and derivatives 4. Trade of Preferences 5. Cash Delivery-Based Trading In fact, trading this way is referred to as "short selling," which is done when there is a chance that the price of the stock will drop.

You can book your profit or loss by selling or buying (if you have opted to engage in short selling) those stocks before the market closes that same evening. In a swing trade or BTST, you are not required to close positions on the same day as you would in an intraday trade because you can hold equities for up to 30 days. If the position is closed on the next trading day, it is referred to as Buy Today Sell Tomorrow (BTST). However, signing up for BTST is not necessary. Swing trades are ones in which you can hold a position for one day or for a month. This means that stocks will be held for a longer period of time than required for intraday deals, but not for as long as required for delivery-based cash trades.

A "Trade in Futures or Derivatives" is just executing an agreement to purchase or sell stocks at a future date, as opposed to investing directly in stocks. "Expiry" designates that time frame. For instance, the term of the Nifty and other equities could be 30 days, but the Bank Nifty term might only be 7. The stocks have to be bought in lots, with each lot having a maximum value of 10 lakh rupees. Furthermore, margin trading capabilities are offered here. As one sort of alternative, insurance is. In this instance, you consent to receive a premium in exchange for buying or selling stocks at a particular date. You are in the black if, on the designated date, the transaction you are selling or buying results in a gain that exceeds the premium amount; if not, you are losing money. Because you can only lose as much as the premium you paid, options are safer than futures.

The sixth kind of trade is Delivery-Based Trade in Cash. After making the final payment for the stocks in this trade, you actually receive ownership of them in your Demat account. In addition, there are two kinds of trading: long-term trading, which involves selling stocks after holding them for a year or more, and short-term trading, which involves selling equities before the end of the year. So, this suggestion basically says that you shouldn't mix and match the five sections described above. Consider this a case study. Rohit purchases an intraday position for 10,000. He plans to report his profit or loss before the market closes.

A 1,500 margin is required of him for this position. Even though Rohit loses 60 on the deal, he does not close his position. He thinks the stock price will go up. Even if the loss reaches 350 by the end of the day, Rohit can't accept it since he thinks the price will surely rise the next day. Why should you suffer a needless 350 loss? Instead of paying the broker the needed '1,500', he pays the full '10,000 in margin, converting his intraday position to a delivery position. Delivery will take two to three days, thus Rohit wants to sell them using BTST trade or Swing trade before delivery. But it's a dreadful day as well; his loss is now 730.

Rohit plans to sell the stock the following day, continuing to brush it off. The stock price increases the next day, but his loss remains unrepaired. In his loss, it comes down to '240. Rohit believes that the price is showing an upward trend, therefore he chooses to take delivery and wait before making a profit through short-term trading. But the stock plummets again. At this point, Rohit expects to lose $1,200. He now invests for the long term instead of the short term. He hopes to make some money out of this transaction, even if he has to hold onto the shares for a while. These investors hold onto their lost stocks for a period of four to five years. Observing Rohit's previous example, what did you notice?

From intraday to BTST, cash, short-term, and finally long-term investing, Rohit shifted his approach. This was a bad idea. This combination of these multiple components is definitely improper. If you are trading intraday, you have to close your position if your loss reaches 5% or book profit if you have won 1%, as stated in earlier recommendations in this book. In this case, Rohit should have taken an intraday position of '10,000 and applied a stop-loss of 1/2%, or '50. After taking this 50 loss, he may have had his margin released and used it to create a new intraday position of 10,000. He might have profited $100, or 1%, from that position, and after deducting his loss, he would have been in the black for the day. He may have even moved up to third position by using that advantage. The main lesson to be learned from this tip is to always draw a distinct boundary between the different stock market groups and to decide on your target, stop-loss, and trading period before making a trade.

According to the author, trading options is better than trading futures, and swing trading is better than intraday trading. By doing this, the chance of loss would be reduced and the likelihood of profit would increase. Swing trading and options trading are covered in great detail in the upcoming chapters.

Control Your Avarice And Fear

Because you have more time for the stock to perform better and the operator cannot prevent your leverage position from being triggered, a swing trade position increases your chances of making money. Averaging out might be a losing strategy in an intraday trade, but in a swing trade, if you do it disciplined, following predetermined criteria and lowering your profit objective with each average out movement, you might be able to quickly exit without incurring a loss.

Because stock delivery is necessary, a swing transaction is considered an investment as opposed to a trade. Even in terms of tax regulations, this income is considered short-term capital gains that you might be able to harvest to lessen your income tax liability rather than speculative income. Later advice would explain the specifics of income tax harvesting. I'll discuss the "Sharegenius" swing trading approach in the upcoming chapter.

The Sharegenius Swing Trading System

The average price of all trades made during that trading day is known as the "Volume Weighted Average Price (VWAP)" for a stock that is traded on an exchange. Let us assume that the volume-weighted average price of TCS stock is $1,948.30 on October 17, 2018. If so, you should place a limit order or after-market order to purchase one share at this average price of $1,948.30. This will ensure that the stock is purchased for you on October 18, 2018, the next trading day, in the event that the price reaches the VWAP of the day before.

I have determined that there is over 90% likelihood that you will be able to buy the stock at the volume-weighted average price of the previous trading day based on my analysis of historical data. You are just buying one stock at the VWAP of the prior day by doing this. You should use this kind of trading only if you maintain your trading account with a bargain broker, where delivery (cash) transactions have no brokerage and the only taxes and duties paid on a $1,000 purchase are one or two rupees. Just keep buying one stock every day.

As soon as you turn a 2.5% profit on the average price of all the stocks you have bought so far, you sell and walk away. That being said, this method ought to be limited to 30 SENSEX stocks or 50 NIFTY stocks. These 30 SENSEX firms or the 50 NIFTY stocks provide the possibility of a 2.5% return, even if they decline gradually for a few days before rising again in a month or two. I will now elaborate further. You will soon have the chance to earn 2.5% to 3% on the average price of all your purchases if you buy one stock every day at the VWAP of the previous day for any of the 30 SENSEX stocks or the 50 NIFTY stocks. This can happen in 4-5 days, 6-7 days, or 10–20 days. If the market goes into a bear phase, this time frame could extend to 30 or 60 days.

In a normal market, a 2.5% return might be obtained in 4 to 20 days. There is an advanced form of this method as well. This involves making four stock orders every day as opposed to just one, with the first being placed at the VWAP of the prior day, the second at 1% less than that VWAP, the third at the low of the prior day, and the fourth at 1% less than that low of the prior day. Assume you purchased four of these TCS shares. In the event that the market fell, all 4 orders would be filled. Whenever the market rises, at least one stock is definitely bought at the VWAP of the prior day; sometimes, two stocks are bought.

When the average price of the stocks you bought is exceeded by 2.5% to 0.5%, you should record the profit and sell your shares. In this case, you should progressively lower your profit target in line with average price. For example, you should book the profit immediately if, on your first day of sales, you are able to make a 2.5% profit. Even if you receive 2% more than the average price of your stock acquisitions, you should book a profit if you don't meet your profit target and keep buying stocks using the same approach. After three consecutive days of averaging, you ought to give up trading with a 1.5% profit target. This would protect you, and you could start fresh agreements with little to no cash when you got your money back.

You should lower your goal to 1% only if, regrettably, even after an average of more than four days, you are still unable to receive the expected return. Even after averaging using the above approach, you should take even a 0.5% profit if, on the fifth day of the week, which is also the last trading day of the week, you are unable to accomplish the profit objective. As I previously stated, brokers such as Zerodha charge a delivery fee of roughly 16 for any amount of stock sales, and the cost of purchasing or selling 2,000 stocks for different things is roughly 4. As a result, after subtracting the previously listed expenses, you can still turn a little net profit even if you sold for a 0.5% profit.

If the stock price has been falling consistently for the last five days, there is a greater chance that it will rebound and reach the 2.5% profit target when the process is resumed the following week.

The basic idea is that you can safely achieve an average weekly return of 1 percent while avoiding losses by trading using the aforementioned strategy and realizing varying degrees of profit—sometimes 2.5 percent, sometimes 2 percent, sometimes 1.5 percent, sometimes 1 percent, and sometimes just 5 percent.

VWAP Technique Breakout

Even if you trade intraday, you can take advantage of VWAP breakouts. To achieve this, just keep a watch on the VWAP for the day and the stock price. If the stock price is higher than the VWAP for the day, wait for the price to drop. The moment the situation shifts, that is, when the stock that is trading above VWAP abruptly drops, you should initiate a short position. You may have noticed that a stock usually decreases by an additional 0.5% to 1% when it sells at a price higher than the day's VWAP. But, on days of erratic trading, the stock can quickly recover, so you should not be overconfident and instead book even a 0.5% return as soon as you receive it.

Likewise, keep an eye out for an increase in the stock if it is currently trading below the day's VWAP. Open a long position immediately if a stock that is currently trading below VWAP suddenly rises. You would observe that a stock usually gains an additional 0.5% to 1% when it trades below the day's VWAP. But on days when there's a lot of volatility, the market can plummet again, so you should book even a 0.5% return as soon as you get it, rather than being greedy. Although this approach is effective in 60 to 80% of cases, it is not perfect. But this is a big part of the art of trading, which is what it is. Stop-loss, etc., can be kept at the 1:2 ratio between stop-loss and profit, as in the previous ideas.

I have found that applying stop-loss raises the possibility of losing money because small stop-losses could be triggered by abrupt fluctuations in price. Then, what ought one to do? You run the risk of losing much more money when you trade without a stop-loss. I've found a solution for the same. It is best to employ the time-bound stop-loss method or the tiny transaction strategy. This is addressed in the tip that follows.

Small Trade Stop-Loss Method

A trader invests $25,000 and establishes a stop-loss of $250, or 1% of the total investment. 500 is the profit he wants to make. If four of these stop-loss scenarios occur, he loses $1,000. Now let's contrast this with our tiny transaction stop-loss strategy. He has the option to trade on margin with 500 and focus on quitting with a 1% profit without utilizing any stop-loss orders, as opposed to taking a 25,000 position. He may open a position for 2,500 using his 500-pound margin and use the VWAP breakout strategy outlined in Tip No. 15 to profit by 1%, or '25.

What could be the biggest loss he could experience in this circumstance? The stock price can only drop by 20% before he loses up to $500, or his margin money, if he didn't set any stop losses. First off, if you are investing in stocks in indices like NIFTY, there is very little chance that their prices will drop by 20% all at once. Secondly, the $500 maximum loss is effectively a stop-loss even if the price does drop. Thirdly, you should use a time restriction in place of the same stop-loss in percentage.

As a result, if you are trading on a Volume Weighted Average Price (VWAP) breakout, you should maintain a small position and mentally decide that you will wait no more than 20 minutes to capture a profit; if you don't, you will quit the trade at the loss. In this scenario, your stop-loss is the loss resulting from the 20-minute time limit; if the breakout is real, a reasonable profit will probably be realized inside those 20 minutes. As previously said, it's okay to lose some of your intraday trades. Just make sure that the gains are always greater than the losses.

Practical Training Before making any real transactions, you should attempt to execute fictitious deals using the previously outlined technique, and you should document those trades on paper. Just record any profit you see inside the initial 20 minutes. If there is a loss on the trade, record the amount lost. Do this activity for a minimum of five days, and then assess the outcome. Kindly let me know how your findings turned out in the YouTube channel or blog comments area.

Mastering The Mentality Of Leveraged Trading

As I have already cautioned, taking a chance due to avaricious desires may be detrimental to your financial security. An especially large investment on the margin is referred to as a "leverage position." Any negative change in the market could result in a significant loss for you. Suppose a trader has $100 in margin available. He is limited to using a maximum of 25 as a margin for a single position by the rules. But, if the trader is successful in doing so and turns a profit, he can get overconfident and think about taking a position with the full $100 margin in an attempt to boost his profits.

He learns that the very nature of his avarice is a curse. As a result, a 4:1 margin to position should always be maintained. The margin-to-position ratio may be new to you, but you may have heard of the profit-to-stop-loss ratio up until now. Permit me to elaborate on this ratio in greater detail. Imagine that you deposit $40,000 as margin when you first start an intraday trading account. Most novice traders in this scenario keep opening trades until all of their margin money is depleted. For instance, they purchase a stock with a margin of $4,000. They take the next spot by a 5,000-point margin. They keep buying shares of different firms in this way until they have used the entire 40,000 as margin. These particular positions are leverage positions; that is, these kinds of trades are what are meant to be considered when all of your margin money is used up.

Now let's examine how a sizable capital loss can occur from neglecting to place stop losses, or even from them not being struck. Suppose you set a stop loss and executed leveraged trades. Now, if you have used up all of the margin funds in your account and there is a big move in the market, your broker can ask for more margin to let you keep your holdings. In this case, your broker would be compelled to terminate all of your leveraged positions due to a shortage of margin, which would result in a substantial loss for you. On the other hand, you can only take positions worth up to one rupee for a total margin of four rupees if you have forty thousand rupees in margin, as per my requirements, which require you to maintain a 4:1 ratio between margin and position.

Since you have '40,000 as margin in this instance, you should only utilize '10,000 to enter intraday trade positions and retain '30,000 in your account. Never forget that the market is open the next day as well. We don't come here to make millionaires overnight. You are only allowed to use 10,000 as margin for intraday trades on that specific day, per this rule. It is important to keep in mind that the remaining cash is reserved for the following day and should never be used for margin on that particular day. You can even make a vow in front of God or a close friend, if needed, promising not to act out of greed and to keep the margin to position ratio at 4:1. Following this advice would keep you from losing your emotional equilibrium. You will only have '38,000 in margin if you use '10,000 as margin and end up losing '2,000 on your transactions that day. Then, you should only enter trades with a "9,500 margin, which is 1/4 of a "38,000," in line with the 4:1 rule.

A similar example would be if you had 10,000 margin and made $2,000 in profit on day one; on day two, you would have 42,000 margin and could use only 10,500 margin for positions. You can avoid taking on leveraged positions by following the 4:1 rule for margin and letting your feelings lead the way. It's possible that you've heard repeatedly that a lot of traders lose all of their money in a single intraday trading day. This only happens because traders have the guts to take on the market and their leveraged holdings. The next piece of advice is about going up against the market.

Take A Break From Competing With The Market

For a trader, greed, fear, and ego are undesirable emotions. You would have to trade like a machine in order to be successful. Don't let your feelings interfere with your task. I know you're wondering why I've become such a preacher at this point. You will understand my lesson after you have read Lalit Prajapat's story. Lalit Prajapat had discovered an excellent trading strategy. As he grew accustomed to shooting in the dark, he actually devised a strategy: "Let me treat the close price of a stock from the previous day as base.

I would not take any positions until the stock remains above that base price, but the moment it comes below that previous day's close price, I would take a short position." This is exactly what he did. He selected four portions. In three of the four stocks he had opportunities in, the stocks had momentarily risen above the previous day's close prices before starting to drop. Lalit started placing short bets as soon as the stock prices dipped below the previous day's close, and he made a sizable profit as the stock prices continued to decline. Lalit attempted the identical strategy with double the margin funds the next day.

As stocks moved above their closing prices, he continued to take "sell" positions, and as soon as they moved below their closing prices, he continued to take "buy" positions for stocks that had started below their closing prices from the day before. On the next day, he too turned a tidy profit. On the third day, he increased his gap even further and followed the same process.

The next week, I would then reassess my viewpoint. In the event that I meet my weekly target returns on a few stocks and my trading account balance goes beyond $20,000, I will withdraw the excess; if that amount is still not enough, I will transfer the required amount. And what if there's only $1,25,000 in capital? A total of $5,000 would be invested each day, with $2,000 going into one NIFTY stock, $2,000 going into one NIFTY midcap stock, and $1,000 going into one small cap firm.

You should divide your daily investment amount by your capital at a ratio of 1:25, so that even if none of your stocks meet your target return for 25 consecutive trading sessions, you will still have sufficient capital. You can invest £2,000 a day, or £150,000 total, in all three equities if you have that much capital. You can invest $3,000 in the NIFTY stock and $2,000 in each of the other two stocks each day, for a total of $7,000, if you have $1,75,000 in funds. I'm hoping that by now you understand how important it is to keep your daily investment amount and your total amount of money at a specific ratio. You should increase the number of stocks by one instead of increasing the investment per stock when your capital reaches '3,75,000' or when your investment per stock reaches '5,000—'5,000—'5,000.

Choose two NIFTY stocks instead if you have '4 lakhs to invest each day: 3,000 in each of the two NIFTY stocks, 5,000 in midcap, and 5,000 in small cap companies. Likewise, if you had much more cash, you could purchase two midcap stocks. You have to take the above-described methodical approach, beginning with '25,000. The following tip will teach you how to set a profit target in this process.

Determining Profit Goals

Here, I'll demonstrate how to set profit targets using an example Zerodha account. If fees increase or you open a trading account with a different brokerage in the future, you can change your goals. I'll discuss the target and profit later; let me first declare the objective rates. Goal for the first week that the stock was bought: S. Profit Target (%): 4.5 S is the No. 1 Stock Average Out at Volume Weighted Average Price Target for the second week at the average price following averaging out. No. 2: Stock Average Out at Volume Weighted Average Price Target at Average Price after Average Outcome (%): 4 S. for the third week. No.: 3 Stock Average Out at Volume Weighted Average Price Target: 3.5 S is the profit target percentage at average price after the fourth week of averaging out. No.: 4 Stock Average Out at Volume Weighted Average Price: Profit Target (%): 2.5 S.

Target for the sixth week at average price after averaging out: Profit Target (%): at the stock's volume-weighted average price. No.: 6 Stock Average Out at Volume Weighted Average Price Target: Profit Target (%): 2 S at average price following the seventh week of averaging out. No.: 7 Stock Average Out at Volume Weighted Average Price Target: 1.5 S is the profit target percentage at average price after the eighth week of averaging out. No.: 8 Stock Average Out at Volume Weighted Average Price Target: after averaging out, target profit (%): 0.5 S for the ninth week or any following week at average price. I will now provide more details. No.: 9 Stock Average Out at Volume Weighted Average Price.

Assume you have Rs. 25,000 in capital. Using a Zerodha account, buy stocks for Rs. 1,000 following the steps outlined in the preceding advice. As of the time this book was written, the only fees assessed at the point of sale are STT and GST, which combined amount to around one rupee. There isn't a relevant brokerage. In a similar manner, '16 is subtracted for transportation costs and an extra Rs. 1 is subtracted for taxes when the stock is sold. Consequently, the entire cost of buying and selling stocks for $1,000 (with cash and carry delivery) is $20, which also includes 15% income tax on profit from short-term capital gains.

However, there may be a way for you to escape having to pay this short-term capital gains tax. We'll talk about this in the income tax harvesting tip section later. You only get around $25 in profit if you make a 4.5% profit on $1,000, or $45. This works out to a 2.5% net return. Whether you sell 1,000 stocks or one item, there is always a delivery charge of about $16. Therefore, if you average out your $2,000 investment over the Book of the next week and make a profit of 4%, $30 would have to be subtracted from costs. You get $50, or a 2.5% net return, if you deduct $30 for fees from 4% of $2,000, or $80. In a similar vein, if you booked a 3.5% profit on $3,000, you would earn $105; your net profit would be $75 after deducting approximately $40 for costs. Keeping with the example, a 3% profit on an investment of $4,000 would yield a net return of roughly 2.5% after expenses are deducted.

Suppose we are still unable to book a profit even after averaging out four times, or for four weeks in a succession. In such a case, we would adjust the profit target to 2.5% after averaging out for the fifth time and determining an investment of $5,000. If the investment amount was raised to $6,000, the profit target would be adjusted to 2%. Once the seven averages were calculated, the goal would stay at 1.5 percent. If profit could still not be booked after a total of eight averages, we would reduce the profit target to 1%. If your stock was very bad and you did not earn even 1% in return after eight averages, you would still be at the minimum profit target of 0.5% after averaging out nine times, or any other number of times after that.

After nine average outs, your initial investment in the stock rises to $9,000, and you leave with a profit of only $45 (0.5%) of the total amount invested. It might be feasible to end at "no profit-no loss" even though this profit is very small after changing the delivery price and other expenses. Making a 0.5% profit would be easy in the end. For example, even exiting at '45.23 would yield a 0.5% profit target if your average price was '45. This would be helpful because most of your swing trades might yield gains between 4.5% and 2.5%. The extremely rare 0.5% profit scenario only materializes when a stock bear market moves significantly and for an extended period of time, or when the market declines significantly.

Nevertheless, the following four advantages exist: 1. Your $9,000 core capital would be released, allowing you to use it for additional swing trades. 2. Even after deducting the delivery charge from 2016 and other expenses from 2018, you are left with '11 as net profit. You are at least not going home empty-handed. This gives you a great deal of mental satisfaction and keeps you from feeling tied to any one thing. 3. You can use this money to make more swing trades and potentially profit. If not, a lot of traders will keep holding onto declining stocks, which could result in them losing half or even a quarter of their capital. They still don't get their money back, even after ten or fifteen years. Within two months, you are free to leave this role. 4. You can select a new, safe investment after selling the stock that has been falling for nine weeks in a row! After nine weeks of declines, just think of how much lower the stock would have gone if you had chosen to make swing trades in the same security!

The next week, if you reinvest $1,000 in that stock, you might even see a 4.5% return. Therefore, there's no need to panic. If you invest just in index stocks and, of those, only Sharegenius top stocks, your odds of finding yourself in a situation where you might have to average out for nine weeks or settle for just 0.5% return become pretty unlikely, in fact nearly nil.

When Swing Trading, Only Utilize Index Stocks

Only equities from the NIFTY 50, NIFTY Midcap 50, Bank NIFTY, BSE Small Cap, etc. should be used for the swing trade that was previously discussed in guidance. Why? You can easily achieve returns of 4.5% to 2.5% on most of these transactions because there may be more volume and swings throughout the day due to the fact that all the main fund companies and foreign investors trade in them as well. For readers who have come to this book from the middle, let me clarify that swing trades, in my opinion, are cash-based transactions that have a holding period of one to thirty days. It is incorrect to classify this as an intraday deal. In any event, even if, unfortunately, while using an index stock, the stock experiences some fundamental change and is taken off the index list, you would still be able to sell in 9 to 10 weeks.

The target in this case would continue to drop until it settled at 0.5%. Once the stock has been removed from the index, you should not trade it. Instead, choose another index stock. The basis is that using the swing trade approach with stocks in the NSE or BSE indices increases the opportunities for early profit booking. There is no chance of getting stuck, not even in the event of a stock plummeting. The scientific feature of this strategy is that it averages out just in a week, and only in strong stocks. As it averages out, you continue to reduce your aim. Ultimately, you manage to walk away with simply your initial investment and perhaps even turn a profit.

Neither Swing Trading Nor Intraday Conversion To BTST

One of my friends paid $300 for 100 Yes Bank shares during an intraday trade. Regretfully, the stock dropped that day and ended at '288. He didn't have the courage to take a $1200 loss, so he moved from intraday to swing trading. He acknowledged the receipt of the materials. Afterwards, the price fell even more, hitting a level of 180, at which he began to invest in long transactions. His trade thus turned into a long-term, profitable investment. All he's doing is waiting for the stock to rise. You must decide on the trading time frame before anything else. That means you have to stick to your decision.

For example, if you bought a stock that you intended to sell after a year, you shouldn't keep checking its market value every day or think about selling it as soon as it starts to decline. As a matter of fact, the main cause of stock market failure is a lack of discipline. Make an attempt to fortify your resolve. Practice is required for the same. You should use caution in your daily life to avoid making frequent changes to your thoughts. Make the decision you have made as firm as you can. Unlike others who frequently alter their decisions and strategies—decisions that the stock market will never forgive—you will be able to succeed as a trader in the stock market because of your strong willpower.

Greed Is The Stock Market's Curse

Greed is the stock market's curse. You have undoubtedly read the phrase "greed is a curse" many times in school when you were younger. But when you trade stocks, you tend to forget this proverb. Most people who trade stocks are always looking for advice that may suddenly make them billionaires. I promise you that this search will never come to an end because the future of any firm is never certain and it takes time for a business to succeed. It takes time for your money to appreciate when you purchase stocks. Therefore, regardless of how precise a tip is or how long you plan to invest for, you should never put a sizable sum of money in stocks at once.

Assume for the moment that you think business "A" would perform brilliantly in the future, that its stock could double, and that it will yield a 100% return. You invest one to two lakhs of rupees in the firm out of avarice. Later, you begin to feel anxious, agitated, and frustrated if the price doesn't increase throughout the next one to two months or, conversely, keeps going down. Rather, you ought to begin by investing merely 25% of your money and keep telling yourself that, before I invest another 25% of my fund, if the company has the guts, it will turn a profit of at least 5%. If the price of the company's stock increases by 10% from where it is now, I would invest an additional 25%, and if it increases by 15%, I would spend the remaining 25%. You might be able to avoid making bad investments by using this kind of strategy.

For additional insight, see my other book, "How Chandu Earned and Chinki Lost in the Stock Market," where I discuss another technique for adjusting large investments based on the 200 DMA.

Is It Possible to Sell a Poor Investment?

I really hope that anyone picking up this book in the middle will first go over the previous swing trading tips in detail before moving on to this tip so that you can understand it. One of my coworkers told me that stock trading was an easy method to make money about 2006. How is that, I questioned." He reasoned that if he traded between '100 and '103 and took a return of 3% every day, he would be able to earn 30% return in a month if he managed to get that return even on ten days in that month.

At the time, the stock of Dabur India was trading around '100. It would rise from '100 to the levels of '105-103-102 or drop back to '98-100. (I am aware that in most cases it is not possible to do this because sometimes the stock breaks its range and if it drops quickly to the level of '80, the entire amount invested for trading at the level of '100 would get blocked; however, what I am about to tell you may help you make money even when the range is broken.) They even succeed in making some money in the beginning, but later they learn of some stories about how so-and-so investors had purchased thousands of stocks some 20 years prior and did not sell them, and that investor is now a multimillionaire.

In fact, all small traders enter the stock market initially to make easy money that way only. They sometimes experience a severe shock when their stocks double after they book their profits, which causes their greed to turn them from traders to long-term investors, and they do not even notice when the market has subtly moved into a bear phase, where all the profits that they had on paper disappear and, on the contrary, the investments go in the red.

Let's say a stock is range-bound between '90 and '110. Someone buys the stock at '95 and sells it at '105 for a few days' profit, but later the stock breaks out and rises to '180, and they regret making those small trades because they believe their investment would have doubled if they had held on to the stocks until that point. However, they are told that there is still time, and if they buy even at '180, the blue They do not book that loss of $20 and instead hope to sell the stock when it rises back to $360. However, the stock drops to '80 and sticks to a range of 80-88 and moves within that range for the following two to three years. In the meantime, the bear phase begins.

The stock rises gradually at first but then drops sharply; in three or four trading sessions, it hits '160. Such investors are horribly shocked by this. This advice is meant to keep these investments alive because, in such cases, their investment at the "180" level becomes dormant and they are left holding it for just three to four years at no profit. Assume you invested $36,000 to buy 200 stocks at a price of $180 a share. The value of your investment dropped to $16,000 when the stock hit 80. The stock you own is fluctuating between 1980 and 1988, but you don't understand why.

To get '1,000, sell the requisite number of stocks at any price between '80 and '88. For instance, you would receive '1,020 if you sold 12 stocks at '85; you would then remove '20 for shipping and brokerage costs, leaving you with '1,000. Just remember that out of your 200 stocks, you are still holding 188 of them and have only registered a loss on 12 of them. Now you invest this $1,000 in stocks of a firm of your choosing from the NIFTY, ETF, or NIFTY 50, applying the swing trading advice from the previous chapters. In other words, you select one of the 50 NIFTY 50 stocks that are priced under $1,000. Repeat the process the next week, setting a limit order for the quantity of stock that can be bought for $1,000 at the VWAP of the day before. When your average holding yields a profit of 4.5% to 0.5%, book your profit and sell it (in the preceding suggestions, we addressed profit targets ranging from 4.5% to 1%).

By undergoing the aforementioned operation, you would profit from: 1. You can book profits in the event that the market rises since you can only record losses in one stock at a time, and those losses are limited to the $1,000 that would profit you. 2. If you begin to make profits in the area of 4.5 to 0.5 percent, you may be able to offset some of the losses from your dead investment. 3. Eventually, the stocks in your investment that were idle would become dividend-paying NIFTY 50 stocks. 4. Instead of making fresh investments, you might use the dormant stocks that have been sitting in your portfolio for a while if you wish to use swing trading entirely for your stock trading in the future.

Put Aside Thoughts Of Bonuses

All of these investors have actually heard countless anecdotes about well-known IT companies. For instance, in 1991, someone might have had 100 shares of a certain company, and the company continued to pay bonuses on a regular basis, growing those shares to 200, 400, 800, and 1,600 shares, respectively. Profiting from the ordinary investor's mindset, even companies with poor fundamentals will sometimes announce bonuses, which drives up the price of the company's stock. This provides an opportunity for corporate promoters to sell their shares.

After hearing such tales, someone is driven by avarice to purchase and hold stock in any company that announces a bonus. One of the best examples of this is the stock of Unitech, which surged from '156.65 to a peak of '14,798.55 in 2006 on the announcement of 12 bonus shares on a single existing stock. Unitech announced a 1:1 bonus share again in 2007, which sent the price plunging even worse. But subsequently, the stock began to decrease, eventually hitting '1.05' in 2019. Actually, the rise in the value of 100 stocks to crores in the case of big IT businesses was not due to incentive payments but rather to higher company earnings. If well-known IT firms like Wipro and Infosys hadn't given out bonuses, the current price of their single shares would have been in the crores, making it extremely difficult for average investors to purchase.

For this reason, bonuses must be paid out on a regular basis to maintain the market price of stocks within the grasp of investors. Bonus shares are issued by a company for a lower income per share, which consequently lowers the market price of the stock. A company's market price increases in proportion to its profits and income as its prospects and income grow. As a result, use caution when making stock investments and base them on the company's earnings and revenue rather than the bonus announcement.

Typical Results Aren't Always Negative

As mentioned in Tip No. 10, you should avoid averaging out a decreasing position. For example, with a mutual fund, you can use the Systematic Investment Plan (SIP) to purchase units for a set monthly amount, which essentially averages out the units alone. This is accurate for intraday positions, but in most cases, averaging out is not detrimental. Similarly, the swing trading strategy outlined in previous suggestions is predicated on a systematic process of averaging out index stocks from NIFTY, etc.

In order to produce returns that range from 4.5% to 0.5% on average costs. To guarantee an average return of about 2.5% and the chance to exit each position safely, all you have to do is keep gradually adding quality dividend-paying index stocks, averaging them out every week or every month.

Either Employ Swing Trading Or Properly Study How To Invest For The Long Term

Readers of my previous book, The Winning Theory in the Stock Market, or my research term on my blog are aware that I prefer to use fundamental ratios, such as base price and net sale per stock, to determine whether a stock is a value before purchasing it. But the 2018 stock market fall made me stop and consider. In fact, if I had purchased Eicher Motors shares in 2007 at a price of around $599 based on these facts while I was trading alone, I never would have experienced any anxiety, anguish, rage, or frustration—not even after the stock fell to about $135 in 2008. Because I had a long-term perspective and used to invest no more than 10% of my monthly income in a single company, I would not have felt trapped either.

At that time, I was making about $15,000 a month, so I could only have invested about $1,500 and could barely have purchased three stocks. Therefore, I wouldn't have been anxious or agitated about losing that $1,500 or about stocks like Eicher Motors being delisted. But after registering as a Research Analyst and beginning to propose companies on a public forum, I've discovered that not all 71,000 of my followers are the same. When the stock drops from ~599 to a level of ~135, they become avaricious and invest lakhs in single lots. They then start teasing me in their remarks. Perhaps it would be acceptable to point out that Eicher Motors, which had fallen from 599 to 135 in 2008, had risen to 32,200 in 2018. Nevertheless, I had to create this swing trading method for my restless followers. We have already discussed swing trading in previous chapters.

The main takeaway from this tip is that you have two options when it comes to investing: either you put small amounts of money—10%

of your monthly income, according to my rules—into your favorite stocks and hold them worry-free for five, ten, or fifteen years, or you wait patiently for the company to perform better—like it did in the case of Eicher Motors—without worrying if your investment loses value and falls below its initial cost. Two, you could opt for a swing trade, which you would never feel trapped in and you would still get your money back if you had to exit with a loss of 0.5% on the average price after several averaging outs. You could then use that money the next week to buy the same stock again at a lower price with a 4.5% profit target.

Why Is Buying Index Stocks Justifiable?

A saying in the stock market goes, "If you can't beat the index, go with the index." Imagine if at 8,000 on the NIFTY, you started your stock market investment career. The NIFTY price right now is 10,800. NIFTY has therefore grown by 30% since you made your investment. If you made more than 30% in profit throughout the Book of your investment, you might be regarded as a competent and skilled investor (the majority of small investors experience a 30% decrease in portfolio value). As a result, even mutual fund managers set their benchmarks against particular indices.

The development of ETFs is based on a similar concept. For example, NIFTY BeES or NIFTY ETFs invest in every stock that comprises the NIFTY Index in the same proportion as their NIFTY component. They therefore trade at prices that are approximately 1/100th or 1/10th (of NIFTY) of NIFTY. Small investors can follow the index by investing in them using a systematic investment plan (SIP), which functions similarly to a mutual fund.

NIFTY Stocks Are An Excellent Choice For Trading And Swing Trading

The futures and options markets for stocks are also where all 50 of the NIFTY 50 stocks are traded. The same stocks are traded by local mutual funds and foreign institutional investors (FIIs). These stocks have appropriate swings and are sufficiently liquid because they make up 80–90% of all trades made on the market. Therefore, I believe that the stocks from the NIFTY 50 should be selected for intraday or swing trading (even the ones to select—that would be covered later).

Second, exchange committees assess firms based on volume, earnings, dividend liability, and other criteria before selecting which ones to include in indexes such as the SENSEX, NIFTY, and so on. Indexes routinely replace stocks that don't meet certain criteria, such market cap, volume, dividends, etc. with new stocks. Because of this, you can use the method outlined in the upcoming chapters to profitably exit stocks that are being subtracted from the NIFTY index and make investments in newly added firms. We'll cover this in more detail in the tip that follows.

Analyze a Plunging Deal

Portfolio that resembles an index As mentioned in the previous advice, there are other factors to consider when choosing stocks for indexes such as NIFTY, SENSEX, and so forth. Renowned economists have created various rules to guarantee that only the best companies are included in such rankings. However, a company that is unable to meet these standards because of its poor performance is removed from the index and replaced with a new company that satisfies those standards following the process of periodic evaluation of index firms. Because of this, if you use the strategy outlined in earlier suggestions to select stocks from NIFTY/SENSEX for your swing trades, and one of your stocks is removed from the index, you should also stop trading in that stock after realizing a profit and select a new stock from NIFTY/SENSEX to replace it.

This implies that you should still average your weekly returns using the VWAP from the prior day, even if the stock that was taken out of the index starts to lose value. Once you have profited by 0.5% on your average price and exited the market without losing money, you can select a new stock from the index to replace the one that was eliminated.

What is my trading strategy for stocks?

The two tactics I would prefer are swing trading, which involves averaging out a stock every week until a return of between 4.5% and 0.5% over average price is achieved, and BTST (buy today, sell tomorrow) over intraday trading. Even though you can only generate an average return of 2% per month, as your older brother, I would even go so far as to recommend that you stick to swing trading exclusively in NIFTY/SENSEX stocks because it is not only safe but also gives you the chance to turn your $10,000 investment into $1.24 crores in 30 years.

We have gone into great detail on this subject in previous chapters. It has already been said to you that in order to swing trade, you have to select stocks from the NIFTY 50. You ought to take the 52-week highs into account for those stocks as well. Stocks that are trading near their 52-week highs, or the year's peak, but no more than 15% down, are the ones you should pick. Why? Because fear and greed are the emotions that drive the stock market. Consequently, investors' stop-loss orders begin to be triggered when a stock falls to its lowest point of the year; even those investors then start selling the shares, which sends it down even more. Another is the notion that the stock market is all-knowing. In the current era of information technology, if a company projects a decline in performance going forward, this information may be leaked inside and reach the market ahead of the official announcement. In the vernacular of the stock market, this is called rumor.

Although it may be considered a rumor, eighty percent of the time it is real, and although it may take up to a year to verify, these rumors are often found to be true. Because of this, it usually happens that a stock that has hit its 52-week low for no obvious reason will keep falling, hitting new lows every 10 to 15 days. The same thing happens when a stock is trading at or near its 52-week high. A stock like that rapidly breaks records. There are several opportunities to routinely earn small profits (4.5% to 0.5%) when trading these stocks. The idea is that faster earnings could be achieved by selecting the top 10-15 NIFTY/SENSEX businesses that are now trading at their year-high levels or within a range of 0% to 15% of those levels. There's a chance that the stock market proverb, "If you buy cheap stocks, you would sell cheap; if you buy premium stocks, you would sell at premium," also applies here.

Perhaps you're asking yourself, "What if I trade close to a high position and become stuck? How would I handle "misfortune in the very first adventure," when the stock might have peaked just after I bought it and then it just keeps going downhill from there? This will be addressed in the ensuing advice.

An Investment Never Declines Abruptly

As demonstrated in the previous tip, rumors leaked to the market by insider business sources persist, causing a firm's stock to fall anywhere from six months to a year before the company really experiences a decline in performance. But when the stock starts to drop after the rumor emerges

When the information becomes public, some avaricious investors start making the same purchases because they think it's too good to miss the chance to buy such a pricey bluechip company at such a low cost. However, even some long-term fundamental investors start out slowly with the same stock because, in the case of a fundamentally good company, even if its performance declines for a year or two, it recovers rather quickly when it does improve. Consequently, the purchases made by long-term fundamental investors who start making these stocks in installments, or the purchases made by small investors who have a tendency to buy stocks that have dropped by 50% (despite the fact that this tendency is incorrect; you have already read in my previous book, "How to Make Profit in Share Market," that the stock having a 52-week high/52-week low ratio over 2 should not be bought for long-term investment), allow the stock to start gaining slowly even slightly.

People think the rumor has been proven false and that they should buy the stock now that it's starting to rise in value. As a result, there is a brief boost in the stock price. But then the stock drops even further than it had gained. To further understand this in action, let's look at Yes Bank and IOC as examples. The NIFTY-listed stocks experienced a significant decrease from their 2018 year-highs. Please review the charts provided. IOC's January 2018 through March 2019 (January 2018 through March 2019; Yes Bank, January 2018 through March 2019) shows that, despite IOC's decline from its peak to a low point, there were obstacles in its path. Like the previous example, Yes Bank's slide chart is not a straight line even though it has decreased from its highest to its lowest point. Interspersed with this are also brief reversals.

You may be wondering why you should be concerned about any of this. The only thing that matters to you is that if you were using those two stocks for swing trades in line with the previously described procedure and averaging out once a week at the VWAP, you could easily exit after booking a profit of 2% to 3% over your average prices by taking advantage of these small bounce backs. After evaluating the companies and determining that they were no longer within 15% of their 52-week highs, you would have selected some other stocks from the NIFTY that were trading near to their 52-week high. I also have a YouTube video on this subject in which I show how the IOC stock dropped by about 65% in a year and how, by using swing trading, you could have profited eight times even during that 65% decline.

Benefits of Purchasing Dividend-Paying Stocks

You should know by now that while trading, I recommend picking large-cap stocks from the SENSEX 30 or NIFTY 50 that are now trading near their 52-week highs. But why is that the way it is? The question "why shouldn't I trade in such small cap or mid cap stocks, suggested by you or any other analyst, that I feel may give a return of 200%-300% in one or two years" has undoubtedly occurred to you.

The answer is that you must be able to hold basic equities first; small investors, as I showed in my previous advice using the example of Eicher Motors, typically lack this ability. Secondly, I'm sure you've heard the story of Sethji; if not, let me tell it to you. There was Sethji, an archetypal miser. He would usually have stale rotis with chili and salt, but no veggies, to save money on produce. But to quench his yearning for vegetables and other delights, after his meal he would close his eyes for 10 minutes and go into a state of meditation, all the while imagining that he was having a sumptuous feast of daal and curries. His appetites used to be satisfied by such contemplations. A bystander who heard him make the sound asked, "Sethji, what happened? "Sethji told him the whole story of how he was eating food in his thoughts and making that sound because he felt his lips burning due to a really hot curry. That guy said, "You stupid Seth, why do you only eat dal and curry if you have to enjoy food in your imagination?"

Another time, when he was in a similar state of concentration, he thought the curry was extremely spicy and started making the sound "Cee-Cee." Consume fresh fruits, kaju-katli, dried fruits, and sweets. If you must imagine yourself eating daal-curry, make sure the chef uses fragrant spices that won't burn your lips during preparation. I'm trying to get across the same point as in the previous paragraph with this suggestion: why invest in risky equities if the returns you can expect are just 4.5% to 0.5%? It is also dangerous to invest in any fundamental stock that has the potential to yield multiple returns in the future.

Any research analyst will recommend a stock, referring to it as a "value stock," if its market price is lower than its "Net Sale Per Share" and its book value. This makes sense, since a stock of this type would only be promoted if it qualified as a "value buy." However, there's a risk associated as well. If certain information concerning a problem that a corporation will face in the future is disclosed into the market before the general public is aware of it, the market price of that stock can drop to the point where we can buy it, assuming it is a value buy. Stocks of Kingfisher, Tantia Construction, Pratibha Industries, Satyam Computers, and other companies were considered fundamental value buys when their market prices dropped below their book values and "Net Sale Per Share" statistics. Such leaked information regarding business issues is referred to as "rumor." However, once information about these businesses became public, the stock prices dropped by 60% to 90%.

As a result, as you have read in my book "," you can invest up to 10% of your monthly income in these fundamental value purchase stocks and, after holding them for two to three years, expect multiple returns. If you wish to hold for a long time and receive a return of 200% to 500%. However, if your goal is to employ swing trading to generate 4.5—0.5% returns over the Book of a day to a month, why should you take a chance? Instead, why not restrict your investment to NIFTY/SENSEX equities that are nearing their annual highs in trading? These stocks are frequently less risky. They also yield dividends and bonuses when retained. They can also be easily obtained, with good volumes and bounce backs for 4.5% to 0.5% profit.

Extracting Taxes on Income to Lower Capital Gains

In this tip, I'll go over how to do income tax farming, or tax harvesting, in the stock market. Sure, it's true that "income tax harvesting," or "income tax farming," is a popular practice in the stock market. Mr. Trump was previously charged with failing to pay the entire income tax on his gains from the stock market while serving in the US government. It was said at the time that he had breached no laws. His actions were referred to as "income tax farming" or "tax harvesting," which is completely lawful and allows people to avoid paying taxes on capital gains from the stock market. You would learn the same tax collection strategies from this tip.

The arithmetic in this is actually very elementary. You stick to the previous recommendations and continue to make little annual investments in reliable dividend-paying stocks. Book profits in the stocks that rise in accordance with your objectives. Retain the remaining stocks and profit from dividends. In the last few days of March, you may go equity harvesting for income tax purposes. This is actually fairly simple. In the final days of March, sell any stocks in your portfolio that are losing money, and document your losses in writing. Purchase the same stocks again in the same number as you did prior to selling them at the same time on the same day. What are you getting out of this? This won't affect the quantity of stocks because we are buying the same number of stocks on the same day and at the same time as those that were sold at a loss.

We would simply have to pay brokerage with cheap brokers, which is usually not too much these days. To avoid paying brokerage, you can even keep a small price difference between your buy and sale; however, the loss we record may be deducted from the earnings for the full year, which would lower the short-term capital gains that arise. What? Let's say that as of March 20th, 2019, you had booked profits totaling '60,000 in a range of stocks. According to income tax legislation, you would have to pay $9,000 in short-term capital gains tax, which is 15% of the total proceeds. Assume for the purposes of this discussion that the stocks we still own as of March 20 show a $45,000 loss. We would sell these stocks and then buy them again in the same amount to make up for any losses.

After deducting this loss of $45,000 from our profit of $60,000, our net profit for the year would only be $15,000. We would have to pay 15% short-term capital gains tax on just this amount, or $2,250. This reduces the tax burden from $9,000 to just $2,250. This is referred to as income tax harvesting. You will save a net of '6,000 in capital gains tax even if the above procedure requires you to spend '750 in brokerage fees. Some readers would argue that selling and purchasing equities on the same day could be viewed as speculative income or intraday trading, in which case they might wonder how we would balance the size of the loss against a temporary loss of capital. This is the reply to the identical. If you choose the cash and carry option while making the order and you already possess the stock, then this kind of selling of shares is not considered intraday trading.

Recently, the stocks you already owned showed a loss. Similar to this, fresh stock is also bought by placing a fresh order and choosing the cash and carry option. In this case, the transaction is considered new as the whole price is paid up front, and the stock is accepted for delivery. If we decide to sell this stock, the tax on the profit will be based on how long we hold it. Therefore, selling stock through a cash and carry order, accepting full payment, and taking delivery of the shares would not be regarded as an intraday deal.

When Trading Options, Apply The 4-Stroke Method

In fact, I've dabbled in a number of different options trading techniques. My next book on options trading will go into greater detail, but for now, I've found that the 4-stroke technique is the best. 80–90% of your option trades could be profitable if you follow this 4-stroke approach. As was previously said, there is no 100% perfect approach for trading the stock market. You may still be a profitable trader even if your technique only has an 80%–90% success rate. Using this method, you can enter positions in NIFTY and Bank NIFTY options. Instead of purchasing calls or putting options on an index, you could, if desired, use this exact approach to purchase options on a particular stock. It is advisable to place options bets in NIFTY or Bank NIFTY rather than any specific stock, though, as there is no liquidity problem with such indices.

This approach is correct, but if you want to invest in a specific stock, you may have problems due to low liquidity. Let me now go over this four-stroke method. Assume that the NIFTY Future closed at $1,873.30 on a certain day when the market closed. Using this method, we would look at the closing price of the future day instead of the NIFTY day's closing price. You now have to prepare for trading the following day in advance depending on this closing price. You have to choose the call or put with the nearest weekly expiry when utilizing this method with Bank NIFTY. For the closest expiry month, you must additionally record the closest "in-the-money call" and "in-the-money out" of this closing price. A futures contract, for example, would have a closest in-the-money call of 10,850 and a closest in-the-money out of 10,900 if its closing price was 10,873.30.

Now you have to note the high and low prices for that call and put that you were trading on that specific day (you may check historical call/put option pricing data by watching my YouTube tutorial). You should record both of those numbers, assuming that the highest and lowest premiums of the day for the call of '10,850 were '163.30 and '86.45, respectively. Note the highest and lowest premiums for the '10,900 out right now. Let us assume that they are 175.35 and 96.40, respectively. Consequently, you now possess four figures (thus the term "4-stroke method"). You are now ready with a chart for the next day. The premium on the '10,850 call at market opening the following day could look like this. If the premium opens above or breaks over the maximum level of '163.30 from the previous day, you should buy the call of '10,850 immediately.

After you have profited '10 on the call, you should sell, thus if you buy at '165.80, you should book profit at '175.80. I've selected 165.80 as an example instead of the high price of 163.30 from the previous day because calls for such breakouts usually rise swiftly, and by the time you open a position, the price would have moved higher by some amount. If it opens or closes below the low of '86.45 the day before, you should short this call of '10,850. Keeping your profit goal at 10 is the ideal Book of action in this situation; for instance, if you opened a short position at 85.50, you should book profits if the price hits 75.50. Since one NIFTY lot is 75 in size, a profit of 10 implies a total profit of 750. Using this 4-stroke method, you can profit by '10' in 5 to 10 minutes when there is a breakout from the previous day's high or low. Similarly, you should buy the '10,900 put and sell it after making a '10 profit if it breaks out above the high of '175.35 on the preceding day. If it starts below or falls below the previous day's low of '96.40,' you should take a short position in the out of '10,900 and sell it after earning a profit of '10.

Bank NIFTY has a lot size of just twenty. Considering that brokerage may also be required, you might keep your profit aim between $15 and $20. In the same way, you may use this four-stroke approach to purchase calls or put options on any specific stock. You can set your profit target at 5% of the premium if you must specify it in terms of the premium. For example, if you are purchasing a call and the high of the previous day was 405.60 and it breaks out at 410, then your target should be 5% of 410, or about 20 rupees. In this case, it is not advisable to get overly greedy because calls and puts decrease at the same rate that they increase. One can wonder, to what extent this technique should use a stop-loss? The maximum stop-loss in this strategy is time-based, therefore if your breakout is true, you should choose a 5-minute stop-loss since you can make 5% or 10-15 rupees in that period.

If you don't meet your profit target in those five minutes, gather your courage and close your position with whatever profit or loss you are making. Time-based stop-loss strategies are what I recommend since close stop-losses are likely to be hit quickly due to the huge and quick swings in call and put pricing. When your target is just 5%, the regulations state that your stop-loss should be half of your target, or 2.5%. There's a chance that your stop-loss will be achieved before your goal is accomplished because the same is too low. It is therefore advised to use a 5-minute stop-loss. Before using this tactic, you ought to have some theoretical instruction. You would learn what the proper stop-loss level is.

Trading In Options Was Launched By The NSE

2001 saw the release of the campaign "Options Trading is Better Than Intraday Trading." Although there wasn't enough volume in the options market at the time, most day traders now trade options instead of intraday contracts. Taking a call-put position in options limits your risks because the most you might lose is the call or put premium. You can utilize more leverage at a lower cost when you trade options intraday. By the way, this book is not about providing in-depth information on options trading; that would take up too much room in a book this small. If you are not familiar with options trading, you can either wait for my next options-specific book or read a book written by another author on the subject.

This advice is merely meant to let you know that if you want to trade a given stock, options trading is a better option than intraday trading. Still, options trading is not for the inexperienced investor. This is something you should only do if you have a lot of money. For example, if Ramesh bought 3,500 shares of Hindalco at $200 intraday, he would have to pay a minimum margin of '1,50,000 on his trade value of '7,00,000, whereas Hitesh could buy a put option on Hindalco for '200 for '9 only, and since its lot size is 3,500, he would only have to pay '31,500 in options premium. If Hitesh were to trade using the previously mentioned 4-stroke approach, he would purchase the call of 200 when it crossed above the high of the previous day. He could profit '3,500 from this trade if he could purchase the call for '9 and sell it at '10. But remember that there is risk involved with both intraday and options trading.

Because of this, the previous advice informed you that a new trader should start with just one lot of Bank NIFTY. Because Bank NIFTY only has a 20 lot size, trading it intraday for 15-20 rupees as advised in the prior advice would not only protect you from the possibility of suffering a big loss, but it would also provide you experience trading options.

Let me stress again that I believe the best Book of action in this situation is swing trading. This would still help you achieve your trading and investment objectives, and as long as you follow the previously outlined steps, there wouldn't be much risk. The second-best technique is to trade options in Bank NIFTY and NIFTY using the 4-stroke procedure. Stock intraday trading falls into the third type. The maximum holding period for options is disclosed in the tip that follows.

Conclusion

The stock market is never driven by the news. It is not necessary for you to follow the incorrect advice given by the so-called experts. They'd say, "The market won't rise now because the American President tweeted about the trade war." An additional time, they might have said, "Now this bear phase is going to be long." At a later period, they may even remark, "We told you in the morning that the market was going to rise today." It almost went too far when some experts said, "Moon became crimson during the lunar eclipse; this is called a "blood moon." This is a rare occurrence, and the color red signals an impending stock market fall. If you keep looking for advice from other people, you will lose. Even disregard my advice.

You should have confidence in both your company and your own skills. You merely need to say this over and over: "There are no good or bad stocks in the market." There are no good or bad markets. All that exists in the market are rising and declining stocks. The market either moves higher or lower. This is the sole regulation in the market. Everything else is not worth it. Remember that there have been and will continue to be ups and downs in the stock market throughout history. So, whether you blame the market's swing on a Trump tweet, a surgical strike, or a "blood moon," it still occurs as the market moves forward. The market's fundamentals consist of ups and downs. How would you trade if there were no ups and downs? You should concentrate on taking advantage of the market's ups and downs rather than putting your hard-earned money into it only based on news and no theory.

Lastly, I conclude by saying that the swing trade formulas I present in this book are the lowest risk and have the potential to produce the biggest returns. An appendix at the end of the book contains a table that shows how $10,000 may become $1.24 crores with just 360 trades and a return of even 2%. Please don't forget to give my book a 5-star rating after perusing that table; doing so will inspire me and allow me to work harder on my next book of choices.

www.ingramcontent.com/pod-product-compliance
Lightning Source LLC
LaVergne TN
LVHW011944060526
838201LV00061B/4201